The Psychobiology
of Depression

The Psychobiology of Depression

Edited by
Joseph Mendels

University of Pennsylvania School of Medicine
and Veterans Administration Hospital, Philadelphia

S P Books Division of
SPECTRUM PUBLICATIONS, INC.
New York

Distributed by Halsted Press
A Division of John Wiley & Sons

New York   Toronto   London   Sydney

Spectrum Publications, Inc.
86-19 Sancho Street, Holliswood, New York 11423

Distributed solely by the Halsted Press Division of John Wiley & Sons, Inc., New York.

Library of Congress Cataloging in Publication Data

Main entry under title:
    Psychobiology of depression

    1. Depression, Mental. — Congresses.
    2. Psychobiology — Congresses.
    I. Mendels, Joseph, 1937 — ed. II. American
Association for the Advancement of Science.
[DNLM: 1. Depression — Congresses. WM 207
A503P 1974]
RC537. P72   616.8'.528   74-26750
ISBN 0-470-59352-0

Printed in the United States of America
123456789

Contributors

ROSS J. BALDESSARINI, M.D.
Department of Psychiatry
Harvard Medical School
Boston, Mass.

BERNARD J. CARROLL, M.D., Ph.D.
Department of Psychiatry
University of Michigan
Mental Health Research Institute
Ann Arbor, Michigan

JONATHAN L. COSTA, M.D.
Laboratory of Clinical Science
National Institutes of Mental Health
Bethesda, Md.

JOHN M. DAVIS, M.D.
Department of Psychiatry
University of Chicago
Chicago, Illinois

ALAN FRAZER, Ph.D.
Department of Pharmacology
University of Pennsylvania
    and
Veterans Administration Hospital
Philadelphia, Pa.

FREDERICK K. GOODWIN, M.D.
Clinical Research Unit
National Institutes of Mental Health
Bethesda, Md.

DAVID JANOWSKY, M.D.
Department of Psychiatry
University of California
San Diego, California

JAMES W. MAAS, M.D.
Department of Psychiatry
Yale University School of Medicine
New Haven, Conn.

JOSEPH MENDELS, M.D.
Department of Psychiatry
University of Pennsylvania
    and
Veterans Administration Hospital
Philadelphia, Pa.

DENNIS L. MURPHY, M.D.
Laboratory of Clinical Science
National Institutes of Mental Health
Bethesda, Md.

ROBERT M. POST, M.D.
Clinical Research Unit
National Institutes of Mental Health
Bethesda, Md.

EDWARD J. SACHAR, M.D.
Department of Psychiatry
Albert Einstein College of Medicine
Bronx, New York

MING T. TSUANG, M.D.
Department of Psychiatry
University of Iowa
Iowa City, Iowa

Contents

FOREWORD

In the mid 1950's I surveyed the systematic research on problems of depression and was appalled by the paucity of such studies. I thought then, as I do now, that these were among the great public health problems of our time. Yet, there was no agreement on the nature of the syndrome(s), nothing beyond intriguing impressions about precipitating factors, abundant speculation, but little checking on predisposing factors, hardly any clues to relevant biological processes and no effective conjunction between psychological and biological approaches. There was a tiny cadre of scientifically well trained investigators, and minimal support for new investigations. In short, a bleak picture of a bleak disorder.

Twenty years later the picture is very different, as the present publication indicates. This difference is in large measure attributable to the remarkably creative endeavors of the National Institute of Mental Health. This agency is at once a vital, dynamic research institute and a wise patron of the sciences. In its *intramural* program, it has vigorously pursued psychobiological research on the nature of mood disorders and their treatment. I had the privilege of fostering this effort in the late 1950's and early 1960's, and have watched its progress with intense interest ever since. The worldwide respect for these studies, and their stimulating impact throughout the field of psychiatry, attest to the quality of this work.

Beyond this *intramural* work, on a larger scale at many centers throughout the United States (and insofar as circumstances permitted, in other countries as well), the *extramural* program has stimulated and supported a very wide range of investigations on possible causes, mechanisms, consequences, treatment, and prevention of depression. Dr. Mendels has wisely selected a representative sample of this work for publication in the present volume.

The impetus for the new wave of research on the depressions came from several sources — the vast, poignant human suffering of these disorders; clinical observations suggesting possible improvements in treatment — both through psychopharmacology and psychotherapy; and basic science — especially biochemical approaches to brain function and animal behavioral studies providing the first useful experimental models of depression. In all of these spheres NIMH staff has been quick to detect promising lines of inquiry and encourage their pursuit; above all, NIMH has insisted on high standards of research method and intellectual discipline — leading to a dependability of evidence virtually unknown 20 years ago.

Today we have anti-depressant medication of reasonable efficacy; a remarkably effective treatment for manic-depressive disorders; useful techniques for intervening in time of personal crisis; a ferment of pharmacological and biochemical research on mood disorders that is almost certain to produce major advances in understanding and treatment in the next decade or two; insights into the interplay of heredity and envirofnment in exacerbating and relieving these disorders. In short, a new day is dawning in the lives of depressed persons, a day far brighter than those they have endured before. In large measure, these well-founded hopes exist because the National Institute of Mental Health has pursued its mission with such dedication, integrity and quality. Most of the advances reported in this fine volume are supported by NIMH. It is fitting that scientists, clinicians and patients take this occasion to express their appreciation.

David A. Hamburg, M.D.
Stanford University School of Medicine

The Psychobiology of Depression

Chapter 1

Clinical Biochemistry and the Choice of the Appropriate Medication for the Psychiatric Patient

JAMES W. MAAS

In the mid 1950's two accidental observations were made which were to have major implications for biological psychiatry. The first of these was that the treatment of hypertensive patients with reserpine in a small but significant number of patients produced a syndrome indistinguishable from clinical endogenous depressions, and the second was that the treatment of patients with tuberculosis with iproniazid led to euphoriant effects which seemed above and beyond that which might be expected from improved physical health. When pharmacological studies indicated that iproniazid, a monoamine oxidase inhibitor, increased the biogenic amines, norepinephrine (NE) and 5-hydroxytryptamine (5-HT), within the central nervous system and that reserpine depleted these amines, there began a series of investigations into the possible role which these amines might have in regulating mood and behavior. Over the next few years the principal investigations were in the area of basic neuropsychopharmacology, but as the interest in this area has grown, an increasing number of clinical studies as to the role which these amines might have in the affective disorders have been published, and these have been summarized in several reviews.[1-5] More

1

recently there has emerged basic neuropharmacological data suggesting a possible role for brain dopamine systems in schizophrenia,[6] and it is anticipated that the thrust of much of the work in the coming decade will be in the area of clinical research dealing with the causes and, if possible, neurobiological bases of the schizophrenias.

In the process of pursuing these lines of clinical investigation, an unanticipated but not unwelcome series of relationships between treatment response or clinical course and pretreatment biochemical variables has emerged. For the most part these relationships have been dealt with in terms of what inferences can be made regarding the biological basis of the illness under scrutiny, but it should not be overlooked that some of these findings may turn out to have pragmatic value for the practitioner whatever the ultimate interpretation as to the processes which underlie them. It would be presumptuous to suggest that any of the findings as of this writing are immediately applicable for use in a general hospital setting, but it seems worthwhile to list a few which have promise for the future.

1. There is evidence that some bipolar depressed patients may respond well to treatment with lithium, and the question arises as to how one might identify the appropriate bipolar, depressed patient for lithium treatment.[7] Mendels and Frazer[8] have developed a reasonably simple method by which such patients may be selected, i.e., they have found that high intracellular (red blood cell) lithium concentrations are associated with improvement in the depressive state, whereas low intracellular lithium concentrations are associated with a failure to improve. Although the original data was obtained from a relatively small number of patients, it should be noted that there was almost no crossover in values for the two groups. This finding, if replicated, could be of particular use for the clinician, as it is known that bipolar depressed patients have a higher incidence of hypomanic reactions when treated with tricyclic antidepressants than do unipolar depressed patients. Further, recent reports indicate that bipolar depressed patients should be maintained prophylactically on lithium rather than a tricyclic antidepressant.[9] Elizur et al.[10] have reported that intracellular (RBC) concentrations of lithium provide a sensitive index of clinical change and are predictive of toxicity. This finding should be of particular interest to the practitioner as plasma levels of lithium provide only a very rough guideline as to toxicity or clinical change.

2. Several groups of investigators have been interested in urinary levels of 3-methoxy-4-hydroxyphenylethylene glycol (MHPG), as this catecholamine metabolite may provide some index of central nervous system norepinephrine metabolism. Whatever the correctness or falsity of this inference,

empirical data from three different groups have led to the finding that those patients who excrete less than normal quantities of MHPG respond well to imipramine or desmethylimipramine, whereas those patients who have high or normal MHPG values have a favorable response to amitriptyline.[11-13] If one could use an assay of MHPG in urine, along with other historical and diagnostic material to select the appropriate antidepressant for a patient, one might save the depressed subject three to four weeks of unnecessary suffering.

3. It has been reported that if one gives patients *d*-amphetamine over a three-day period on a double blind basis one is able to predict those patients who will respond to treatment with imipramine or desmethylimipramine, i.e., those patients who respond to *d*-amphetamine are those who have a mood elevation when given this drug. Although it was not specifically tested, the inference also is that those patients who fail to respond to *d*-amphetamine with a mood elevation would be more likely to respond to amitriptyline.[14-15] This *d*-amphetamine test when coupled with the MHPG urinary assay offers the possibility as noted before of selecting the appropriate tricyclic antidepressant and saving the patient needless time on a drug which will be without benefit.

4. It has been noted that pretreatment cerebrospinal fluid (CSF) 5-hydroxyindoleacetic acids (5-HIAA), the major metabolic product of 5-hydroxytryptamine, when present in concentrations below 15 ng/ml, predict a failure to respond to nortriptyline, while CSF levels above 15 ng/ml predict a favorable response to this drug.[16]

5. Depressed patients who have minimal increases in CSF 5-HIAA after probenecid do not respond to amitriptyline and those depressed patients who respond therapeutically to 5-HTP have low increases in CSF 5-HIAA with probenecid administration.[17 18]

6. Schizophrenic patients who have poor premorbid socialization and marked affective blunting show relatively small increases in CSF HVA after probenecid and require more medication for an optimal response.[19]

This type of finding may be prototypical of much information which will be generated from future studies of the relationship of dopamine systems to schizophrenia, i.e., it is anticipated that relationships among a variety of pretreatment biochemical variables, clinical outcome, type, and quantity of medication will emerge.

Several of the findings noted above at this time are provocative leads and need replication under stringent conditions which are available only on research metabolic units. Assuming, however, that some of these findings are replicated, the question then arises as to what requirements must be satisfied before a given technique can be expected to find general acceptance as an aid to the selection of the appropriate medication for a particular psychiatric patient. First, the analytical techniques by which a given compound is assayed must be sufficiently sensitive and specific and, further, the performance of the assays both in terms of time and equipment needed, must be within the reach of at least large hospitals. For example, in the studies mentioned above, assays of lithium, urinary MHPG, and CSF HVA can be performed with conventional laboratory equipment, whereas the CSF MHPG and 5-HIAA assays, if at all possible, should be performed using a mass fragmentographic method. This requirement would probably preclude its use in hospitals which were not located in large biomedical complexes where such instrumentation might be available.

Given the availability of the necessary analytical techniques, a further and most difficult requirement must be met before any biochemical test can be routinely accepted, i.e., a pilot trial in a general hospital setting, not a research metabolic unit, is necessary. A few comments about this last seemingly obvious point are needed. Most of the biochemical parameters which may prove to have relevance to the choice of medication will in themselves be affected by previous medication. The degree to which this confounding variable will cloud the utility of the measure is unknown. On research metabolic units this problem is avoided by opting for adequate washout periods. Such lengthy times off medication are generally not feasible in the general hospital setting because of bed costs, and a variety of, at times irrational, pressures to begin some form of treatment as soon as possible. Finally, another problem is that funding is oftentimes possible for studies done on the research metabolic unit but is difficult to obtain for pilot investigations in the general hospital setting in that lack of a clearly demonstrated advantage to the patient prohibits the charge for the assay to the patient or through third party payments, and large-scale applied projects do not generally fare well with funding agencies. In this regard it would seem that psychiatry is much less adventurous and open to empirical testing than other medical specialties. To my knowledge there are no biochemical tests presently in use in psychiatric hospitals which have entered into, much less passed, this important phase of testing the applicability of a given biochemical test for the selection of treatment in the general psychiatric hospital. It is hoped and expected, however, that in the coming decade the situation will change.

No mention has been made here of the use of measures of blood levels of psychotrophic and antidepressant medications because the focus has been principally on the use of pretreatment biochemical variables and subsequent response, but nevertheless it is clear that this area of clinical psychopharmacology will also have a major part in our treatment of patients, and it is likely that the biochemical laboratories of future modern psychiatric hospitals will have facilities for both sophisticated assays of drug levels, as well as methods for assaying appropriate substances which may aid in the selection of appropriate medication.

References

1. Bunney, W.E., Jr., and Davis, J.M.: *Arch. Gen. Psychiat.*, 13:483, 1965.
2. Schildkraut, J.J.: *Amer. J. Psychiat.* 122:509, 1965.
3. Himwich, H.: *In* "Biochemistry, Schizophrenia, and Affective Illness" (H. Himwich, ed.), pp. 230-282. Williams and Wilkins, Baltimore (1970).
4. Maas, J.W.: *In* "Catecholamines and Behavior" (A. Friedhoff, ed.), Plenum Press, New York, in press.
5. van Praag, H.M., Korf, J., and Schut, D.: *Arch. Gen. Psychiat.* 28:827-831, 1973.
6. Maas, J.W. and Garver, D.: Linkages of basic neuro-pharmacology and clinical psychopharmacology, "American Handbook of Psychiatry," in press.
7. Mendels, J.: *In* "Lithium" (S. Gershon and B. Shopsin, Eds.), pp. 253-276. Plenum Press, New York, 1973.
8. Mendels, J., and Frazer, A.: *J. Psychiat. Res.* 10:9-18, 1973.
9. Prien, R.F., Klett, C.J., and Caffey, E.M.: *Arch. Gen. Psychiat.* 29:420-425, 1973.
10. Elizur, A., Shopsin, B., Gershon, S., and Elenberger, A.: *Clin. Pharmacal. Therap.* 13:947-952, 1972.
11. Maas, J.W., Fawcett, J., and Dekirmenjian, H.: *Arch. Gen. Psychiat.* 26:252-262, 1972.
12. Schildkraut, J.J.; *Amer. J. Psychiat.* 130:695, 1973.
13. Beckman, H., Jones, C.C., and Goodwin, F.K.: Presented at American Psychiatric Association meeting, Detroit, Michigan, May 1974.
14. Fawcett, J., and Siomopoulous, V.: *Arch. Gen. Psychiat.* 25:247, 1971.
15. Fawcett, J., Maas, J.W., and Dekirmenjian, H.: *Arch. Gen. Psychiat.* 26:246, 1972.
16. Asberg, M., Bertilsson, L., Tuck, D., Cronholm, B., and Sjoqvist, F.: *Clin. Pharmacal. Therap.* 14:227-286, 1973.
17. Bowers, M.: Personal communication.
18. van Praag, H.M., and Korf, J.: *Int. Pharmacopsychiat* 9:35-51, 1974.
19. Bowers, M.: *Arch. Gen. Psychiat.*, in press.

Chapter 2

Adrenergic Responses in Depression: Implications for a Receptor Defect*

ALAN FRAZER

Investigations of Biogenic Amines in Affective Illnesses

It has been hypothesized that affective illnesses are a reflection of some disturbance in biogenic amine function, [1-3] depression being associated with an absolute or relative deficiency of biogenic amines, such as norepinephrine (NE), dopamine (DA), or serotonin, at some important functional site in the brain. These theories have generated much research and it is clear that our understanding of monoamine systems in the brain has advanced considerably during the last ten years.

To evaluate these hypotheses, most investigators have studied amines or their metabolites in blood, urine, or lumbar fluid. The thrust of clinical studies concerned with biogenic amines in affective illness is indicated in Fig. 1.

At the top of the figure, a schema of a catecholaminergic neuron (presynaptic side) impinging on an effector cell (postsynaptic side) is indicated.

---

*Presented at 140th Annual Meeting of AAAS, San Francisco, California, February 27, 1974.

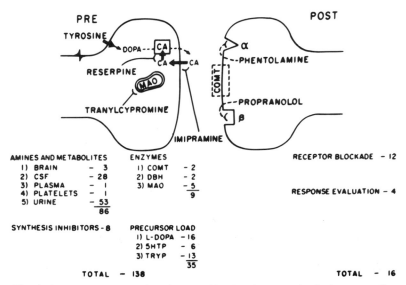

Fig. 1. Schematic representation of a catecholaminergic neuron impinging on an effector cell. Sites of action of drugs which can modify such synaptic transmission are indicated. At the bottom of the figure is listed the number of original clinical investigations concerned with some aspect of DA, NE, or serotonin function in mania or depression.

Also shown is the number of original clinical investigations involved with some aspect of monoamine function in affective illness; they have been separated, somewhat arbitrarily, into two types of investigations: (1) those concerned primarily with presynaptic events, and (2) those dealing with postsynaptic processes. The list is not comprehensive; for example, review articles are not included. Also, only one paper was selected when investigators published more than one study covering much the same data. Although the neuron presented is catecholaminergic, investigations of serotonin or its precursors or metabolites are listed as well.

It can be seen that there have been numerous investigations of the concentration of amines or their metabolites in several different body fluids or tissues. A total of 138 such "presynaptic" investigations are listed. In contrast, it is apparent that there have been relatively few investigations concerned with "postsynaptic" events. In fact, there appears to be only four investigations evaluating amine-induced or amine precursor responses in depression.

Prange et al.[4] examined the systolic blood pressure rise produced by an infusion of NE in 38 depressed patients. They reported that depressed patients upon improvement, regardless of the type of treatment, had a greater systolic blood pressure response to NE than when ill. As a nondepressed control group was not included in this study, it could not be concluded, as the authors themselves emphasize, that depressive illness *per se* is associated with decreased reactivity to NE.

More recently, Sachar and his colleagues[5][6] measured changes in plasma growth hormone (GH) and prolactin concentrations produced by administration of the catecholamine precursor, L-dihydroxyphenylalanine (L-dopa) to depressed patients and to normal controls. These studies are discussed later.

The investigations reported here represent, then, only the fourth study of amine-induced responses in patients with affective disorders.

The dearth of investigations measuring amine responses may be caused, in part, by the difficulty in quantifying central nervous system responses evoked by monoamines. Yet, it seems important to attempt to evaluate monoamine-induced responses in patients with affective disorders for several reasons:

(1) The type of information that is gained from studies of amines or their metabolite concentrations *per se* is somewhat limited. There need not necessarily be a correlation between amine concentrations and their functional effects. A rise in amine or metabolite concentrations or an increase in amine "turnover" can occur as a consequence of receptor blockade[7]; in this instance, though, the postsynaptic effect of the amine would be diminished.

(2) It might be possible by receptor activation evaluation to detect a malfunction that is not located primarily at the receptor but rather in a neuronal system with input into the receptor. The intensity of an effect in an end organ is related both to the amount of neurotransmitter released and to the responsiveness of the postsynaptic receptor to its agonist. It appears that there is an interrelationship between these parameters. Deguchi and Axelrod[8] have shown recently, using the rat pineal gland, that end organ responsiveness to adrenergic agonists depends on the amount of prior exposure of its adrenergic receptor to catecholamines. In situations with excessive previous exposure to catecholamines, the subsequent response to catecholamines was diminished (i.e., there is subsensitivity). The converse effect, or supersensitivity, was observed when there was reduced prior exposure to catecholamines. In other words, a defect in presynaptic neurotransmitter synthesis or release can cause an alteration in postsynaptic receptor sensitivity. This alteration should be detectable using direct-acting agents. This alteration in receptor sensitivity does complicate interpretation of response data, insofar as it may not give information regarding the primary site of the lesion. However, it enhances the utility of the strategy

since an abnormality existing at one of several different sites could be detected by measuring the end response.

It had been suggested some years ago[2] that one possible way to produce an amine deficiency would be by altered postsynaptic receptor sensitivity. More recently, Ashcroft and his colleagues[9] have amplified on this idea of a change in aminergic receptor sensitivity in depression. Adequate testing of this has not yet been conducted.

We decided, therefore, to measure catecholaminergic responses in depressed patients and in nondepressed control subjects. Two separate studies were done. In one investigation, a biochemical response was measured in platelets *in vitro* to a direct acting adrenergic agonist. In the second investigation, a neuroendocrine response was measured *in vivo* both to a direct acting agonist and to an indirect acting agent.

Before presenting the results of these studies, one point deserves emphasis. While we are interested in evaluating the interaction of the agonist with the receptor, it should be noted that what is being measured is the response produced as a result of receptor activation. Receptors may be defined anatomically as membrane components that interact transiently with an appropriate agonist to elicit a specific change of state — or response — of the tissue. However, receptors are usually defined operationally in terms of the cellular responses which they initiate. This is what has been done in the present investigations. However, there may be numerous steps between the activation of the receptor and the measured response (Fig. 2), any one of which may not be functioning properly. Thus, an abnormal response to an agonist need not necessarily imply abnormal receptor sensitivity. With this in mind, it seemed appropriate to measure a response that most nearly approximates the response of the receptor.

Platelet Adenylate Cyclase Responses in Depressed Patients

To this end, the response measured in the first study to be presented was the NE-induced decrease in radioactive adenosine $3'$, $5'$ -monophosphate (cyclic AMP) in platelets. This biochemical response to NE was chosen as it appears that adrenergic receptors are closely related to, and may even be a

$$\text{AGONIST} \longrightarrow \text{RECEPTOR} \longrightarrow N_1, N_2, \cdots N_n \longrightarrow \text{RESPONSE}$$

Fig. 2. Schematic representation of the interaction of an agonist with its receptor leading through numerous intermediate steps to the observed response.

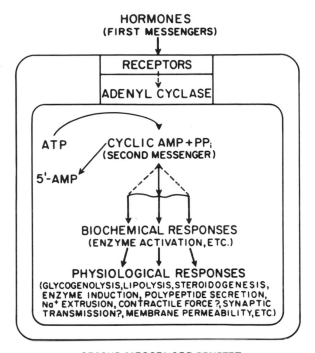

SECOND MESSENGER CONCEPT

Fig. 3. Schematic representation of the "second messenger" concept of Sutherland and Rall.

part of, adenylate cyclase,[10] the enzyme which catalyzes the conversion of adenosine triphosphate (ATP) to cyclic AMP[11].

A diagrammatic representation of the "second messenger" hypothesis of Sutherland and Rall[11] is show in Fig. 3. These investigators suggested that a variety of hormones, including the catecholamines, act as "first messengers" to deliver information to their target cells. These hormones cause activation of adenylate cyclase, located in the plasma membrane of the cell, such that there is an increase in the intracellular concentration of cyclic AMP. The cyclic necleotide, functioning as a "second messenger," then catalyzes reactions which ultimately result in the final response produced by the hormone.

The response of platelet adenylate cyclase to prostaglandin E_1 (PGE₁) and to NE in 11 male depressed patients who were hospitalized on a clinical research ward was studied. Some of the characteristics of these patients are noted in Table I. They all had a syndrome of depression, without any

TABLE I

Clinical Characteristics of the Depressed Patients Studied

Patient	Diagnosis	Age	Depression Rating Scale Hamilton	Beck
HI	Unipolar depression	48	18	15
BO	Unipolar depression	40	26	19
MI	Unipolar depression	56	27	27
DO	Unipolar depression	63	35	41
MC	Bipolar depression	44	23	–
DU	Bipolar depression	63	28	41
OR	Bipolar depression	54	36	35
CO	Depressive neurosis	42	10	12
BE	Depressive neurosis	58	16	10
GR	Depressive neurosis	30	20	30
OD	Depressive neurosis	53	28	32
	Mean	50	24	26
	SEM	3	2	4

history or current clinical features suggestive of any other psychiatric disorder: schizophrenia, drug abuse, alcoholism, or organic brain syndrome. The severity of the depression was characterized both on the Hamilton Rating Scale[12] and on the Beck Depression Inventory.[13] The depressed patients were subdivided into several categories: Three patients were characterized as being bipolar depressives, i.e., recurrent depressive episodes with a history of a clear-cut manic or hypomanic episode in the past; four patients as unipolar depressive, i.e., recurrent depressive episodes without a history of mania or hypomania; and four patients as having a depressive neurosis — these were a group of patients with a history of mild-moderate chronic symptomatology usually associated with an "inadequate" personality.

Eight healthy male control subjects were also studied. Their mean age of 40 years is somewhat lower than the average age of the patient population, but not significantly so. All patients and subjects were drug-free for at least two weeks prior to evaluation of platelet adenylate cyclase activity.

Platelet adenylate cyclase was estimated by incubation of platelet rich plasma obtained from each subject with ³H-adenine. Adenine is taken up by tissues and incorporated into adenine nucleotides,[14] [15] so that it is possible, using this method, to label a portion of the endogenous pool of platelet ATP. The labeled ATP is then converted to labeled cyclic AMP, and the rate of this conversion can be altered by compounds such as PGE₁ or NE. The labeled cyclic AMP produced was isolated and purified by the method of Krishna *et al.*[16]

For initial statistical analysis of the data obtained, comparisons were made by analysis of variance[17] between the bipolar and the unipolar patients and also between the patients with depressive neurosis and the other seven patients. No difference in the response to either PGE₁ or to NE between the different subgroups was noted. Also, no significant correlations in the response to either PGE₁ or to NE with either age or the severity of the depression was noted. Therefore, for purposes of this report, the patients were combined into one group of 11 for comparison with the group of eight control subjects.

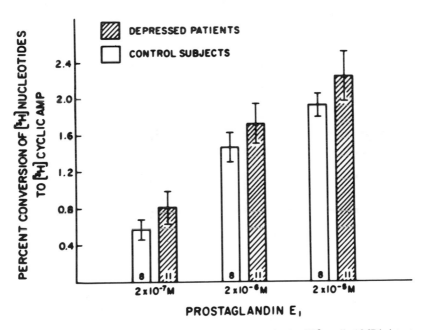

Fig. 4. Stimulatory effect of PGE₁ *in vitro* on the net synthesis of H³-cyclic AMP in intact platelets obtained from depressed patients and control subjects. The bars and brackets represent the means and SEM, respectively; the number of subjects is indicated in each bar.

The basal percent conversion of ^{3}H-nucleotides to ^{3}H-cyclic AMP in the control subjects (0.10%) was not significantly different from that measured in the 11 depressed patients (0.09%; $p > 0.9$).

The stimulation of radioactive cyclic AMP net synthesis by PGE$_1$ in the control subjects and in the depressed patients is shown in Fig. 4.

PGE$_1$ caused a dose-dependent increase in the accumulation of ^{3}H-cyclic AMP in both the control subjects and in the depressed patients. No difference in the magnitude of this stimulation was observed between the two subject populations.

We next evaluated the inhibition produced by NE on the maximal stimulatory response produced by PGE$_1$, which in our system occurred at a concentration of $2 \times 10^{-5} M$. NE produced a dose-dependent reduction in the stimulation caused by PGE$_1$, both in the control and depressed patients

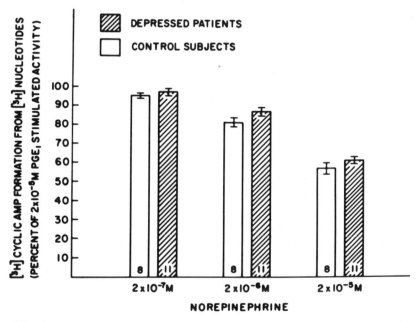

Fig. 5. Inhibitory effect of NE *in vitro* on 2×10^{-5} PGE$_1$-stimulated H^3-cyclic AMP formation in intact platelets obtained from depressed patients and control subjects. The response to PGE$_1$ has been taken as 100%. In control subjects, the net synthesis of ^{3}H-cyclic AMP was 1.92 ± 0.13% in the presence of PGE$_1$, whereas it was 2.24 ± 0.27% in the depressed patients ($p \rangle 0.3$). This represents, approximately, a twentyfold stimulation over basal values. The bars and brackets represent the means and SEM, respectively; the number of subjects is indicated in each bar.

(Fig. 5). It is apparent that there is no significant difference in the magnitude of this effect between the two subject populations.

It deserves to be emphasized that the data presented were obtained using male patients. The sparse data available which have been interpreted in favor of a receptor abnormality in depression have, in the main, been obtained in female patients. In this regard, it is interesting that while we were conducting these studies, Murphy and his colleagues at NIMH were also investigating the effect of NE on platelet ^{3}H-cyclic AMP net synthesis.[18] These investigators studied female patients as well as male depressives and noted no difference in the response elicited as a function of sex. Also, NE reduced PGE$_1$-induced stimulation of ^{3}H-cyclic AMP to the same extent (about 60%) in nine unipolar depressed patients, in eight bipolar depressed patients, and in 11 controls.

These two studies, then, are in very good agreement. In a discipline where inability to confirm is often the rule rather than the exception, this point seems worth emphasizing.

Conclusions

Several factors must be borne in mind when evaluating these results, which are clearly negative; that is, the stimulation of ^{3}H-cyclic AMP production by PGE$_1$ and the reduction in enzyme activity caused by NE were the same in the depressed patients and in the control subjects. The first factor to consider is that while the platelet obviously does not provide a measure of neuronal sensitivity, the system used does have several advantages: (1) Platelets are readily obtainable; (2) they are a homogenous cell population; and most importantly, (3) they provide an *in vitro* system for measuring response. When response is measured *in vitro*, factors such as drug absorption, distribution, elimination, and metabolism which can alter the final response obtained *in vivo* are controlled. Nevertheless, as with many peripheral measures, it is difficult to extrapolate from these results to the brain as there are differences between the response of platelet adenylate cyclase and brain adenylate cyclase to NE. Catecholamines increase brain cyclic AMP concentrations,[19][20] while we measured the ability of NE to decrease platelet adenylate cyclase activity stimulated by PGE$_1$. Further, in brain, the increase in cyclic AMP produced by catecholamines is due primarily to β-adrenergic receptors,[21-23] although α-receptors are involved as well.[25][25] In contrast to this, reduction of the PGE$_1$ response caused by NE platelets is mediated by α-adrenergic receptors.[26-28] Thus, some decrease in the central response of adenylate cyclase to NE may exist in depression which would not have been detected by the study of the platelet system. On the other hand, it can be said that the results obtained make it unlikely that there is a generalized decrease in peripheral α-adrenergic responsiveness in depressed male or female patients.

Growth Hormone Release in Depressed and Manic Patients

In view of the negative results obtained in the preceding *in vitro* study of a peripheral adrenergic response, it seemed important to attempt to evaluate, in depressed patients, a central response mediated by catecholamines. To do this, we chose to measure a neuroendocrine response in which catecholamines are known to be involved, namely the release of growth hormone (GH).

There is general agreement that the secretion of the six major tropic hormones of the anterior lobe of the pitutary is under central nervous system (CNS) control. Such control originates, in particular, from that portion of the hypothalamus termed the hypophysiotropic area,[29] an area rich in different monoamine systems.[30] By modifying the activity of these monoamine systems, it is possible to elicit the release of the anterior pitutary hormones so that their concentrations in blood are altered. However, as Wurtman[31] has noted, there are about a half-dozen different loci at which monoamines might act to alter release of hormones from the anterior lobe of the pituitary, so that interpretation of such studies must be cautious. Further caution must be exercised as the drugs are administered *in vivo,* so that factors such as differing rates of drug absorption, metabolism, or excretion could conceivably account for any differences in response observed. One tries to minimize the importance of such factors in different ways, for example, by the selection of a proper control group. Obviously, though, there is a limit to which this can be done.

While it is clear that catecholamines are involved in the regulation of GH release in mammals (see 32 and 33), the relative importance of NE and of DA in eliciting such release is controversial.[34-39] It appears that both DA and NE are involved in GH release and act, perhaps, at different anatomical sites. As dopaminergic neurons are found in high density at the site of release of growth hormone-releasing factor, it was decided to use the dopamine receptor-stimulating agent apomorphine (APO) to elicit GH release. The effect of the catecholamine precursor, L-dihydroxphenylalanine (L-dopa), in eliciting GH release was investigated as well. Sachar *et al.*[5] [6]

have already published reports on the ability of L-dopa to stimulate GH release in depressed patients, but we believe we are the first to evaluate the effectiveness of APO in causing such release in depressed patients. While this work was in progress, two other groups of investigators showed that APO elicited GH release in normal controls.[40-42]

Two important features of apomorphine's mechanism of action deserve emphasis:

(1) Practically all available evidence suggests that APO can stimulate DA receptors directly. Stored or newly synthesized DA does not appear to be needed for its effects to be observed,[43-48] nor does APO change the steady-state concentration of brain NE, DA, or serotonin.[49 50]

(2) APO appears to act specifically on dopamine receptors. For example, it has little demonstrable effect on a NE-mediated response in the spinal cord.[44] Furthermore, APO does not alter the "turnover" of brain NE, whereas the synthesis of DA is reduced.[44 49 51] Reduction of amine "turnover" is observed in response to amine receptor stimulants.

Thus, it seems reasonable to conclude that the GH response elicited by apomorphine is due to stimulation of central dopaminergic receptors, probably at the level of the external layer of the median eminence.

With L-dopa, the situation is somewhat more complicated as this agent is a precursor of both DA and NE and can alter responses thought to be mediated by either monoamine.[44 52] In addition, L-dopa can have effects on other biogenic amine systems, such as serotonergic ones (see 53). For these reasons, and the fact that it is an indirectly acting agent, considerable caution must be exercised when interpreting results obtained with this drug. However, it is clear that L-dopa can produce GH release in man[54-56] and, as mentioned, Sachar and his colleagues have evaluated the stimulatory effect of this agent on GH release in depressed patients.[5 6]

As in the previous study, only male subjects were used for this investigation of GH release. All patients and control subjects were drug-free for at least ten days prior to testing. The test was started between 8:00 and 9:00 AM after an overnight fast. At 20-minute intervals, about 5 ml of blood was obtained from a cannula inserted into the antecubital vein over a total period of 210 minutes. The drug was always given immediately after the third blood drawing. In each subject, then, three base line values were obtained before GH release was stimulated. The data obtained for a test was not used if any of the three base line values exceeded 3 ng/ml, since there may be feed-back regulation of GH release.[57 58] This occurred several times, particularly in some younger control subjects, and may reflect a stress response.[59-61]

TABLE II

Growth Hormone (HGH) Response to Apomorphine in "Younger" and in "Older" Control Populations

Control Group	N	Age (years)	Weight (pounds)	HGH (ng/ml)
Younger	9	21 ± 1 [a] (18-28) [b]	166 ± 9 (122-205)	21 ± 3 (12-31)
Older	9	47 ± 3 (36-64)	165 ± 7 (133-195)	11 ± 1 (7-14)
P	-	<.001	NS	<.005

[a] $\bar{X}$ ± SEM
[b] range of values

The growth hormone concentration in the plasma was measured by radioimmuonassay, using ^{125}I-HGH.[62]

In a preliminary study, it was found that 250 mg L-dopa, given orally, produced an equivalent peak GH response to that observed after 500 mg of the amino acid. Since we are concerned with the sensitivity of the system to amines, rather than its maximum capacity, we reasoned that the lower dose of L-dopa would be better to use to study GH release in the patients.

In a second preliminary study, we evaluated the effect of age on the GH response elicited by APO (Table II). Apomorphine (0.75 mg, injected subcutaneously) elicited a mean peak GH response in younger subjects almost twice as high as that observed in older subjects. This was not due to a weight difference between the subject populations.

This age-dependent effect of APO in eliciting GH release is similar to that reported by Sachar *et al.*[5] on GH release caused by 500 mg L-dopa. Among the possible explanations for this phenomenon, it seems reasonable to suggest that this diminished GH response to APO with increasing age reflects a reduced sensitivity of DA receptors to stimulation. While further research is needed to investigate this idea, it seems to us to be of sufficient importance to merit additional study. For example, could this be, in part, an explanation for the higher spontaneous secretory rate of GH seen in young adults as compared with older subjects?[63]

To evaluate the adequacy of the GH response in the patients, it was decided that the GH concentration measured after APO should be at least 7 ng/ml; this value is two standard deviations lower than the mean response seen in our older control subjects.[64] Values in the patients that did not reach this concentration are indicated as being an inadequate response. The same value (7 ng/ml) was used as the adequate response to L-dopa. The GH response results obtained in patients subdivided according to the criteria mentioned previously are shown in Tables III–IV. When both tests, APO and L-dopa, are indicated for the same patient, they were done within three days of each other.

Only one of seven unipolar depressed patients had an inadequate GH response to APO, and one of four such patients had a poor response to L-dopa (Table III). This latter patient had an adequate response to APO.

The results obtained in bipolar male patients, either depressed or hypomanic, are summarized in Table IV. Among the bipolar depressed patients, only one patient had an inadequate response, and this was both to APO and to L-dopa. The hypomanic patients show an interesting trend. All three of these patients had an adequate response to APO, whereas two of these patients exhibited a diminished response to L-dopa.

Among patients diagnosed as having a depressive neurosis, seven received L-dopa; of these, three had an inadequate response (Table V). Of five such patients receiving APO, two had a diminished response. One patient had an inadequate response to both APO and to L-dopa, whereas two patients had a poor response to L-dopa but not to APO. In this group, there was one patient (CO) who had a sufficient response to L-dopa but not to APO.

TABLE III

Growth Hormone Response to Apomorphine (0.75 mg, s.c.) or to L-Dopa (250 mg, p.o.)

Unipolar Depression

Patient	BDI[a]	HRS[b]	Growth Hormone (ng/ml) APO	L-DOPA
DO	41	35	9	3*
SP	30	23	19	–
HU	29	25	7	–
MI	27	18	15	10
GR	19	30	–	16
HA	19	7	22	8
LO	18	–	3*	–
SL	14	13	7	–

[a]Beck Depression Inventory
[b]Hamilton Rating Scale
*inadequate response

TABLE IV

Growth Hormone Response to Apomorphine (0.75 mg, s.c.) or to L-Dopa (250 mg, p.o.)

Patients	BDI	HRS	APO	L-DOPA
A) Bipolar-Depressed				
DU	41	28	7	10
ST	38	38	-	20
OR	35	36	4*	6*
MA	22	16	9	-
WI	15	11	25	-
B) Bipolar-Hypomanic				
LE	-	-	7	8
SO	-	-	21	3*
GO	-	-	19	1*

* inadequate response

TABLE V

Growth Hormone Response to Apomorphine (0.75 mg, s.c.) or to L-Dopa (250 mg, p.o.)

Depressive Reaction			Growth Hormone (ng/ml)	
Patient	BDI	HRS	APO	L-DOPA
AR	41	-	-	10
GR	30	20	7	1*
BO	22	22	-	22
BE	17	7	8	34
HI	13	18	8	4*
CO	12	-	5*	10
BO	7	-	4*	1*

*inadequate response

To summarize these data: 19 patients were given APO and, of these, four (or 21%) had an inadequate GH response. Among the diagnostic subgroups, these inadequate responses occurred in one of seven patients with unipolar depression; one of four bipolar depressives; none of three hypomanics; and two of five patients with a depressive neurosis.

Of 17 patients given L-dopa, seven (or 41%) had an inadequate response. The inadequate responses to L-dopa were distributed across the diagnostic subgroups as follows: one of four patients with unipolar depression; one of three bipolar depressives; two of three hypomanics; and three of seven patients with a depressive neurosis.

When L-dopa and APO were administered to the same patient, more inadequate GH responses were observed with L-dopa as compared to APO (Table VI). Of 13 patients given both drugs, seven had an inadequate response to L-dopa, whereas just three patients had a poor response to APO. Two patients showed a poor response to both drugs and one patient had a poor response to APO but an adequate response to L-dopa. However, five of the patients with an inadequate response to L-dopa exhibited a sufficient response to APO.

TABLE VI

Growth Hormone Response to Apomorphine (0.75 mg, s.c.) or to L-Dopa (250 mg, p.o.) in Depressed Patients

| Patient | Growth Hormone (ng/ml) | |
	Apomorphine	L-Dopa
HA (54)	22	8
DO (63)	9	3*
MI (56)	15	10
DU (56)	7	10
OR (54)	4*	6*
LE (54)	7	8
SO (47)	21	3*
GO (30)	19	1*
CO (42)	5*	10
BE (58)	8	34
HI (48)	8	4*
GR (30)	7	1*
BO (40)	4*	1*

*inadequate response

Conclusions

Since the number of patients studied is small, especially when placed into different diagnostic subclasses, it would be premature to make any definitive conclusions from the data obtained in this latter study. A few observations may be in order, however. First, the number of patients showing an inadequate GH response to the direct acting agent, APO, is relatively small, about 20% of those studied. Also, there did not seem to be a tendency for these inadequate responses to occur in any specific diagnostic subgroup. If there were a receptor mediated, or perhaps more properly some GH response abnormality in depression, this might be expected to occur predominantly in the bipolar depressives, according to the schema of Ashcroft and his colleagues.[9] This was not the case.

It might appear that there were a reasonable percentage of inadequate responses to L-dopa — about 40% of the patients tested had an inadequate response. Unfortunately, we do not have, as yet, our own control group for direct comparison. The data of Sachar and his co-workers[6] on the GH response elicited by 500 mg L-dopa indicates that 33% of their male control subjects (over 45 years of age) had an inadequate response by our criterion. This value is similar to that which we found in our depressed patients, which leads us to believe that the GH response to L-dopa in our male depressed patients was not that different from normal. Certainly, we did not observe the high percentage of inadequate responses in our unipolar patients that was noted by Sachar et al.,[6] in their male unipolar depressive population. The reason for this difference is unclear.

Our results do suggest a trend for more inadequate responses to L-dopa than to APO. Five of 13 patients tested both with APO and L-dopa, showed an inadequate response to the indirectly acting agent but not to APO. In contrast, only one patient showed a poor response to APO and an adequate response to L-dopa. This trend tended to be most obvious in the hypomanic patients. We think additional research of this trend is warranted before speculation as to its cause would be meaningful.

In summary, then, we have measured two responses produced by stimulation of amine receptors—the first being a peripheral αadrenergic response elicited by NE. The decrease in cyclic AMP was measured *in vitro* in platelets obtained from male depressed patients. The results obtained provide no evidence that the response elicited was abnormal in depressives.

In the second study, a neuroendocrine response induced *in vivo* by a single dose of the direct-acting dopamine receptor-stimulating agent apomorphine was assessed in depressive and in hypomanic patients. The results obtained to date with this system do not suggest any consistent abnormality in patients with affective illnesses. These data, also, do not support the idea of a generalized amine receptor or response abnormality in depression.

Negative data, however, must be interpreted cautiously. These results certainly do not eliminate the possibility of an amine receptor defect in affective diseases. It may be that the receptors mediating GH release are functioning normally in depressives, whereas amine receptors activating other responses (e.g., pleasure, anger, motor activity) are not. Attention must be focused on responses mediated by limbic system activation, for example. To do this, clearer understanding of the ways in which amines modify such responses are needed, as are improved techniques to quantify such behaviors in man.

In addition, examination should be made of responses elicited by endogenously released amines (caused, for example, by physiological and psychological stresses and stimuli) as opposed to those caused by exogenous agonists. If, indeed, there is an abnormality of amine systems in depression, proper evaluation must be made of the functional consequences of such abnormalities. This can only be done, ultimately, by evaluating the responses produced by activation of these systems. Further research, then, should be directed to this end.

Acknowledgments

The encouragement, advice, and assistance of the following investigators throughout the course of these investigations is gratefully acknowledged: Drs. Bernard J. Carroll, Iradj Maany, Joe Mendels, Ghanshyam Pandey, and Yao-Chun Wang. These investigations were supported in part by research funds from the Veterans Administration.

References

1. Prange, A.J., Jr: The pharmacology and biochemistry of depression. *Dis. Nerv. System.* 25:217–221, 1964.
2. Schildkraut, J.J.: The catecholamine hypothesis of affective disorders: A review of supporting evidence. *Amer. J. Psychiat.* 122:509–522, 1965.
3. Coppen, A: The biochemistry of affective disorders. *Brit. J. Psychiat.* 113:1237–1264, 1967.
4. Prange, A.J., Jr., McCurdy, R.L., and Cochrane, C.M.: The systolic blood pressure response of depressed patients to infused norepinephrine. *J. Psychiat. Res.* 5:1-13, 1967.
5. Sachar, E.J., Mushrush, G., Perlow, M. *et al.*: Growth hormone responses to L-dopa in depressed patients. *Science.* 178:1304–1305, 1972.

6.   Sachar, E.J., Frantz, A.G., Altman, W., *et al.:* Growth hormone and prolactin in unipolar and bipolar depressed patients: Responses to hypoglycemia and L-dopa. *Amer. J. Psychiat.* 130:1362–1367, 1973.

7.   Anden, N-E., Butcher, S.G., Corrodi, H., *et al.:* Receptor activity and turnover of dopamine and noradrenaline after neuroleptics. *Europ. J. Pharmacol.* 11:303-314, 1970.

8.   Deguchi, T., and Axelrod, J.: Supersensitivity and subsensitivity of the β-adrenergic receptor in pineal gland regulated by catecholamine transmitter. *Proc. Nat. Acad Sci. U.S.A.* 70:2411-2414, 1973.

9.   Ashcroft, G.W., Eccleston, D., Murray, L.G., *et al.:* Modified amine hypothesis for the aetiology of affective illness. *Lancet* ii: 573–577, 1972.

10.   Robinson, G.A., Butcher, R.W., and Sutherland, E.W.: On the relation of hormone receptors to adenyl cyclase, *in* ''Fundamental Concepts in Drug–Receptor Interactions'' (J.F. Danielli, J.F. Moran, and D.J. Triggle, Eds.), pp. 59-81, Academic Press, New York (1969).

11.   Sutherland, E.W., and Rall, T.W.: The relation of adenosine-3', 5'-phosphate and phosphorylase to the actions of catecholamines and other hormones. *Pharmacol. Rev.* 12:265-299, 1960.

12.   Hamilton, M.: A rating scale for depression. *J. Neurol. Neurosurg. Psychiat.* 23:56–62, 1960.

13.   Beck, A.T., Ward, C.H., Mendelson, M., *et al.:* An inventory for measuring depression. *Arch. Gen. Psychiat.* 4:561–571, 1961.

14.   Kuo, J.F., and DeRenzo, E.C.: A comparison of the effects of lipolytic and antilipolytic agents on adenosine 3',5'-monophosphate levels in adipose cells as determined by prior labelling with adenine-8[14] *C. J. Biol. Chem.* 244:2252-2260, 1969.

15.   Shimizu, H., Daly, J.W., and Creveling, C.R.: A radioisotopic method for measuring the formation of adenosine 3',5'-monophosphate in incubated slices of brain. *J. Neurochem.* 16:1609–1619, 1969.

16.   Krishna, G., Weiss, B., and Brodie, B.B.: A simple, sensitive method for the assay of adenyl cyclase. *J. Pharmacol. Exp. Therap.* 163:379–385, 1968.

17.   Lindquist, E.F.: ''Design and Analysis,'' pp.266–273; Houghton Mifflin Co., Boston (1956).

18.   Murphy, D.L., Donnelly, C., and Moskowitz, J.: Catecholamine receptor function in depressed patients. *Amer. J. Psychiat.*; in press.

19.   Kakiuchi, S., and Rall, T.W.: The influence of chemical agents on the accumulation of adenosine 3',5'-phosphate in slices of rabbit cerebellum. *Mol. Pharmacol.* 4:367–378, 1968a.

20.   Burkard, W.P.: Catecholamine induced increase of cyclic adenosine 3',5'-monophosphate in rat brain *in vivo. J. Neurochem.* 19:2615–2619, 1972.

21.   Kakiuchi, S., and Rall, T.W.: Studies on adenosine 3',5'-phosphate in rabbit cerebral cortex. *Mol. Pharmacol.* 4:379–388, 1968b.

22.   Shimizu, H., Tanaka, S., Suzuki, T., *et al.:* The response of human cerebrum adenyl cyclase to biogenic amines. *J. Neurochem.* 18:1157–1161, 1971.

23.   Kodama, T., Matsukado, Y. and Shimizu, H.: The cyclic AMP system of human brain. *Brain Res.* 50:135–146, 1973.

24.   Chasin, M., Rivikin, I., Mamrak, F., *et al.:* α- and β-adrenergic receptors as mediators of accumulation of cyclic adenosine 3',5'–monophosphate in specific areas of guinea pig brain. *J. Biol. Chem.* 246:3037–3041, 1971.

25.   Perkins, J.P., and Moore, M.M.: Characterization of the adrenergic receptors mediating a rise in cyclic 3',5'-adenosine monophosphate in rat cerebral cortex. *J. Pharm. Exper. Ther.* 185:371–378, 1973.

26. Robison, G.A., Arnold, A., and Hartman, R.C.: Divergent effects of epinephrine and prostaglandin E₁ on the level of cyclic AMP in human blood platelets. *Pharm. Res. Commun.* 1:325–332, 1969.

27. Marquis, N.R.; Becker, J.A., and Vigdahl, R.L.: Platelet aggregation. 3. An epinephrine induced decrease in cyclic AMP synthesis. *Biochem. Biophys. Res. Commun.* 39:783–789, 1970.

28. Wang, Y.-C., Pandey, G.N., Mendels, J., *et al.:* The effect of lithium on prostaglandin E₁-stimulated adenylate cyclase activity of human platelets. *Biochem. Pharmacol.* 23:845–855, 1974.

29. Halasz, B., Pupp, L., and Uhlarik, S.: Hypophysiotrophic area in the hypothalamus. *J. Endocrinol.* 25:147–154, 1962.

30. Jansson, G., Fuxe, K., and Hokfelt, T.: On the catecholamine innervation of the hypothalamus with special reference to the median eminence. *Brain Res* 40:271–281, 1972.

31. Wurtman, R.J.: Brain monoamines and endocrine function. *Neurosci. Res. Prog. Bull.* 9:172–297, 1971.

32. Martin, J.B.: Neural regulation of growth hormone secretion. *New Engl. J. Med.* 288:1384–1393, 1973.

33. Müller, E.E.: Nervous control of growth hormone secretion. *Neuroendocrinology* 11:338–369, 1973.

34. Müller, E.E., DalPra, P., and Pecile, A.: Influence of brain neurohumors injected into lateral ventricles of the rat on growth hormone release. *Endocrinology* 83:893–896, 1968.

35. Fuxe, K., and Hökfelt, T.: Catecholamines in the hypothalamus and the pituitary gland *in* "Frontiers in Neuroendocrinology" (W.F. Ganong and L. Martini, Eds.), pp.47-96. Oxford Univ. Press, New York (1969).

36. Müller, E.E., Pecile, A., Felici, M., *et al.:* Norepinephrine and dopamine injection into lateral brain ventrical of the rat and growth hormone-releasing activity in the hypothalamus and plasma. *Endocrinology* 86:1376–1382, 1970.

37. Clementi, F., Ceccarelli, B., Cerati, E., *et al.:* Subcellular localization of neurotransmittors and releasing factors in the rat median eminence. *J. Endocrinol.* 48:205–213, 1970.

38. Björkland, A., Falck, B., Hromek, F., *et al.:* Identification and terminal distribution of the tubero-hypophyseal monoamine fibre systems in the rat by means of stereotaxic and microspectrofluorimetric techniques. *Brain Res.* 17:1–23, 1970.

39. Toivola, P.T.K., and Gale, C.C.: Central adrenergic regulation of growth-hormone secretion in baboons. *Intern. J. Neurosci.* 4:53–63, 1972.

40. Lal, S., Sourkes, T.S., Friesen, H.G.: Effect of apomorphine on human-growth-hormone secretion. *Lancet* ii:661, 1972.

41. Brown, W.A., Van Woert, M.H., and Ambani, L.M.: Effect of apomorphine on growth hormone release in humans. *J. Clin. Endocrinol.* 37:463–465, 1973.

42. Lal, S., DeLaVega, C.E., Sourkes, T.L., *et al.:* Effect of apomorphine on growth hormone, prolactin, luteinizing hormone and follicle-stimulating hormone levels in human serum. *J. Clin. Endocrinol. Metab.* 37:719–724, 1973.

43. Ernst, A.M.: Mode of action of apomorphine and dexamphetamine on gnawing compulsion in rats. *Psychopharmacologia* 10:316–323, 1967.

44. Anden, N.E., Rubenson, A., Fuxe, K., *et al.:* Evidence for dopamine receptor stimulation by apomorphine. *J. Pharm. Pharmacol.* 19:627–629, 1967.

45. Ungerstedt, U., Butcher, L.L., Butcher, S.G., *et al.:* Direct chemical stimulation of dopaminergic mechanisms in the neostriatum of the rat. *Brain Res.* 14:461–471, 1969.

46. Kebabian, J.W., Petzold, G.L. and Greengard, P.: Dopamine-sensitive adenylate cyc-

lase in caudate necleus of rat brain, and its similarity to the "dopamine receptor." *Proc. Nat. Aca. Sci. U.S.* 69:2145–2149, 1972.

47. Nymark, M.: Apomorphine provoked stereotype in the dog. *Psychopharmacologia* 26:361–368, 1972.

48. Bunney, B.S., Aghajanian, G.K., and Roth, R.H.: Comparison of effects of L-dopa, amphetamine and apomorphine on firing rate of rat dopaminergic neurones. *Nature (New Biol)* 245:123–125, 1973.

49. Butcher, L.L., and Anden, N.E.: Effects of apomorphine and amphetamine on schedule-controlled behavior: Reversal of tetrabenazine suppression and dopaminergic correlates. *Eur. J. Pharmacol.* 6:255–264, 1969.

50. Tagliamonte, A., Tagliamonte, P., Perez-Cruet, J., *et al.*: Effect of psychotropic drugs on tryptophan concentration in the rat brain. *J. Pharmacol. Exp. Therap.* 177:475–480, 1971.

51. Roos, B.E.: Decrease in homovanillic acid as evidence for dopamine receptor stimulation by apomorphine in the neostriatum of the rat. *J. Pharm. Pharmacol.* 21:263–264, 1969.

52. Ernst. A.M.: Relation between the action of dopamine and apomorphine and their O-methylated derivatives upon the CNS. *Psychopharmacologia* 7:391–399, 1965.

53. Wurtman, R.J., and Romero, J.A.: Effects of levodopa on nondopaminergic brain neurons. *Neurology* 22:72–81, 1972.

54. Boyd, III, A.E., Lebovitz, H.E., and Pfeiffer, J.B.: Stimulation of human growth hormone secretion by L-dopa. *New Engl. J. Med.* 283:1425–1429, 1970.

55. Kansal, P.C., Buse, J., Talbert, O.R. *et al.*: The effect of L-dopa on plasma growth hormone, insulin, and thyroxine. *J. Clin. Endocrinol. Metab.* 34:99–105, 1972.

56. Perlow, M.J., Sassin, J.F., Boyar, R., *et al.*: Release of human growth hormone, follicle stimulating hormone, and luteinizing hormone in response to L-dihydroxy-phenylalanine (L-dopa) in normal man. *Dis. Nerv. Syst.* 33:804–810, 1972.

57. Yates, F.E., Russell, S.M., and Maran, J.W.: Brain-adenohypophysial communication in mammals. *Ann. Rev. Physiol.* 33:393-444, 1971.

58. Hagen, T.C., Lawrence, A.M., and Kirsteins, L.: Autoregulation of growth hormone secretion in normal subjects. *Metabolism* 21:603–610, 1972.

59. Copinschi, G., Hartog, M., Earll, J.M., *et al.*: Effect of various blood sampling procedures on serum levels of immunoreactive human growth hormone. *Metabolism* 16:402–409, 1967.

60. Greene, W.A., Conron, G., Schalch, D.S., *et al.*: Psychological correlates of growth hormone and adrenal secretory responses in patients undergoing cardiac catheterization. *Psychosom. Med.* 31:450, 1969.

61. Glick, S.M.: The regulation of growth hormone secretion, *in* "Frontiers in Neuroendocrinology" (W.F. Ganong, and L. Martini, Eds.), pp.141-182. Oxford Univ. Press, New York (1969).

62. Molinatti, G.M., Massara, F., Strumia, E., *et al.*: Radioimmunoassay of human growth hormone. *J. Nucl. Biol. Med.* 13:26–36, 1969.

63. Finkelstein, J.W., Roffwarg, H.P., Boyar, R.M., *et al.*: Age-related change in the twenty-four-hour spontaneous secretion of growth hormone. *J. Clin. Endocrinol.* 35:665–670, 1972.

64. Parker, M.L., Hammond, J.M., and Daughaday, W.H.: The arginine provocative test: An aid in the diagnosis of hyposomatotropism. *J. Clin. Endocrinol.* 27:1129–1136, 1967.

Chapter 3

Utilization of Cellular Studies of Neurotransmitter-Related Enzymes and Transport Processes in Man for the Investigation of Biological Factors in Behavioral Disorders

DENNIS L. MURPHY

and

JONATHAN L. COSTA

Some cells outside the central nervous system (CNS) contain neurotransmitter-related enzymes and carry out metabolic sequences very similar to those found in CNS neurons. Studies of certain metabolic and neurological disorders in man have been aided by the identification and measurement of enzyme activities and metabolic processes in leukocytes and erythrocytes from blood and in fibroblasts obtained by skin biopsy.[1][2] The utilization of these peripheral cell model systems has only recently been applied in the field of behavioral disorders. In attempts to evaluate individual differences in psychoactive drug responses in man and to search for distinctive biological characteristics of individuals with behavioral disor-

This Chapter is written under the auspices of and funded by the Federal Government and is not subject to copyright.

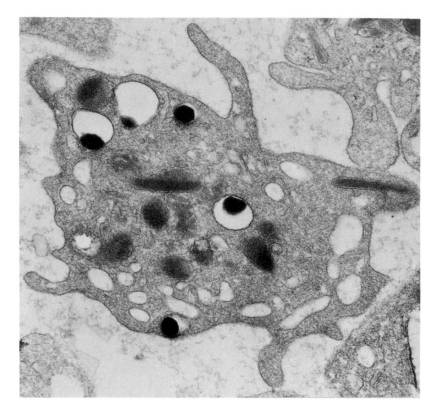

Fig. 1. Electron micrograph of a cat platelet. The platelet contains several "dense bodies" with eccentrically-located, and very electron-dense cores, scattered α-granules and mitochondria, and electron-lucent channels of the "open canilicular system." X56,000

ders, some recent studies in man have focused on cellular studies of enzymes and of the cellular membrane transport and storage processes involved in the regulation of neurotransmitter function. This presentation will review recent studies utilizing these approaches in man, presenting examples from work done in our laboratory.

The human cell which has been most investigated as a model for neurotransmitter-related transport, metabolic, and enzyme activities is the human platelet[3-6] (Fig. 1). These cells accumulate biogenic amines via high affinity transport mechanisms in the cell membrane and store them in membrane-bound vesicles[7][8] (Table I). Platelets release stored amines from vesicles by exocytosis—the same mechanism utilized in the release of neurotransmitters at synapses. Platelets contain monoamine oxidase and indole-N-methyl transferase,[9-11] two enzymes involved in the metabolism of biogenic amines. They also exhibit physiological changes[12] which correlate with changes in cyclic AMP levels in response to norepinephrine and some other biogenic amines; these responses are blocked by phentolamine and appear to have many similarities to α-adrenergic receptor responses studied in other tissues.[13 14] Although other blood cells have not been as extensively studied as the human platelet for biogenic amine-related functions, neither leukocytes nor erythrocytes appear to accumulate or store biogenic amines to a comparable extent.[8]

Biogenic Amine Storage in Platelets

Serotonin and perhaps other amines are complexed in high concentrations in membrane-bound vesicles with ATP, calcium, and probably a small amount of protein.[15] Intravesicular serotonin storage has many similarities to the vesicular storage mechanisms for biogenic amines in the adrenal medulla and in the peripheral and central nervous system.[8] Platelet serotonin content is reduced by reserpine and by tricyclic antidepressant drugs such as imipramine which decrease serotonin uptake across the external cell membrane of the platelet.[3 8 16] Serotonin storage can also be reduced by other

TABLE I

Biogenic Amine-Related Characteristics
of the Human Platelet

Amine uptake: Saturable active transport system for serotonin, with $K_m = 3 \times 10^{-7}$ M.

Amine storage: Vesicles which bind serotonin, dopamines, and other amines with C_i/C_o gradients @ 1000:1.

Amine metabolism: Monoamine oxidase, indoleamine N-methyltransferase, and other enzymes.

Amine receptor function: Norepinephrine, epinephrine, and dopamine reduce cyclic AMP formation; amine effects are blocked by phentolamine.

---

amines such as tyramine, dopamine, and octopamine, which enter the cell and apparently displace endogenous serotonin.[17]

A recently completed electron microscopic study of some of the quantitative characteristics of serotonin storage in platelets indicated that there appears to be a rather closely maintained number of amine storage bodies per platelet; these storage bodies are similar in size to storage vesicles in the adrenal medulla, although they are somewhat larger (198 nm in diameter) than the amine storage vesicles reported in noradrenergic nerve terminals (50 nm in diameter) (Table II).[18]

Biogenic Amine Uptake in Platelets

The cell membrane transport processes for biogenic amines have been a point of special interest in psychopharmacology. Neurotransmitter amines released at synapses are principally inactivated by these processes, rather than by enzymatic degradation as in the case of acetylcholine. Furthermore, the drug group with the widest spectrum of antidepressant efficacy, the tricyclic antidepressants, has been thought to act by inhibiting the synaptic amine reuptake processes.[19] [20]

The prototypical tricyclic antidepressants like imipramine, amitriptyline, desipramine, and their congeners are all effective amine uptake inhibitors. In contrast, the antipsychotic phenothiazines, despite their structural

TABLE II
Serotonin Storage in Human and Cat Platelets

	Human (N=9)	Cat (N=6)
Storage body		
Number per platelet	6.4 ± 0.3	12.1 ± 0.6
Diameter (nm)	198 ± 6	293 ± 7
Volume (10^3 nm^3)	6,690 ± 770	16,300 ± 1.100
Serotonin		
Molecules per platelet (x 10^3)	3,650 ± 280	35,400 ± 4,100
Molecules per storage body (x 10^3)	523 ± 69	3,120 ± 640

similarities, require 10-fold or higher concentrations to reduce amine uptake.[19] [20] However, two recent bodies of data have complicated the predominant interpretation relating the clinical antidepressant efficacy of the tricyclic drugs to their amine uptake-inhibiting properties.

Several careful studies have demonstrated equal antidepressant efficacies for two phenothiazines (thioridazine and chlorpromazine) compared to the classic tricyclic drugs.[21] [22] In addition, newer tricyclic drugs such as iprindole and several other compounds which, like the phenothiazines, are less effective amine uptake inhibitors have also been reported to have antidepressant efficacy equal to that of the tricyclics.[23] [24] Furthermore, these other drugs also share some of the behavioral activating effects of the original tricyclic drugs (e.g., the enhancement of motor activity in rodents)[23] [24] — effects which had previously been thought to result from uptake inhibition.

In studies of amine uptake in platelets from patients receiving tricyclic antidepressants and phenothiazines under ordinary clinical conditions, we observed that serotonin uptake was markedly inhibited (over 60%) by imipramine, while amitriptyline had lesser effects, and chlorpromazine had negligible uptake-inhibiting effects[26] (Table III). Similarly, iprindole has been reported to have negligible effects on platelet serotonin content[23]; this drug is also a poor uptake inhibitor in brain tissue preparations.[23] [25]

A second finding tending to negate the original suggestions that the efficacy of tricyclic antidepressants could be understood in terms of their uptake-inhibiting properties comes from studies with lithium carbonate. This drug enhances serotonin and metaraminol uptake in platelets [26] [27] (Table III) and norepinephrine uptake in brain tissue preparations.[28] Enhanced uptake with lithium treatment was considered as possibly relevant to the most dramatic clinical action of lithium, its use as an antimanic agent. However, a number of subsequent studies have demonstrated that lithium also has antidepressant effects.[29] [30] Thus, antidepressant activity appears to be associated not only with drugs like the tricyclics which inhibit amine uptake but also with other drugs like iprindole and lithium which either do not inhibit uptake or actually enhance it.

Furthermore, even among the classic tricyclic drugs, there is a rather poor correlation between uptake inhibiting efficacy and clinical efficacy, with drugs such as desipramine being the most effective inhibitors of norepinephrine uptake, but apparently somewhat less effective clinically than amitriptyline and imipramine, which have less uptake-inhibiting efficacy for norepinephrine.[25] [31] [32] While there appears to be some tendency for drugs with preferential serotonin uptake-inhibiting potency such as chlorimi-

TABLE III
Psychoactive Drug Effects *In Vivo*
on ^{14}C-5-Hydroxytryptamine Uptake in Human Platelets

	N	^{14}C-5HT uptake (ng/mg protein/3 min)	P
Controls	24	237 ± 19	
Imipramine (75-250 mg/day)	13	92 ± 13	@0.001
Amitriptyline (100-300 mg/day)	8	164 ± 39	@0.05
Chlorpromazine (200-1000 mg/day)	9	221 ± 34	@N.S.
Phenelzine (40-60 mg/day)	6	217 ± 43	N.S.
Litthium	19	328 ± 24	@0.01

pramine and imipramine to be generally more effective clinically, the single most effective tricyclic drug, amitriptyline, appears to have a relatively less serotonin uptake-inhibiting effect in man (Table III). Thus, the apparent uptake-enhancing properties of lithium, the lack of uptake-inhibiting effects of other tricyclic drugs like iprindole, and the rather low correlation between norepinephrine or serotonin uptake inhibition and clinical efficacy constitutes evidence against a simple cause-effect relationship between amine uptake inhibition and clinical antidepressant efficacy.

The tricyclic antidepressant agents affect biogenic amine storage, release, metabolism, and receptor function[8] [33--35] in addition to their effects on amine uptake. Data from animal studies and studies of human platelets indicate that uptake inhibition occurs rapidly, within 1–2 days of the initiation of treatment; in contrast, antidepressant effects often do not become apparent for 2 to 3 weeks.[26] While a "psychological change lag period" or delayed accumulation of the drugs in brain are plausible explanations, it is certainly as likely that other delayed actions of the drugs may be involved in their behavioral actions, including, for example, direct effects of the drugs on amine storage or receptor functions, or indirect compensatory or adaptive changes such as those on amine synthesis previously demonstrated for other psychoactive drugs given chronically.[35]

Another major group of antidepressant drugs, the monoamine oxidase inhibitors, have also been suggested to produce their behavioral effects by affecting biogenic amine uptake. Hendley and Snyder[36] noted that among monoamine oxidase-inhibiting drugs, like tranylcypromine, phenelzine, iproniazid, and isocarboxazid, a closer correlation occurred between clinical efficacy and amine uptake inhibition potency rather than MAO-inhibiting potency. However, the MAO-inhibiting drugs require 100-fold higher concentrations *in vitro* to achieve uptake inhibition compared to imipramine and amitriptyline, while the MAO-inhibiting drugs are given clinically in smaller doses. *In vivo,* platelets from patients receiving one MAO inhibitor, phenelzine, exhibited no evidence of uptake inhibition (Table III). It remains an open question whether uptake inhibition may contribute to the action of these drugs. Tranylcypromine has been demonstrated to possess amine-releasing effects like the amphetamines,[37] and it seems likely that MAO-inhibiting drugs may affect behavior through a variety of mechanisms.

Our studies of the effects of psychoactive drugs on amine uptake afforded us the opportunity to compare the initial rate of amine uptake in depressed patients versus normal controls. As indicated in Table IV, there were no

TABLE IV
[14]C-Serotonin Accumulation in Platelets
from Depressed Patients and Controls

	^{14}C-Serotonin uptake (ug/mg protein/hr)
Depressed patients	
Bipolar (N = 16)	4.54 ± 0.63
Unipolar (N = 19)	4.37 ± 0.52
Depressed patients--improved	
Bipolar (N = 7)	4.66 ± 1.01
Unipolar (N = 9)	3.92 ± 0.85
Normal controls	
(N = 12)	4.26 ± 0.78

differences in the unipolar and bipolar patient subgroups compared to controls, or in depressed patients compared before and after recovery. These data do not support suggestions that an alteration in amine uptake might occur in patients with affective disorders.[38] However, a lack of alteration in serotonin uptake in platelets certainly does not reflect on the possibility that the uptake of norepinephrine or other neurotransmitters in brain might be altered in these patients.

Biogenic Amine Receptor Function in Platelets

Platelets respond to norepinephrine, epinephrine, and, to some degree, to dopamine and serotonin with changes in platelet aggregation and, under some circumstances, with altered cyclic adenosine monophosphate (AMP) formation.[12-14 39] The cyclic AMP and aggregation responses to norepinephrine and epinephrine are blocked by phentolamine but not by propranolol and hence fall in the category of α-adrenergic responses.[13 14]

One psychoactive drug, lithium carbonate, inhibits the platelet cyclic AMP responses to prostaglandin E_1 and to norepinephrine in a dose-dependent fashion *in vitro*.[39 40] In addition, platelets obtained from patients receiving lithium were found to have diminished responses to prostaglandin E_1 and norepinephrine (Table V).[39] In other studies complementary to

TABLE V
^{3}-H-Cyclic AMP Formation in Platelets
from Depressed Patients and Normal Controls
in Response to Prostaglandin E_1
and Norepinephrine Administration

	Depressed patients (N=17)		Normal controls (N=11)
	Unipolar (N=9)	Bipolar (N=11)	
^{3}H-Cyclic AMP formed (cpm/mg protein/5 min) PGE$_1$ (2×10^{-6} M)	674 ± 82	646 ± 91	663 ± 77
PGE$_1$ + norepinephrine (10^{-4} M)	263 ± 36	233 ± 39	279 ± 28
% Norepinephrine inhibition	61	64	58
^{3}H-Adenine incorporation (cpm/mg protein/30 min)	4.3 ± 0.6	4.4 ± 0.8	4.3 ± 0.8

those reported recently by Wang *et al.*,[41] no differences in the platelet cyclic AMP production responses to norepinephrine in either bipolar or unipolar depressed patients of either sex were observed.[42] This would argue against a generalized α-adrenergic receptor deficit during depression which had been hypothesized to exist on the basis of other data.[43-45]

Monoamine Oxidase Activity in Human Platelets

Recent interest has developed in measuring biogenic-amine related enzymes in blood cells and plasma, and studies of monoamine oxidase (MAO), dopamine-β-hydroxylase, catechol-*O*-methyl transferase, and indole-*N*-methyl transferase have been accomplished.[9-11 46-54] Unfortunately, the platelet and other blood cells do not contain any of the enzymes involved in the synthesis of the catecholamines, serotonin, or γ-aminobutyric acid (GABA).[55-57] The major amine degradatory enzyme, monoamine oxidase, is found in human platelets. Because monoamine oxidase-inhibiting drugs have been successfully used as antidepressants, and also possess other behavioral effects, we have been studying this enzyme over the past several years.

Unlike the plasma MAO — which is a quite different enzyme, with a different cofactor, and different inhibitor-related characteristics[58] — the platelet MAO is a mitochondrial enzyme, like the MAO's in other tissue, and appears very similar in its characteristics to the so-called "B" form of MAO found in brain and other tissues[9 10 46 54] (Table VI). In fact, on the basis of the simple sigmoid curves we have observed in response to both the relatively specific inhibitor of the "B" form, deprenyl, and the "A" form inhibitor, clorgyline,[54] it would seem that the platelet may have only a single form of the enzyme present rather than the two to five possible forms suggested to be present in other tissues, including brain, on the basis of electrophoretic evidence.[59 60]

Our initial studies were directed toward the correlation of the clinical antidepressant effects of MAO inhibitors with the degree of platelet MAO inhibition achieved in individual patients.[47 61] Platelet MAO activity is markedly inhibited by MAO-inhibiting drugs used as antidepressants[10 47] (Table VI). Because of the marked MAO inhibition oberved in almost all of the patients, and the very modest antidepressant effects observed in our group of severely depressed, hospitalized patients, this correlational study is not yet complete.[61]

However, in beginning these studies of the effects of MAO-inhibiting drugs, we observed some differences between the bipolar and unipolar

TABLE VI
Comparison of Human Platelet
versus Plasma Monoamine Oxidases

	Human platelet MAO	Human plasma MAO
Localization:	Mitochondria	Soluble
Substrates:	Primary, secondary, and tertiary amines	Primary amines only
Cofactor:	Probably flavin adenine dinucleotide	Pyridoxal
K_m (x10^{-4} M):		
Tyramine	0.5	1.8
Benzylamine	1.0	1.0-3.0
Inhibitors ID_{50} (M) :		
Pargyline	2×10^{-8}	@ 10^{-3}
Tranylcpromine	1×10^{-6}	1×10^{-3}
Iproniazid	2×10^{-6}	1×10^{-3}
Isoniazid	@ 10^{-3}	1×10^{-3}
KCN	@ 10	5×10^{-4}

subgroups of depressed patients.[47] The bipolar patients manifested an approximate 50% reduction in platelet MAO as a group characteristic (Fig. 2). Age and sex did not appear to be important variables in this sample, although in a larger sample of normals we verified the reports by Robinson et al.[62] and concluded that platelet MAO tended to be slightly higher in females, although in our data this difference was insignificant over age 20 and under age 50.

The clinical state of the patients did not appear to correlate with platelet MAO activity, as patients sampled when depressed and improved or when manic and improved did not exhibit altered MAO activity (Table VII). Drugs other than MAO inhibitors also appeared to have minimal effects on enzyme activity.[47] [48]

Because these findings suggested that platelet MAO activity might represent a rather stable characteristic of the individual, we examined enzyme activity levels in twin samples from normal and patient populations. Among normal individuals, monozygotic twins were found to have an intraclass correlation coefficient about twice as great as that of dizygotic twins (Table VIII).[6] [63] This difference was highly significant when examined by analysis of variance ($p < 0.001$). The use of the Osbourne formula for the calculation of hereditability suggested the existence of a high degree of genetic influence on interindividual differences in enzyme activity (Table VIII). Data from same-sex siblings and random pairs matched for age and sex support this conclusion (Table IX).[6] Similarly high intraclass correlation coefficients were found for a monozygotic twin group discordant for schizophrenia [64] and also in a continuing study of bipolar twin pairs[6] (Table IX).

These findings have some implications for future studies. Because platelet MAO activity apparently represents a relatively stable, genetically influenced characteristic of the individual, it may be useful in correlating and perhaps eventually predicting some other characteristics which have been suggested to be influenced by familial and possibly genetic factors. For example, Pare and his colleagues in England have reported data suggesting a familial clustering of differential responsivity to tricyclic antidepressants versus MAO-inhibiting antidepressants.[65] [66]

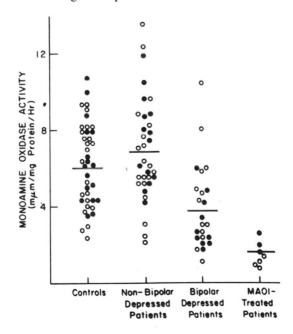

TABLE VII
Platelet Monoamine Oxidase Activity
in Relation to Clinical State
in Depressed and Manic Patients

	N	MAO activity (nM/mg protein/hr)	
		Depressed or manic	Improved
Depressed pateints			
Bipolar	13	3.08 ± 0.52	3.61 ± 0.66
Unipolar	12	5.67 ± 0.78	5.38 ± 0.85
Manic patients	16	3.19 ± 0.83	3.53 ± 0.74

In addition, a number of clinical, psychological, biological, and pharmacological response characteristics have been described as differentiating bipolar from unipolar depressed patients.[47] We are currently examining a number of these diagnosis-related characteristics from the vantage point of their correlation with MAO activity. Some characteristics of potential interest such as EEG patterns and tricyclic antidepressant blood levels are already known from other twin studies to be heavily genetically influenced,[67] [68] and may prove to be of special interest.

As drugs inhibiting MAO have psychoactive effects with marked influence on behavior in animals and man, there is some potential that MAO activity measurements may represent not only biological marker,[64] but might also reflect differences in biogenic amine metabolic patterns related to behavior in different individuals. However, MAO inhibition is associated with a complex sequence of biochemical changes in brain, including increased accumulation of several neuroamines thought to function as neurotransmitters, an increased accumulation of other amines (such as phenethylamine, tyramine, octopamine, and tryptamine whose functions are less certain), as well as some other changes, including effects on amine synthesis, all of which factors may affect behavior (Table X).[69] Furthermore, the existence of different molecular forms of MAO, and the fact that different inhibiting drugs do not have equal effects on the different MAO forms further complicate interpretation of the possible effects of alterations in MAO activity. While the MAO inhibitiors used as psychoactive drugs all markedly affect the human platelet MAO, any attempt to directly relate the endogenous platelet enzyme activity to MAO activity in other tissues, including brain, will require more information than is yet available on the characteristics of these enzymes in platelets and brain.

One biological correlation with MAO inhibition observed in man followed from the discovery of a sensitive enzymatic assay for octopamine.[70] Octopamine is a naturally occurring amine formed from tyramine which can be stored in amine storage vesicles in nerve endings which has been demonstrated to be released from cells in response to nerve stimulation.[71][72] We observed that platelets incubated with radioactively labeled octopamine *in vitro* accumulated and stored it, achieving concentration gradients of about 30:1.[73] MAO-inhibiting drugs have previously been demonstrated to increase octopamine concentrations in brain and heart tissue and to elevate levels of octopamine and its metabolite, *p*-hydroxy mandelic acid, in urine.[73][74]

Octopamine had not previously been demonstrated to be present in human cells; in our studies, only small amounts were found in platelets from four of 17 normal individuals, and these amounts were at the limits of sensitivity of the assay. However, platelets from six depressed patients receiving MAO-inhibiting drugs were all found to have measurable octopamine, with values ranging up to 100-fold those found in the normal individuals.[73] This occurr-

TABLE VIII

Platelet Monoamine Oxidase Activity in
Monozygotic and Dizygotic Twins

		MONOZYGOTIC TWINS					DIZYGOTIC TWINS		
Sex	Age	MAO Activity (nM/mg protein/hr)		Δ	Sex	Age	MAO Activity (nM/mg protein/hr)		Δ
F	20	5.55,	6.35	0.80	F	20	1.59,	5.42	3.83
F	20	16.04,	17.69	1.65	F	21	6.74,	9.80	3.06
F	21	4.96,	7.57	2.61	F	24	4.59,	10.36	4.59
F	27	4.07,	6.82	2.75	F	30	2.56,	7.25	4.69
F	39	1.80,	2.96	1.16	F	48	1.91,	6.01	4.10
M	20	2.49,	3.11	0.62	M	18	9.92,	12.73	2.81
M	22	4.61,	5.13	0.52	M	18	0.68,	1.86	1.18
M	46	3.32,	3.60	0.28	M	20	0.47,	4.58	4.11
M	52	4.45,	5.19	0.74	M	45	4.18,	7.01	2.83
					M	53	1.04,	2.02	0.98

$\bar{X}$ = 5.87 ΣΔ = 11.13

$\bar{X}_\Delta$ = 1.24

$\bar{X}_\Delta/\bar{X}$ = 0.211

$\bar{X}$ = 5.04 ΣΔ = 33.36

$\bar{X}_\Delta$ = 3.34

$\bar{X}_\Delta/\bar{X}$ = 0.662

Intraclass
Correlation Coefficient r_{i_c} = 0.88
$(r = \Sigma(X-a)(y-a)/ns^2)$

r_{i_c} = 0.45

Heredability (Osborne) $H = \dfrac{\Sigma_{DZ}(\Delta)^2/2n - \Sigma_{MZ}(\Delta)^2/2n}{\Sigma_{DZ}(\Delta)^2/2n}$ = 0.83

Mann-Whitney U = 7, p < .001

TABLE IX

Apparent Genetic Influence on Monoamine Oxidase Activity:
Intraclass Correlations for Platelet Monoamine Oxidase Activity
in Normal, Schizophrenic, and Bipolar Twins

	N (pairs)	Intraclass correlation
Normals		
Monozygotic twins	9	0.88
Dizygotic twins, same sex	10	0.45
Sib pairs, same sex	37	0.28
Random pairs matched for age and sex	37	0.12
Monozygotic twins discordant for schizophrenia	13	0.65
Monozygotic twins concordant for bipolar manic-depressive disorder	3	0.83

ence of octopamine in platelets did seem to be a drug effect, as unipolar depressed patients with normal MAO levels had no higher octopamine levels than the normals. There was some indication, however, that octopamine levels were elevated in bipolar patients who were found, as before, to have moderately reduced platelet MAO activity levels. These quantities of octopamine are quite small, even in the MAO-inhibited individuals. The implication, though, is that if octopamine is increased in human platelets in response to MAO inhibition, then it seems more plausible to consider that it or other similar "false transmitter" amines might be involved, as other studies have suggested,[75] in some of the side effects of MAO inhibition such as hypotension, or perhaps even in some of the behavioral effects of MAO inhibition.[17]

Conclusion

This survey of some of the biogenic amine-related characterisitics of the platelet illustrates ways in which this model can be utilized in the study of psychoactive drug effects and behavior (Table XI). It seems possible to monitor individual differences in response to drugs, and to correlate these differences with both biological changes (as noted in the case of octopamine) and with clinical changes in patients' behavior.

There are many additional factors which need to be examined in regard to other biological interactions with drug effects — for example, the sex and age differences which appear to influence such disparate parameters as platelet MAO activity and the clinical antidepressant response to tricyclic antidepressants. Other studies have demonstrated that thyroid hormones and estrogens may interact with the tricyclic antidepressant drugs, and developing evidence suggests the occurrence of interactions between sex hormones and amine uptake mechanisms as well as with MAO activity.

Finally, as illustrated in the studies of platelet MAO activity, it may prove possible to correlate some genetically based differences in enzyme activity with some individual differences in psychological and biological characteristics in patient subgroups.

TABLE X

Examples of the Biological Effects of Mao-Inhibiting Drugs
Relevant to Neurotransmitter Function and Behavior

I. Accumulation of Neurotransmitter amines (norepinephrine, dopamine, serotonin)

    A. Unequal effects on different amines
    B. Different MAOI produce different effects

II. Accumulation of other amines (tyramine, octopamine, phenethylamine, tryptamine(--"false transmitters"

    A. Endogenous amine depletion
    B. Release of other amines having lesser effects at synapses
    C. Inhibition of endogenous amine synthesis
    D. Increased likelihood of occurence and/or potentiation of (a) methylated amine metabolites, (b) dimethyl tryptamine, (c) 6-hydroxydopamine, 5,6-dihydroxytryptamine

III. Decreased formation of aldehydes from biogenic amines

IV. Decreased synthesis of biogenic amines via feedback mechanisms

---

TABLE XI

Applications of the Study of Biogenic Amine-Related
Characteristics of the Human Platelet

I. Monitor individual differences in response to druqs:

        MAO-inhibiting drugs
        reserpine   Resperpine
        Tricyclic antidepressants
        Lithium

II. Study other factors influencing platelet amine uptake, storaqe, release, metabolism, and receptor function (e.g., hormones)

III. Evaluate genetically- based or otherwise altered differences in enzyme activity and membrane protein-related functions in individuals for possible correlation with behavior

---

References

1. Hsia, D.Y.Y.: Utilization of leukocytes for the study of inborn errors of metabolism. *Enzyme* 13:161–168, 1972.
2. Harris, H.: "The Principles of Human Biochemical Genetics," Elsevier, New York (1971).
3. Pletscher, A.: Metabolism, transfer, and storage of 5-hydroxytryptamine in blood platelets. *Brit. J. Pharmacol.* 32:1–16, 1968.
4. Born, G.V.R., and Smith, J.B.: Uptake and release of [^{3}H]-adrenaline by human platelets. *Brit. J. Pharmacol.* 39:765–778, 1970.
5. Paasonen, M.K., Ahtee, L., and Solatunturi, E.: Blood platelet as a model for monoaminergic neurons, *in* "Progress in Brain Research" Ed., E. Eranko, Vol. 34, pp. 269-279. Elsevier, Amsterdam (1971).
6. Murphy, D.L.: Technical strategies for the study of catecholamines in man, *in* "Frontiers in Catecholamine Research" (E. Usdin, and S. Snyder, Eds.) pp. 1077–1082. Pergamon Press, Oxford, 1974.
7. Da Prada, M., and Pletscher, A.: Differential uptake of biogenic amines by isolated 5-hydroxytryptamine organelles of blood platelets. *Life Sci.* 8:65–72, 1969.
8. Murphy, D.L., and Kopin, I.J.: The transport of biogenic amines, *in* "Metabolic Transport" (L.E. Hokin, Ed.) pp. 503–542. Academic Press, New York (1972).
9. Paasonen, M.K., and Solatunturi, E.: Monoamine oxidase in mammalian blood platelets. Ann. Med. Exp. Biol. Fenn. 43:98–100, 1965.
10. Robinson, D.S., Lovenberg, W., Keiser, H., *et al.:* Effect of drugs on human blood

platelet and plasma amine oxidase activity *in vitro* and *in vivo. Biochem. Parmacol.* 17:109–119, 1968.

11. Wyatt, R.J., Saavedra, J.M., and Axelrod, J.: A dimethyltryptamine-forming enzyme in human blood. *Amer. J. Psychiat.* 130:754–760, 1973.

12. Mustard, J.F., and Packham, M.A.: Factors influencing platelet function: Adhesion, release and aggregation. *Pharmacol. Rev.* 22:97–187, 1970.

13. Moskowitz, J., Harwood, JP., Reid, WD., *et al.:* The interaction of norepinephrine and prostaglandin E_1 on the adenyl cyclase system of human and rabbit blood platelets. *Biochim. Biophys. Acta.,* 230:279-285, 1971.

14. Johnson, M., and Ramwell, P.W.: Implications of prostaglandins in hematology, *in* "Prostaglandins and Cyclic AMP" (R.H. Kahn and W.E. Lands, Eds). Academic Press, New York (1973).

15. Pletscher, A., Da Prada, M., Berneis, K.H., *et al.:* New aspects on the storage of 5-hydroxytryptamine in blood platelets. *Experientia* 27:993–1002, 1971.

16. Todrick, A., and Tait, A.C.: The inhibition of human platelet 5-hydroxytryptamine uptake by tricyclic antidepressive drugs. The relation between structure and potency. *J. Pharm. Pharmacol.* 21:751–762, 1969.

17. Murphy, D.L.: Amine precursors, amines and false neurotransmitters in depressed patients. *Amer. J. Psychiat.* 129:141–148, 1972.

18. Costa, J.L., Reese, T.S., and Murphy, D.L.: Serotonin storage in platelets: Estimation of storage-packet size. *Science* 183:537–538, 1974.

19. Glowinski, J., and Axelrod, J.: Inhibition of uptake by tritiated noradrenaline in the intact rat brain by imipramine and structurally related compounds. *Nature (London)* 204:1318–1319, 1964.

20. Gyermek, L.: The pharmacology of imipramine and related antidepressants. *Int. Rev. Neurobiol.* 9:95-143, 1966.

21. Overall, J.E., Hollister, L.E., Meyer, F., *et al.:* Imipramine and thioridazine in depressed and schizophrenic patients: are there specific antidepressant drugs? *J. Amer. Med. Ass.* 189:605–608, 1964.

22. Wheatley, D.: Comparative effects of propranolol and chlordiazepoxide in anxiety states. *Brit. J. Psychiat.* 115:1411–1412, 1969.

23. Fann, W.E., Davis, J.M., Janowsky, D.S., *et al.:* Effect of iprindole on amine uptake in man. *Arch. Gen. Psychiat.* 26:158–162, 1972.

24. Carlsson, A., Fuxe, K., Hamberger, B., *et al.:* Effect of a new series on bicyclic compounds with potential thymoleptic properties on the reserpine-resistant uptake mechanism of central and peripheral monoamine neurones *in vivo* and *in vitro. Brit. J. Pharmacol.* 36:18–28, 1969.

25. Lahti, R.A., and Maickel, R.P.: The tricyclic antidepressants — inhibition of norepinephrine uptake as related to potentiation of norepinephrine and clinical efficacy. *Biochem. Pharmacol.* 20:482–486, 1971.

26. Murphy, D.L., Colburn, R.W., Davis, J.M., *et al.:* Imipramine and lithium effects on biogenic amine transport. *Amer. J. Psychiat.* 127:339–345, 1970.

27. Murphy, D.L., Colburn, R.W., Davis, J.M., *et al.:* Stimulation by lithium of monoamine uptake in human platelets. *Life Sci.* 8:1187–1193, 1969.

28. Colburn, R.W., Goodwin, F.K., Bunney, W.E. Jr., *et al.:* Effect of lithium on the uptake of noradrenaline by synaptosomes. *Nature (London)* 215:1395–1397, 1967.

29. Goodwin, F.K., Murphy, D.L., and Bunney, W.E., Jr.: Lithium carbonate treatment in depression and mania. *Arch. Gen. Psychiat.* 21:486–496, 1969.

30. Mendels, J.: Lithium and depression, *in* "Lithium: Its Role in Psychiatric Research and Treatment" (S. Gershon and B. Shopsin, Eds.), pp. 253-267. Plenum Press, New York (1973).

31. Carlsson, A.: Structural specificity for inhibition of (^{14}C)-5-hydroxytryptamine uptake by cerebral slices. *J. Pharm. Pharmacol.* 22:729–732, 1970.

32. Kannengiesser, M.H., Hunt, P., and Raynaud, J.P.: An *in vitro* model for the study of psychotropic drugs and as a criterion of antidepressant activity. *Biochem. Pharmacol.* 22:73–84, 1973.

33. Schanberg, S.M., Schildkraut, J.J., and Kopin, I.J.: The effects of psychoactive drugs on norepinephrine-^{3}H metabolism in brain. *Biochem. Pharmacol.* 16:393–399, 1967.

34. Reid, W.D., Stefano, F.J.E., Kurzepa, S., *et al.:* Tricyclic antidepressants: Evidence for an intraneuronal site of action. *Science* 164:439–439, 1969.

35. Mandell, A.J., Segal, D.S., Kuczenski, R.T., *et al.:* Some macromolecular mechanisms in CNS neurotransmitter pharmacology and their physiological organizations, *in* "The Chemistry of Mood, Motivation and Memory" (J. McGaugh, Ed.) pp. 105-148. Plenum Press, New York (1972).

36. Hendley, E.D., and Snyder, S.H.: Relationship between the action of monoamine oxidase inhibitors on the noradrenaline uptake system and their antidepressant efficacy. *Nature (London)* 220:1330–1331, 1968.

37. Horn, A.S., and Synder, S.H.: Steric requirements for catecholamine uptake by rat brain synaptosomes: Studies with rigid analogs of amphetamine. *J. Pharmacol. Exp. Ther.* 180:523–530, 1972.

38. Bunney, W.E., Jr., Goodwin, F.K. and Murphy, D.L.: The "switch process" in manic-depressive illness. III. Theoretical implications. *Arch. Gen. Psychiat.* 27:312–317, 1972.

39. Murphy, D.L., Donnelly, C., and Moskowitz, J.: Inhibition by lithium of prostaglandin E_1 and norepinephrine effects on cyclic adenosine monophosphate production in human platelets. *Clin. Pharmacol. Ther.* 14:810–814, 1973.

40. Wang, Y.C., Pandey, G.N., Mendels, J., *et al.:* The effect of lithium on prostaglandin E_1-stimulated adenylate cyclase activity of human platelets. *Biochem. Pharmacol.* 23:845–855, 1974.

41. Wang, Y.C., Pandey, G.N., Mendels, J., *et al.:* Platelet adenylate cyclase responses in depression: Implications for a receptor defect. *Psychopharmacologia,* in press.

42. Murphy. D.L., Donnelly, C., and Moskowitz, J.: Catecholamine receptor function in depressed patients. *Amer. J. Psychiat.,* in press.

43. Prange, A.J., McCurdy, R.L., and Cochrane, C.M.: The systolic blood pressure response of depressed patients to infused norepinephrine. *J. Psychiat. Res.* 5:1–13, 1967.

44. Prange, A.J., Jr., Wilson, I.C., Nox, A.E., *et al.:* Thyroid-imipramine clinical and chemical interaction: Evidence for a receptor deficit in depression. *J. Psychiat. Res.* 9:187–205, 1972.

45. MRC Brain Metabolism Unit Report. Modified amine hypothesis for the etiology of affective disorders. *Lancet* 2:253–257, 1972.

46. Collins, G.G.S., and Sandler, M.: Human blood platelet monoamine oxidase. *Biochem. Pharmacol.,* 20:289–296, 1971.

47. Murphy, D.L., and Weiss, R.: Reduced monoamine oxidase activity in blood platelets from bipolar depressed patients. *Amer. J. Psychiat.* 128:1351–1357, 1972.

48. Murphy, D.L., and Wyatt, R.J.: Reduced monoamine oxidase activity in blood platelets from schizophrenic patients. *Nature (London)* 238:225–226, 1972.

49. Cohn, C.K., Dunner, D.L. and Axelrod, J.: Reduced catechol-*O*-methyltransferase activity in red blood cells of women with primary affective disorder. *Science* 170:1323–1342, 1970.

50. Weinshilboum, R., and Axelrod, J.: Serum dopamine-beta-hydroxylase activity. *Circ. Res.* 28:307–315, 1971.

51. Weinshilboum, R.M., and Axelrod, J.: Reduced plasma dopamine-β-hydroxylase activity in familial dysautonomia. *New Engl. J. Med.* 285:938–942, 1971.

52. Wooten, G.F., Eldridge, R., Axelrod, J., *et al.:* Elevated plasma dopamine-β-hydroxylase activity in autosomal dominant torsion dystonia. *New Engl. J. Med.* 288:284–287, 1973.

53. Lamprecht, F., Wyatt, R.J., Belmaker, R., *et al.:* Plasma dopamine-beta-hydroxylase in identical twins discordant for schizophrenia, *in* "Frontiers in Catecholamine Research"(F. Usdin and S. Snyder, Eds.), Pergamon Press, New York, (1973).

54. Murphy, D.L., and Donnelly, C.H.: Monoamine oxidase in man: Enzyme characteristics in human platelets, plasma and other human tissues, *in* "Neuropsycholpharmacology of Monoamines and Their Regulatory Enzymes" (E. Usdin, Ed.), pp. 71-85. Raven Press, New York (1974).

55. Lovenberg, W.: Personal communication.

56. Kizer, S., Zivin, J., Saavedra, J., *et al.:* A sensitive microassay for tryptophan hydroxylase. *J. Neurochem.*, 1974, in press.

57. Evans, M.K., Martin, D.L., and Murphy, D.L.: Glutamate decarboxylation in human platelets. *New Eng. J. Med.* 290:165–166, 1974.

58. McEwen, C.M., Jr.: The soluble monoamine oxidase of human plasma and serum, *in* "Advances in Biochemical Psychopharmacology," Vol. 5, pp. 151–165, Raven Press, New York, 1972.

59. Youdium, M.B.H.: Multiple forms of monoamine oxidase and their properties, *in* "Advances in Biochemical Psychopharmacology" (E. Costa and P. Greengard, Eds.), Vol. 5, p. 67. Raven Press, New York (1972).

60. Sandler, M., and Youdim, M.B.H.: Multiple forms of monoamine oxidase: Functional significance. *Pharmacol. Rev.* 24:331–348, 1972.

61. Murphy, D.L., Brand, E., Baker, M., *et al.:* Phenelzine effects in hospitalized unipolar and bipolar depressed patients: Behavioral and biochemical relationships. *Proc. Coll. Int. Neuropsychopharmacol.*, 1974, in press.

62. Robinson, D.S., Davis, J.M., Nies, A., *et al.:* Relation of sex and age to monoamine oxidase activity of human brain, plasma and platelets. *Arch. Gen. Psychiat.* 24:536–539, 1971.

63. Nies, A., Robinson, D.S., Lamborn, K.R., *et al.:* Genetic control of platelet and plasma monoamine oxidase activity. *Arch. Gen. Psychiat.* 28:834–838, 1973.

64. Wyatt, R.J., Murphy, D.L., Belmaker, R., *et al.:* Reduced monoamine oxidase activity in platelets: A possible genetic marker for vulnerability to schizophrenia. *Science* 179:916–918, 1973.

65. Pare, C.M.B., Rees, L., and Sainsbury, M.J.: Differentiation of two genetically specific types of depression by the response to anti-depressants. *Lancet* 2:1340–1343, 1962.

66. Pare, C.M.B., and Mack, J.W.: Differentiation of two genetically specific types of depression by the response to antidepressant drugs. *J. Med. Gent.* 8:306–309, 1971.

67. Buchsbaum, M.S.: Average evoked response and stimulus intensity in identical and fraternal twins. *Physiol. Psychol.*, in press.

68. Alexanderson, B., Sjoqvist, F. and Prince Evans, D.A.: Steady-state plasma levels of

nortriptyline in twins. Influence of genetic factors and drug therapy. *Brit. Med. J.* 4:764–768, 1969.

69.   Murphy, D.L., Belmarker, R., and Wyatt, R.J.: Monoamine oxidase in schizophrenia and other behavioral disorders, *in* "Catecholamines and Their Enzymes in Relation to Neuropathology of Schizophrenia." (S.S. Kety, and S. Mathysse, Eds.).

70.   Molinoff, P.B., Landsberg, L., and Axelrod, J.: An enzymatic assay for octopamine and other β-hydroxylated phenylethylamines. *J. Pharmacol. Exp. Ther.* 170:253–261, 1939.

71.   Kopin, I.J., Fischer, J.E., Musacchio, J., *et al.:* Evidence for a false neurochemical transmitter as a mechanism for the hypotensive effect of monoamine oxidase inhibitors. *Biochemistry* 52:716–721, 1964.

72.   Molinoff, P.B., and Axelrod, J.: Distribution and turnover of octopamine in tissues. *J. Neurochem.* 19:157–163, 1972.

73.   Murphy, D.L., Cahan, D.H., and Molinoff, P.B.: Occurrence, transport and storage of octopamine in human blood platelets. *Clin. Pharmacol. Ther.,* in press.

74.   Kakimoto, Y., and Armstrong, M.D.: On the identification of octopamine in mammals. *J. Biol. Chem.* 237:422–427, 1962.

75.   Kopin, I.J.: False neurotransmitters in the mechanism of action of central nervous system and cardiovascular drugs, *in* "Biogenic Amines and Physiological Membranes" (J.H. Biel and L.G. Abood, Eds.) Vol. 5/B, pp. 329–353. Marcel Dekker, New York (1971).

Chapter 4

Studies of Cerebrospinal Fluid Amine Metabolites in Depressed Patients: Conceptual Problems and Theoretical Implications

ROBERT M. POST
and
FREDERICK K. GOODWIN

Introduction

The science of direct measurement of amine metabolism in patients with affective illness has progressed from its primitive initial stages to a more sophisticated plateau. Accompanying this progress is a shift from a primary emphasis on issues of methodology, validity of techniques, and the replicability of the data itself to issues of interpretation, conceptualization, and implications for treatment.

The original formulations of the catecholamine[1] [2] and indoleamine hypotheses[3] [4] of affective illness, while of enormous heuristic value, now seem overly simplified and inadequate to deal with the complexity of the field,[5] and modifications and elaborations of these hypotheses have become more attractive.[6-11] Since the amine theories of affective illness were

47

largely based on studies in animals, direct assessment of amine function in man became essential to hypothesis testing. The cerebrospinal fluid (CSF), with its contiguity to brain and partial isolation from the periphery, thus became a focus for study of amine metabolites.

In CSF investigations in Europe and the United States, approximately one-half of all base line studies of depressed patients compared to controls have demonstrated decreased levels of either 5-hydroxyindoleacetic acid (5HIAA), homovanillic acid (HVA) (reviewed in footnote 12), or 3-methoxy-4-hydroxyphenyl glycol (MHPG),[13-15] major metabolites of serotonin, dopamine, and norepinephrine, respectively. Differences in assay procedures volume of CSF, degree of prior bed rest, activity and position of patients, diagnostic criteria, prior treatment, severity and duration of illness, and appropriateness of control group appear important in explaining some of the different results obtained and are discussed in detail elsewhere.[12 16 17]

Similarly, critical questions of the central origins of CSF metabolites have been explored, yielding the general conclusion that most HVA is derived from rostral sources in the brain[18-20] while significant amounts of 5HIAA and MHPG are also derived from sources in the spinal cord.[19-22]

In the second phase of CSF investigation, probenecid has been utilized to measure "turnover" of serotonin and dopamine. Probenecid blocks transport of 5HIAA and HVA out of CSF resulting in elevation of the metabolites proportional to the amounts of amine synthesized and metabolized.[23] Results of investigators employing different methods of probenecid administration, with few exceptions,[24] have tended to show decreases in 5HIAA and HVA in depressed patients compared to controls (Table I).[25-30] Again, initial methodological studies have supported the idea that the probenecid technique can provide a measure of central amine turnover,[23 29 31-38] that the results are not artifacts of differences in blood or CSF levels of probenecid,[28 30 39 40] and that metabolism from rostral sources in the brain is more likely to be reflected after probenecid blockade.[41]

Thus, there is wide agreement that CSF amine metabolite techniques can provide a "window" into central nervous system metabolism and that one or more amine neurotransmitters may be altered in affective illness. Results from our group at NIMH will be reviewed briefly and newer findings presented as a background to a discussion of some current conceptual problems in the field. If several amine systems are altered in affective illness, are these changes primary and etiological, or a secondary consequence of the illness or some of its symptoms? Why do the effects of antide-

TABLE I

5HIAA and HVA following Probenecid in Depressed Patients

	Accumulations in depressed patients as percent of controls			
	5HIAA (%)	N	HVA (%)	N
Sjostrom and Roos, 1972 (70)	41[a]	(24)	40[a]	(10)
Bowers, 1974 (40)	109	(11)	138	(10)[b]
Goodwin, Post, et al., 1973 (29)	80	(6)	47[a]	(6)
van Praag and Korf, 1973 (30)	69[a]	(28)	75[a]	(28)
Sjostrom, 1974[c] (39)	low[a]	(22)	low[a]	(22)

[a]Significant, p< 0.05.

[b]Minus one patient treated with CPZ.

[c]CSF probenecid levels equal in patients and controls.

pressant treatments appear paradoxical? Are the changes specific to affective illness? Could they reflect predisposing factors? Are there biologically identifiable subgroups of depressed patients which have clinical relevance particularly in relation to the predication of response to specific drugs? And, finally what do these findings suggest for future work and model building?

Methods

Patients with affective illness diagnosed by criteria similar to that of Fieghner et al.[42] were admitted to a 12-bed clinical treatment and research unit at NIMH for three to five months. Methods, described in detail elsewhere,[29][43] included lumbar punctures performed at 9:00 AM (base line) and at 3:00 PM the next day after 18 hours of prior probenecid administration (100 mg/kg in four divided doses). Patients remained at bed rest from midnight until each lumbar puncture. For these drug-free studies, patients were off medications for at least two weeks. Similar procedures were followed for studies during treatment with tricyclic antidepressants (imipramine, amitriptyline) and lithium and after electroconvulsive shock

TABLE II

Base Line Levels of Amine Metabolites in Affective Illness and Experimental Hyperactivity

	5HIAA	HVA	MHPG
Normal and neurological controls	27.3 ± 2.2 (29)	22.4 ± 2.4 (28)	16.1 ± 2.2 (10)
Depression	25.6 ± 1.2 (72)	19.7 ± 2.3 (65)	10.3 ± .9 (40)[b]
Hypomania	25.4 ± 2.2 (9)	13.9 ± 3.8 (8)	11.6 ± 1.9 (5)
Mania	33.3 ± 3.8 (11)	26.2 ± 5.8 (12)	16.6 ± 3.4 (8)
Hyperactivity (for 4 hr in depressed patients)	39.7 ± 4.0[c] (11)	42.7 ± 5.1[c] (9)	16.4 ± 2.4[c] (8)

[a] Values = ng/ml ± SEM (number of subjects).

[b] Depressed vs. controls: 5HIAA and HVA, n.s.; MHPG, $p < 0.01$.

[c] Hyperactive vs. depressed: 5HIAA and HVA, $p < 0.001$; MHPG, $p < 0.05$.

therapy (ECT). For special studies, such as simulation of manic hyperactivity and sleep deprivation, appropriate modifications of the procedure were employed.[12] [44] Neurological controls and normal parents of neurological patients were studied under similar conditions in collaboration with T.N. Chase.[45] Acute schizophrenic patients were studied in collaboration with E. Fink and W. Carpenter.[46] 5HIAA, HVA and MHPG were determined by methods of Ashcroft and Sharman,[47] Gerbode and Bowers,[48] Anden *et al.*,[49] and Gordon and Oliver.[50] Duplicate samples were also assayed for HVA and MHPG by mass fragmentographic methods by Edna Gordon and co-workers[51] although only fluorometric and gas chromatographic assays will be reported here. In this paper, non-probenecid amine metabolite values will be referred to as *levels,* while probenecid-induced increases will be labeled *accumulations.*

Major Findings

Diagnostic Groups

In depressed patients, base line 5HIAA levels did not differ significantly from normal or neurological controls, acute schizophrenic, or manic patients (Table II). However, in a small group of depressed patients studied nine hours, rather than 18 hours, after probenecid administration, accumulations tended to be lower in neurological patients studied under similar conditions (Fig. 1). An appropriate control group assessed 18 hours after probenecid is now being studied to test the significance of the trend for lower 5HIAA accumulations in depression. 5HIAA accumulations after 18 hours in depressed patients were not significantly lower than in manic patients, however.

Base line HVA levels also do not significantly differ among normal control, neurological controls, depressed, or manic groups (Table II). However, HVA accumulations after nine hours of probenecid are significantly lower in depressed patients than in controls ($p < 0.01$). HVA's in depressed patients do not significantly differ from those in manic patients studied 18 hours after probenecid (Fig. 2).

Levels of MHPG in the CSF of depressed patients were significantly lower than other groups studied including normals ($p < 0.01$), mixed neurological patients ($p < 0.05$), Parkinsonian patients ($p < 0.01$), schizophrenic ($p < 0.01$), and manic patients ($p < 0.05$) (Table II). Accumulations of MHPG after probenecid paralleled the base lines, again revealing lower·

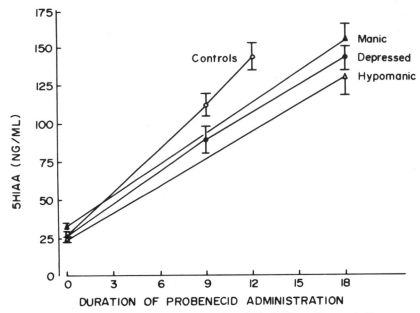

Fig. 1. Accumulation of 5HIAA after Probenecid in Different Diagnostic Groups

MHPG in depressed patients. While small, significant increases in total MHPG did occur after probenecid in all groups tested, they were not of the magnitude demonstrated for 5HIAA and HVA. In our patients the increase in MHPG is accounted for by free MHPG and not the sulfate conjugate[52] as reported in the rabbit[53] and rat.[54] Thus, in man increases in MHPG after probenecid do not appear related to a specific blockade of transport out of CSF. While these MHPG increases are thus not likely to reflect nonrepine-phrine turnover, values after probenecid lumbar punctures do serve as an independent replication of our base line MHPG results.

Clinical Correlations

Individually the three metabolites 5HIAA, HVA, and MHPG do not correlate significantly with individual clinical characteristics of affective illness, such as severity, presence of psychosis, absence of endogenous characteristics, or prior history of mania (bipolar). However, there were trends for lower levels of MHPG after probenecid to be associated with severity of depression and presence of endogenous symptoms. While there seemed to be a small cluster of depressed patients with very low MHPG's, they do not appear to represent a clinically separable subgroup. Although patients with very low MHPG's did tend to have lower 5HIAA accumulations after probenecid, there was no overall correlation of base line MHPG with 5HIAA, ($r = 0.18$) or HVA ($r = 0.14$) accumulation after probenecid (Fig. 3). Age was not a significant determinant of amine metabolite values.

Females had significantly higher probenecid-induced accumulations of 5HIAA and HVA (Table III) in spite of receiving a lower absolute dose of probenecid (administered on a mg/kg basis). The base line levels of 5HIAA and HVA were also higher, but not significantly, in females than in males. The trend was reversed for MHPG levels; females had nonsignificantly lower MHPG's than males.

Neither base line nor probenecid amine metabolite concentrations in drug-free depressed patients were significant predictors of subsequent clinical response to tricyclic or lithium antidepressant treatment although the trend for lower values to predict a therapeutic lithium response as reported earlier[29] continued.

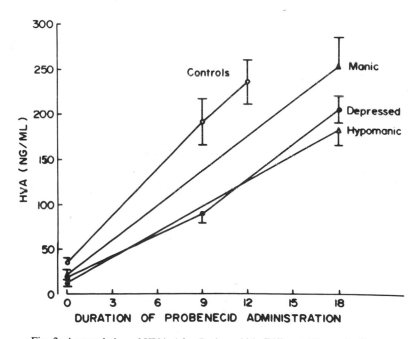

Fig. 2. Accumulation of HVA After Probenecid in Different Diagnostic Groups.

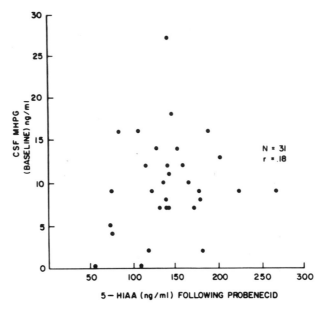

Fig. 3. Correlation between CSF 5-HIAA and MHPG in Depressed Patients

Effect of Motor Activity

All three metabolites, 5HIAA, HVA, and MHPG, increased significantly when depressed patients simulated manic hyperactivity for four hours prior to lumbar puncture (Table II). In depressed patients, afternoon lumbar punctures (2:00–4:00 PM) after milder degrees of activity (normal daily routine about ward with no bed rest) were associated with intermediate values for HVA and MHPG (Fig. 4). However, 5HIAA levels were significantly lower ($p < 0.05$) in the afternoon (18.3 ± 1.3, $n = 11$), than at 9:00 AM (25.6 ± 1.2, $n = 72$), perhaps reflecting a diurnal variation in serotonin metabolism that overrides a smaller activity effect.

Sleep Deprivation

Fourteen patients deprived of sleep for 26 to 34 hours tended to have increased 5HIAA's ($p < 0.10$), but MHPG and HVA remained unchanged. Of a total of 17 patients, nine experienced clear-cut mood improvement usually confined to the day after sleep deprivation, four showed equivocal clinical improvement, while four experienced negative effects such as increased fatigue, irritability, and depression. Antidepressant response to sleep deprivation was closely paralleled by subsequent antidepressant response to other therapeutic modalities (tricyclics, lithium, and ECT) ($p<0.05$, Chi square, Maxwell correction for small cell size). Base line levels of amine metabolites or changes in them after sleep deprivation were not significantly related to type of clinical response, although larger increases in 5HIAA tended to occur in the nonresponders rather than responders.

Effects of Antidepressant Treatments

Approximately three weeks of tricyclic (imipramine and amitriptyline) treatment significantly lowered probenecid-induced accumulations of 5HIAA, and ECT and lithium antidepressant treatment tended to do likewise[43][55][56] (Table IV). That is, 5HIAA accumulations which already may be low in depressed patients, decreased still further with successful (and in a few cases unsuccessful) antidepressant treatment. HVA was not significantly affected by tricyclics, lithium, or ECT.

TABLE III

Sex Differences in CSF Amine Metabolites in Affective Illness

	Males	Females	Significance
Baseline			
5HIAA	22.7 ± 3.5 (17)	26.5 + 1.3 (55)	n.s.
HVA	13.4 ± 2.5 (16)	21.7 · 3.0 (49)	n.s.
MHPG	11.7 ± 3.1 (7)	9.8 + 1.0 (30)	n.s.
Probenecid			
5HIAA	107 ± 11 (10)	153 + 9 (37)	p<0.05
HVA	154 ± 18 (9)	230 + 17 (36)	p· 0.05
MHPG	17.2 ± 2.7 (10)	14.7 + 1.6 (28)	n.s.

Base line and probenecid MHPG's remained low and did not significantly increase in depressed patients who improved clinically during tricyclic, lithium, or after ECT treatment or in a small improved group studied medication-free (Figs. 5 and 6). These preliminary findings require confirmation with a larger sample, but suggest that MHPG's may not return to normal levels with remission. However, in patients studied during tricyclic treatment there appeared to be an interaction of MHPG level with clinical response: Those patients who improved most with tricyclic treatment had slight increases in MHPG while those who did not improve had decreases in MHPG (Fig. 7). (Tricyclic responders and equivocal responders are included in the improved group in Figs. 5 and 6, above.)

The duration of psychotropic drug treatment may be a significant variable in determining amine changes. For example, the phenothiazines, chlorpromazine and thioridazine, induce large increases in HVA accumulation acutely, but after three weeks of administration, HVA accumulations are no longer elevated.[57] Such alterations in dopamine metabolism might provide a close correlation of time-course of biochemical effects and onset of maximum therapeutic efficacy.

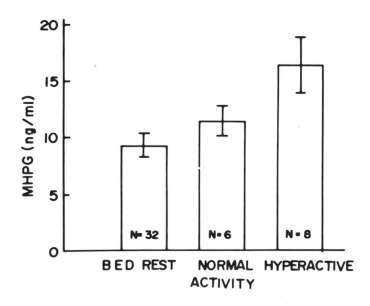

Fig. 4. Effect of Activity on Spinal Fluid MHPG in Depressed Patients

TABLE IV

Treatments of Depression: Effects on 5HIAA and HVA Accumulations

	Probenecid 5HIAA[a] N	Percent baseline	p	Probenecid HVA[a] N	Percent baseline	p
Depressed, med-free	143 ± 8 (50)	100		214 ± 14 (14)	100	
Amitriptyline	100 ± 12 (8)	70	0.05	213 ± 33 (7)	99	ns
Imiprimine	99 ± 15 (10)	70	0.05	224 ± 37 (10)	105	ns
Lithium	126 ± 13 (14)	89	ns	209 ± 21 (14)	98	ns
ECT	87 ± 17 (4)	61	0.05	121 ± 28 (4)	56	0.10
Improved, med-free	114 ± 12 (10)	80	ns	213 ± 28 (9)	99	ns

[a]Values = ng/ml ± S.E.M.

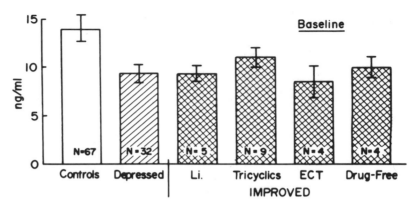

Fig. 5. CSF MHPG During Depression and After Recovery: Baseline

Discussion

Role of Amine Changes in Depression

The results, at first view, appear paradoxical; apparent amine metabolite changes in depression are not reversed by treatment, but in some cases, are exacerbated. The findings of low MHPG in depressed patients, which do not appear to increase with improvement on or off drugs, suggest an underlying biochemical alteration — one which might predispose to affective illness. This could reflect a genetic or early environmental-experiential change, or both. Such a deficit might represent a biochemical marker for increased vulnerability to affective illness, possibly reflecting an altered sensitivity to psychological and biochemical stress. It is also possible the MHPG is lowered in more immediate temporal proximity to the depressive episode, but the deficit is not immediately reversed and perhaps requires months to return to normal. In either case, if the MHPG findings are replicated, they would be inconsistent with the simple catecholamine hypothesis postulating a decrease in norepinephrine metabolism associated with depression per se.

It is puzzling that 5HIAA accumulations, which may initially be low during depression, decrease still further with treatment. One explanation is that the tricyclics, lithium, and ECT may, by different mechanisms, increase activity of the postsynaptic neuron and, via a feedback mechanism, turn off presynaptic synthetic activity resulting in a decrease in serotonin turnover. This result would be similar to the effects of a drug which stimulates dopamine receptors (such as ET-495) — it is effective in Parkinson's disease yet decreases already low HVA values in CSF still further.[58]

A less parsimonious and anti-intuitive alternate explanation could be that the pathophysiology of depression involves an increase in serotonin receptor activity and that any decrease in serotonin turnover measured in patients represents the operation of feedback mechanisms attempting to restore balance. By direct action on the presynaptic neuron,[59] antidepressant treatment might further reduce serotonin turnover enough to decrease postsynaptic activity as well. Recent studies by Sheard, Aghajanian, Bunney, and their co-workers, in which electrical recordings of single aminergic neurons are obtained, should aid in separating direct and reflex presynaptic and postsynaptic events.[60] [61] Tricyclic and monoamine oxidase inhibitor antidepressants, which decrease 5HIAA accumulations in CSF, also inhibit firing of presynaptic serotonergic neurons in the raphe system.[60]

A tentative, working formulation would then link some antidepressant treatment modalities to decreases in serotonin turnover. Conversely, we have recently examined the neurohormone melatonin, which increases serotonin turnover, and found that it exacerbates depressive symp-

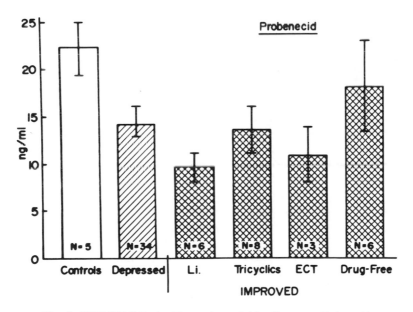

Fig. 6. CSF MHPG During Depression and After Recovery: Probenecid

tomatology.[62] [In studies at NIMH, we have not found tryptophan, the amino acid precursor of serotonin, to be a particularly effective antidepressant especially in unipolar patients.[63]] Furthermore, it is intriguing to speculate that the 40% higher 5HIAA levels at 9:00 AM compared to those in the afternoon could correlate with the early morning exacerbation of mood and symptomatology in some depressed patients. Finally, the higher levels and accumulations of 5HIAA (and HVA) in females than in males could ultimately relate to sex differences in susceptibility to depressive illness.

Dopamine metabolism as reflected in HVA values in CSF, may also be altered in depression (Table II, Fig. 2). Is it then reasonable to postulate a specific role for dopamine in depression? Or is it not more likely that changes in dopamine metabolism may be symptomatic of the depressive

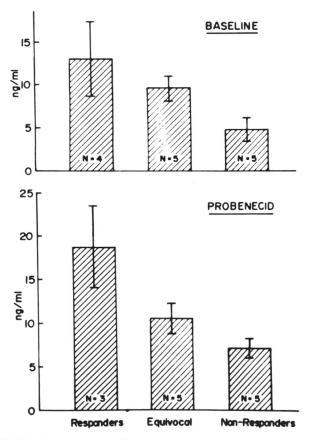

Fig. 7. CSF MHPG in Patients on Tricyclics: Relationship to Antidepressant Response

process or, more specifically, related to particular symptom configurations in affective illness, such as the clinical spectra of arousal and activity?[8] [17] The large changes in HVA with experimental hyperactivity argue in favor of this notion. Probenecid-induced accumulations of HVA are higher, but not significantly so, in manic (156 ± 13) compared to either hypomanic (131 ± 12) or depressed patients (143 ± 8) who are less active.

Our recent study of acute schizophrenic patients[46] demonstrated that their probenecid-induced accumulations of 5HIAA and HVA did not differ significantly from patients with depressive or manic illness. To the extent that acute schizophrenics can be considered a control group for patients with affective illness, the data suggest that serotonin and dopamine turnover may not be specifically altered in affective illness. Even if it is eventually demonstrated that all our psychiatric patient groups have lower metabolite accumulations than appropriate normal control groups, a specific or etiological role for these amines in any one psychiatric illness would still not be supported by the data. Some general illness-related variable, such as stress, arousal, psychic disorganization, sleep disturbance, hospitalization, etc., potentially could be mediating the alterations in amine metabolism.[17]

Implications

Based on the CSF data presented and more extensive reviews,[5-11] it appears that the concept of any one neurotransmitter abnormality providing a sufficient explanation of depressive illness is not supported. Rather, a more fruitful line of inquiry and conceptualization seems organized around the idea that multiple biological alterations may occur and potentially reflect such factors as underlying genetic-experiential predispositions, changes etiologically involved in the specific episode, and an array of nonspecific, symptom-like changes.

It is also possible that rather than multiple amine systems being altered in affective illness, there may be subgroups of patients whose depressions relate predominantly to alterations in one amine and not another. The idea that there may be biological as well as clinical heterogeneity in the affective disorders receives some support from the CSF findings; but it is disappointing, however, that all three amine metabolites in this study fail to predict subsequent drug responsiveness at a high level of statistical significance. More sophisticated statistical techniques such as discriminant function analysis may be helpful in defining clinical subtypes and predicting drug response on the basis of several metabolite alterations. Drug responders do appear to be separable on the basis of various clinical criteria and procedures such as sleep deprivation. There is an impressive correlation between antidepressant response to sleep deprivation and response to other treatment modalities. Those who improve after sleep deprivation also respond to other treatments (tricyclics, lithium, ECT).

New Directions

While metabolites measured to date appear to reflect presynaptic events, either primary or on a feedback basis, no measures of postsynaptic neuronal activity are available. However, it is possible that postsynaptic function and sensitivity might be assessed from measurements in CSF, such as that of C-AMP. An initial study of C-AMP in depression,[64] now substantiated by further data,[65] has shown that C-AMP is not decreased as reported in urinary studies and may even be elevated in CSF of depressed patients. In speculating far beyond the data available, it is conceivable that these levels could reflect an altered postsynaptic sensitivity in depressed patients and that this change, in addition to altered norepinephrine metabolism (low MHPG), might correlate with increased vulnerability to stress and psychological loss and subsequently to depression.

Methodological advances in mass fragmentography and radioimmunoassay presage the continued development of new CSF assays of neurotransmitters themselves (especially acetylcholine) in addition to their metabolites and the enzymes in their metabolic pathways, as well as assays of hormones and hypothalmic releasing factors in CSF. Another area for further investigation and clarification is the role of heavy metals and electrolytes and their influence on enzyme and neurotransmitter systems. For example, Carman et al.[66] have recently demonstrated consistent decreases in calcium concentrations in CSF (as well as serum) following ECT and several other antidepressant responses. Ultimately, the assessment of new transmitters and their regulators should lead to a more clear delineation of the complex interactions and feedback adjustments involved in depression and its treatment.

In the study of switch into and out of manic and depressive states rapid behavioral and biochemical changes have been stressed.[67] An equally rich avenue of investigation now appears to be the slow, tonic changes which may underlie and reach critical thresholds necessary for the occurence of sudden psychobiological shifts. Slow changes in EEG-monitored sleep parameters, evoked potentials, physical activity, amine metabolites, and vital signs have been documented in a patient with regular, approximately, three-week cycles between mania and depression.[68] Concepts of threshold, altered set-point, receptor supersensitivity, and altered biological rhythms are ripe for exploration and already appear within the limits of our techniques. Studies are now in progress at NIMH which explore different biochemical and psychological reactivity to psychological and physiological stresses.[69]

The time-limited changes in amine metabolism suggested by data on HVA accumulations during phenothiazine treatment[57] appear to offer new potential in understanding the relationship of biochemical change to clinical response. Alterations in amine systems that are manifest after three weeks of treatment may better correlate with the time-course of onset of maximal clinical antipsychotic or antidepressant effects (usually two to three weeks) than acute biochemical changes. The regulatory and long-term compensatory mechanisms within and between neurotransmitter systems may be crucially related to the pathophysiology of abnormal behavior and its therapies.

Thus, instead of a model suggesting a single biochemical abnormality in mania or depression, the thrust of newer, direct biological data in man would suggest the rewards of considering multiple alterations, subtle but critical changes in neurotransmitter ratios and sensitivities, and multiple feedback adjustments to psychoactive stimuli and drugs.

References

1. Bunney, W.E., Jr., and Davis, J.M.: Norepinephrine in depressive reactions. *Arch. Gen Psychiat.* 13: 483–494, 1965.
2. Schildkraut, J.J.: The catecholamine hypothesis of affective disorders: A review of supporting evidence. *Amer. J. Psychiat.* 122: 509–522, 1965.
3. Lapin, I.P., and Oxenkrug, G.F.: Intensification of the central serotonergic processes as a possible determinant of thymoleptic effect. *Lancet* i: 132–136, 1969.
4. Coppen, A.J.: The biochemistry of affective disorder. *Brit. J. Psychiat.* 113: 1237, 1969.
5. Goodwin, F.K., and Sack, R.L.: Affective Disorders: The catecholamine hypothesis revisited, *in* "Frontiers in Catecholamine Research" E Usdin and S. Snyder, eds. Pergamon Press, Oxford (1973).
6. Kety, S.: Brain amines and affective disorders *in* "Brain Chemistry and Mental Disease" B.T. Ho and W.M. McIsaac, Eds., pp. 237-244, Plenum Press, New York (1971).
7. Prange, A.J., Jr., Lipton, M., and Wilson, T.: Balance and permission as principles in the relationship between neurotransmitters and mental disease. Presented at the American College of Neuropsychopharmacology, December 1973.

8. Murphy, D.L.: L-DOPA, behavioral activation and psychopathology, *in* "Neurotransmitters," Kopin, I.J. (Ed.) — Res. Publ. Assoc. Res. Nerv. Ment. Dis. Vol. 50, pp. 472-493, (1972).

9. Janowski, D.S., Davis, J.M., El-Yousef, M.K., and Sekerke, H.J.: A cholinergic-adrenergic hypothesis of manic and depressions. *Lancet* ii, 632–635, 1972.

10. Post, R.M.: Multiple psychiatric syndromes related to a single pharmacological agent. Annual Meeting, American Psychiatric Association, Detroit, Michigan, May, 1974.

11. Goodwin, F.K., and Bunney, W.E., Jr.: A psychobiological approach to affective illness. *Psychiat. Ann.* 3:19–56, 1973.

12. Post, R.M., Kotin, J., Goodwin, F.K., and Gordon, E.K.: Psychomotor activity and cerebrospinal fluid amine metabolites in affective illness. *Amer. J. Psychiat.* 130: 67–72, 1973.

13. Post, R.M., Gordon, E.K., Goodwin, F.K., and Bunney, W.E., Jr.: Central norepinephrine metabolism in affective illness: MHPG in the cerebrospinal fluid. *Science* 179: 1002–1003, 1973.

14. Shaw, D.M., O'Keefe, R., MacSweeney, D.A., Brooksbank, B.W.L., Noguera,R., and Coppen, A., *et al.*: 3-Methoxy-4-hydroxyphenylglycol in depression. *Psychol. Med.* 3: 333-336, 1973.

15. Shopsin, B., Wilk, S., Gershon, S., Davis, K., and Suhl, M.: An assessment of norepinephrine metabolism in affective disorders. *Arch. Gen. Psychiat.* 28: 230–233, 1973.

16. Moir, A.T.B., Ashcroft, G.W., Crawford, T.B.B., *et al.*: Central metabolites in cerebrospinal fluid as a biochemical approach to the brain. *Brain* 93: 357–368, 1969.

17. Post, R.M., and Goodwin, F.K.: Simulated behavior states: An approach to specificity in psychobiological research. *Biol. Psychiat.* 7: 237–254, 1973.

18. Papeschi, R., Sourkes, T.L., Poirier, J.K., and Boucher, R.: On the intracerebral origin of homovanillic acid of the cerebrospinal fluid of experimental animals. *Brain Res.* 28: 527–533, 1971.

19. Curzon, G., Gumpert, E.J.W., and Sharpe, D.M.: Amine metabolites in the lumbar cerebrospinal fluid of humans with restricted flow of cerebrospinal fluid. *Nature New Biol.* 231: 189–191, 1971.

20. Post, R.M., Goodwin, F.K., Gordon, E.K., and Watkins, D.: Amine metabolites in human cerebrospinal fluid: Effects of cord transection and spinal fluid block. *Science* 179: 897–899, 1973.

21. Bulat, M., and Zivokiv, B.: Origin of 5-hydroxyindoleacetic acid in the spinal fluid. *Science* 173: 738–740, 1971.

22. Weir, R., Chase, T.N., Ng, L.K.Y., and Kopin, I.J.: 5-Hydroxyindoleacetic acid in spinal fluid: Relative contributions from brain and spinal cord. *Brain Res.* 52: 409–412, 1973.

23. Neff, N.H., Tozer, T.N., and Brodie, B.B.: Application of steady-state kinetics to studies of the transfer of 5-hydroxyindoleacetic acid from brain to plasma. *J. Pharmacol. Exp. Ther.* 158: 214–218, 1967.

24. Bowers, M.B.: Cerebrospinal fluid 5-hydroxyindoleacetic acid (5HIAA) and homovanillic acid (HVA) following probenecid in unipolar depressives treated with amitriptyline. *Psychopharmacologia (Berlin)* 23:26-33, 1972.

25. Roos, B.E., and Sjostrom, R.: 5-Hydroxyindoleacetic acid (and homovanillic acid) levels in the CSF after probenecid application in patients with manic-depressive psychosis. *Pharmacol. Clin* 1:153–155, 1969.

26. Van Praag,.H.M., and Korf, J.: A pilot study of some kinetic aspects of the metabolism of 5-hydroxytryptamine in depression. *Biol. Psychiat.* 3:105–112, 1971.

27. Van Praag, H.M., and Korf, J.: Retarded depression and the dopamine metabolism. *Psychopharmacologia (Berlin)* 19:199–203, 1971.

28. Sjostrom, R.: Steady-state levels of probenecid and their relation to acid monoamine metabolites in human cerebrospinal fluid. *Psychopharmacologia (Berlin)* 25:96–100, 1972.

29. Goodwin, F.K., Post, R.M., Dunner, D.L., and Gordon, E.K.: Cerebrospinal fluid amine metabolites in affective illness: The probenecid technique. *Amer. J. Psychiat.* 130:73–79, 1973.

30. Van Praag, H.M., Korf, J., and Schut, D.: Cerebral monoamines and depression. *Arch. Gen. Psychiat.* 28:827–833, 1973.

31. Tamarkin, N.R., Goodwin, F.K., and Axelrod, J.: Rapid elevation of biogenic amine metabolites in human CSF following probenecid. *Life Sci.* 9: 1397–1408, 1970.

32. Bowers, M.B., Jr.: Clinical measurements of central dopamine and 5-hydroxytryptamine metabolism: Reliability and interpretation of cerebrospinal fluid acid monoamine metabolite measures. Neuropharmacology 11: 101–111, 1972.

33. Sjostrom, R.: Steady-state levels of probenecid and their relation ot acid monoamine metabolites in human cerebrospinal fluid. *Psychopharmacologia (Berlin)* 28: 96–100, 1972.

34. Korf, J., and Van Praag, H.M.: Amine metabolism in the human brain: Further evaluation of the probenecid test. *Brain Res.* 35: 221–230, 1971.

35. Bulat, M., and Zivkovic, B.: Penetration of 5-hydroxyindoleacetic acid across the blood-cerebrospinal fluid barrier. *J. Pharm. Pharmacol.* 25: 178–179, 1973.

36. Korf, J., Van Praag, H.M., and Sebens, J.B.: Serum tryptophan decreased, brain tryptophan increased and brain serotonin synthesis unchanges after probenecid loading. *Brain Res.* 42: 239–242, 1972.

37. Van Praag, H.M., Flentge, F., Korf, J., Dols, L.C.W., and Schut, F.: The influence of probenecid on the metabolism of serotonin, dopamine and their precursors in man. *Psychopharmacologia (Berlin)* 33: 141–151, 1972.

38. Perel, J.M., Levitt, M., and Dunner, D.: Plasma and cerebrospinal fluid probenecid concentrations as related to accumulation of acidic biogenic amine metabolites in man. *Psychopharmacology* 35: 83–90, 1974.

39. Sjostrom, R.: Diagnosis of manic-depressive psychosis from cerebrospinal fluid concentration of 5-hydroxyindoleacetic acid, *in* "Serotonin—New Vistas," Biochemistry and Behavioral and Clinical Studies, E. Costa, G.L. Gessa, and M. Sandler, Eds., Vol 11. Raven, New York (1974).

40. Bowers, M.B.: Amitriptyline in man: Decreased formation of central 5-hydroxyindoleacetic acid. *Clin. Pharm. Therap.* 15: 167–170, 1974.

41. Post, R.M., Allen, F.H., and Ommaya, A.K.: Cerebrospinal fluid and iodide[131] transport in the spinal subarachnoid space. *Life Sci.,* 14: 1885-1894, 1974.

42. Feighner, J.P., Robins, E., Guze, S.B., Woodruff, R.W., Jr., Winobur, G., and Munoz, R.: Diagnostic criteria for use in psychiatric research. *Arch. Gen. Psychiat.* 26: 57–63, 1972.

43. Post, R.M., and Goodwin, F.K.: Effects of amitriptyline and imipramine on amine metabolites in the cerebrospinal fluid of depressed patients. *Arch. Gen. Psychiat.* 30: 234–239, 1974.

44. Post, R.M., Kotin, J., and Goodwin, F.K.: Effects of sleep deprivation on mood and

CSF amine metabolites in depressed patients, in *"Sleep Research"* M.H. Chase, W.C. Stern, and P.L. Walter, Eds., Vol. 2, p. 171, Bram Information Service, Univ. Calif., Los Angeles (1973).

45. Chase, Y.N. Gordon, E.K., and Ng, L.K.Y.: Norepinephrine metabolism in the central nervous system of man: Studies using 3-methoxy-4-hydroxyphenylethylene glycol levels in cerebrospinal fluid. *J. Neurochem.* 20: 1–7, 1973.

46. Fink, E., Post, R.M., Carpenter, W., and Goodwin, F.K.: CSF amine metabolites in acute schizophrenia. Presented at the Annual Meetings, American Psychiatric Association, Detroit, May 6–10, 1974.

47. Ashcroft, G.W., and Sharman, D.F.: Measurement of acid monoamine metabolites in human CSF. *Brit. J. Pharmacol.* 19: 153–160, 1962.

48. Gerbode, F., and Bowers, M.D.: Measurement of acid monoamine metabolites in human and animal cerebrospinal fluid. *J. Neurochem.* 15: 1053–1055, 1968.

49. Anden, N.E., Roos, B.E., and Werdinius, B.: The occurrence of homovanillic acid in brain and cerebrospinal fluid and its determination by a fluorimetric method. *Life Sci.* 2: 448–458, 1963.

50. Gordon, E.K., and Oliver, J.: 3-Methoxy-4-hydroxyphenylethylene glycol in human cerebrospinal fluid. *Clin. Chim. Acta* 35: 145–150, 1971.

51. Gordon, E.K., Oliver, J., Black, K.E., and Kopin, I.J.: Simultaneous assay by mass fragmentography of VMA, HVA and MHPG in CSF and urine, *Biochem. Med.*, 1974, in press.

52. Gordon, E.K., Oliver, J., Goodwin, F.K., Chase, T.N., and Post, R.M.: Effect of probenecid on free 3-methoxy-4-hydroxyphenylethylene glycol (MHPG) and its sulfate in human cerebrospinal fluid. *Neuropharmacology* 12: 391–396, 1973.

53. Extein, T., Korf, J., Roth, R.H., and Bowers, M.B., Jr.: Accumulation of 3-methoxy-4-hydroxyphenylglycol-sulfate in rabbit cerebrospinal fluid following probenecid. *Brain Res.* 54: 403–407, 1973.

54. Meek, J.L., and Neff, N.H.: Acidic and neutral metabolites of norepinephrine: Their metabolism and transport from brain. *J. Pharmacol. Exp. Ther.* 181: 457–462, 1972.

55. Goodwin, F.K., Post, R.M., and Murphy, D.L.: Cerebrospinal fluid amine metabolites and therapies for depression. Presented at the Annual Meeting, American Psychiatric Association, Honolulu, Hawaii, May 1973.

56. Post, R.M., and Goodwin, F.K.: Electroconvulsive shock therapy and amine metabolites in CSF of depressed patients, unpublished manuscript.

57. Post, R.M., and Goodwin, F.K.: Phenothiazines: Dopamine turnover and onset of antipsychotic effects. Letter to *Lancet,* 1974, in press.

58. Chase, T.N., Woods, A.C., and Glaubiger, G.A.: Parkinson disease treated with a suspected dopamine receptor agonist. *Arch. Neurol.* 30: 383–386, 1974.

59. Bruinvels, J.: Inhibition of the biosynthesis of 5-hydroxytryptamine in rat brain by imipramine. *Eur. J. Pharmacol.* 20: 231–127, 1972.

60. Sheard, M.H., Zolovick, A., and Aghajanian, G.K.: Raphe neurons: Effects of tricyclic antidepressant drugs. *Brain Res.* 43: 690–694, 1972.

61. Bunney, B.S., and Aghajanian, G.K.: Central dopaminergic neurons: A model for predicting the efficacy of putative antipsychotic drugs, in *"The Use of Model Systems in Biological Psychiatry"* D. Ingle and H. Shein, Eds., M.I.T. Press, Cambridge (1974), in press.

62. Carman, J.S., Post, R.M., Buswell, R., and Goodwin, F.K.: Melatonin and mood, unpublished data.

63. Murphy, D.L., Baker, M., Kotin, J., and Bunney, W.E., Jr.: Behavioral and metabolic effects of L-tryptophan in unipolar depressed patients, in "Serotonin and Behavior" J. Brachas and E. Usdin, Eds., Academic Press, New York (1972).

64. Cramer, H., Goodwin, F.K., Post, R.M., and Bunney, W.E., Jr.: Effect of probenecid and exercise on cerebrospinal fluid cyclic AMP in affective illness. *Lancet* ii: 1346–1347, 1972.

65. Cramer, H., Post, R.M., and Goodwin, F.K., unpublished data.

66. Carman, J., Post, R.M., Goodwin, F.K., Bunney, W.E., Jr., and Teplitz, T.A.: Calcium, ECT, lithium, and mood. Presented at the Annual Meetings, American Psychiatric Association, Detroit, May, 1974.

67. Bunney, W.E., Jr., Goodwin, F.K., and Murphy, D.L.: The 'Switch Process' in manic-depressive illness. I, II, and III. *Arch. Gen. Psychiat.* 27: 295–317, 1972.

68. Stoddard, F.J., Post, R.M., Gillin, J.C., Buchsbaum, M.S., Carman, J.S., and Bunney, W.E., Jr.: Phasic changes in manic depressive illness. Presented at the Annual Meeting, American Psychiatric Association, Detroit, May, 1974.

69. Goodwin, F.K., Beckman, H., and Buchsbaum, M.: Effects of stress on urinary MHPG in depressed patients and normal controls. Unpublished data, 1974.

70. Sjostrom, R., and Roos, B.E.: 5-Hydroxyindoleacetic acid and homovanillic acid in cerebrospinal fluid in manic-depressive psychosis. *Eur. J. Clin. Pharmacol.* 4: 170–176, 1972.

Chapter 5

An Overview of the Basis
for Amine Hypotheses
in Affective Illness*

ROSS J. BALDESSARINI

One of the most widely discussed current ideas concerning a possible biological basis of the affective disorders is that the metabolism of biogenic amines may be disturbed in these conditions.[1-8] A series of similar hypotheses have derived from the theory that biologically active monoamines, known to affect smooth muscle and other peripheral tissues, function in the central nervous system (CNS) as neurotransmitters at chemically mediated synapses, or otherwise as neurohumors modulating the activity of central neurons which are involved in the regulation of mood and behavior. The amines usually discussed in this context are the catecholamines, dopamine and norepinephrine, and the idoleamine, 5-hydroxytryptamine, or serotonin, as well as the quarternary amine, acetylcholine. In their simplest form, the hypotheses suggest that depression is associated with altered availability

*Partially supported by U.S. Public Health Service (NIMH) Grant MH-16674 and U.S.P.H.S. (NIMH) Career Development Award, MH-74370.

of one or another of these amines at functionally important sites, or "receptors" and conversely, that mania is associated with an alteration opposite to the present in depression.

The general idea that affective illnesses might be due to a derangement of the metabolic chemistry of the patient is at least as old as classical antiquity since the Hippocratic tradition included the notion that melancholia represented a disorder of behavior and feeling associated with an excess of a humor, black bile. With the rise of modern scientific medicine, such ideas have persisted and expanded. Several features of affective illnesses are usually cited as supporting a biological hypothesis. These include the association of somatic symptoms with depression (disturbances of sleep, appetite, gastrointestinal function, sex drive, and sensation) and the diurnal pattern of depression, as well as the frequent association of depression with medical illness, including endocrine and other metabolic disorders. Also, the growing impression that there may be a familial-genetic aspect of the major affective disorders gives further support for the existence of a biological component in their etiology. Finally. the apparent lack of association with obvious external "stress factors" in the initiation of many serious depressions or elations suggests that they may arise from an internal dysfunction.

In addition to these general features of affective disorders suggestive of a biological etiology, the development of effective organic therapies for the disorders with the rise of modern psychopharmacology in recent decades has given more substantial and specific support to hypotheses relating affective disturbances to disorders of neurotransmitter function. Perhaps the most influential developments in this century which suggested that physical treatments could have specific and profound effects on major endogenous or idiopathic psychiatric illnesses was the introduction of the "shock" therapies (insulin coma, 1933; chemically induced seizures, 1934; and electroshock, 1937). Most of these treatments are now only of historical interest, and while the popularity of electroconvulsive therapies (ECT) also waned following the appearance of antidepressant and antipsychotic drug therapies in the 1950's, modern ECT remains the most effective and a very safe form of treatment of severe depressive illness. By the late 1950's, psychiatry had available at least three kinds of drugs which were effective in mania (lithium salts, reserpine, and the phenothiazines and their relatives) and two types of antidepressants (the inhibitors of monoamine oxidase (MAO) and the "tricyclic" agents such as imipramine). These groups of drugs were found to be, respectively, antagonistic or agonistic to the monoamine neurons in the CNS. In addition, it was realized that antiad-

TABLE I

Effects of Drugs on the Metabolism of Amines in the CNS

Type of Drug	Drug	Actions	Behavioral Effects
Precursors	L-Dopa	DA increased	Antiparkinsonian, dyskinesia, psychotogenic
	Tryptophan 5HTP	5HT increased	Sedative usually, antimanic?
Inhibitors of Synthesis	α-Me-*p*-Tyrosine (AMPT)	Blocks tyrosine hydroxylase, lowers CA levels	Sedative, antihypertensive
	α-Me-DOPA (Aldomet)	Blocks decarboxylase	Sedative, antihypertensive, depressant
	Disulfiram (Antabuse)	Blocks β-hydroxylase, lowers NE	Little effect, some depression, some excitement on withdrawal
	p-Cl-Phenylalanine (PCPA)	Blocks tryptophan hydroxylase, lowers 5HT	Aggression, hypersexuality, insomnia
Decrease retention	α-Me-DOPA	False transmitter replaces endogenous CA	Sedative, antihypertensive, depressant
	Reserpine, tetrabenazine	Block storage in vesicles, lower amine levels	Sedative, depressant
Alter membrane crossing	Amphetamines	Increase release, decrease re-uptake (some MAO inhibition)	Stimulant, anorexic, psychotogenic
	Cocaine	Decreases re uptake	Stimulant, euphoriant
	Tricyclic antidepressants (e.g., imipramine)	Mainly block re-uptake (some MAO inhibition)	Antidepressant
	Lithium salts	Decrease release and storage	Antimanic, mood stabilizing
Block receptors	Neuroleptics e.g., phenothiazines, butyrophenones)	Mainly CA-receptor-blockade	Antimanic, neuroleptic, antipsychotic, sedative
	Lithium salts	Block adenyl cyclase	Antimanic, mood stabilizing
	Methysergide	Mainly indoleaminc-receptor blockade	Antimanic? (doubtful)
Inhibitors of Catabolism	MAO inhibitors	Block MAO, increase amine levels	Antidepressant, euphoriant
	Polyphenols (e.g., butylgallate)	Block COMT	Little effect or toxic

Abbreviations and symbols used: DA. dopamine; NE. norepinephrine; CA. catecholamine; 5HT. serotonin; 5HTP. 5-hydroxytryptophan; Me. methyl; MAO. monoamineoxidase; COMT. catechol-*O*-methytransferase.

renergic drugs, including reserpine and other related amine-depleting agents, as well as the methylated analogs of amino acid precursors of the catecholamines (such as α-methyl-dopa) were sometimes associated with depressive syndromes in patients receiving the drugs for hypertension (see Table I). Interestingly, each of the therapeutic discoveries in clinical psychopharmacology occurred by serendipity or lucky accident without the benefit of the now current theories of their effects on the metabolism of central neurotransmitters, and certainly without the benefit of an amine hypothesis of the affective disorders.

By the late 1950's the time was ripe for specific formulations of such amine hypotheses, which started to appear [1] [2] and to affect clinical experimentation[9] [10] by 1959, although Weil-Malherbe had begun to study the metabolism of catecholamines and serotonin in the body fluids of psychiatric patients several years earlier.[11] Since that time, specific hypotheses have been presented and discussed repeatedly. In this country, the catecholamines and particularly norepinephrine have been emphasized, while many European investigators have been very interested in serotonin. These hypotheses arose in an era of optimism of the 1950's and 1960's, which accompanied enormous strides in basic and applied biochemistry, including the description of several genetic errors of metabolism, and the impressive empirical successes of the psychopharmaceutical industry. The various amine hypotheses have often been called "heuristic," and it is true that they have kept many investigators busy testing them. Sadly, to date, they have not led to a coherent basic biological theory of abnormal human behavior, nor have they led to the rational development of more powerful or safer therapies than those available nearly 20 years ago through the benefits of empiricism and simple good luck.

An important preliminary question is why have pharmacologists directed so much effort and attention to the synapse as a likely site of action of drugs used in psychiatry and as a likely site of abnormality in psychiatric illness? There appear to be at least two reasons. First, it is likely that the synapse represents a particularly vulnerable point of neuronal function where relatively selective and specific metabolic derangements or drug mechanisms might occur. In contrast, based on comparison with known instances of organic brain dysfunction, it seems likely that a disturbance of the metabolism of neurons affecting, for example, energy production, impulse conduction, or the structure of the cell or its myelin sheath would lead to a rather generalized dysfunction such as coma or dementia, or might produce a visible histological neuropathology, none of which occurs in depression or mania. A second reason is that the development of modern neuropharmacology has been heavily influenced by concepts and methods developed for the more classic pharmacology of the peripheral autonomic nervous system, which have been very fruitfully applied to studies of the actions of psychopharamaca on the CNS.

In the past decade, a great deal of neurohistological, biochemical, and behavioral work in the mammalian brain have contributed a considerable body of knowledge bearing on the location and probable functions of monoamine-containing neuronal pathways in the CNS.[8][12][13] Several conclusions based on that work are now evolving. In general, it seems probable that many important functions of the brainstem and diencephalon subserving crucial autonomic and homeostatic mechanisms are partially regulated by neurons which synthesize and secrete monoamine neurotransmitters. It is clear that the very diffuse and widespread distribution of terminals arising from the cell bodies of serotonin- and norepinephrine-containing neurons is well suited to their serving generalized functions having a relatively leisurely time course. Such functions might include levels of arousal or consciousness, the tonic regulation of autonomic functions and their phasic responses to challenge and stress, and possibly affect, either as a discrete function or as a condition of arousal or autonomic function; other functions might include the regulation of muscular tone and posture through the extrapyramidal motor system, and quite possibly, the regulation of timing of other functions. It almost seems as if monoaminergic systems of the CNS represent an homologous analog of the peripheral autonomic nervous system, except that the "end-organ" is the CNS itself. It seems very unlikely that monoaminergic systems would be involved in very precise, rapidly changing functions subserving sensation or the central control of the phasic contraction of skeletal muscles. It is also clear that monoamine systems, arising from a mere few thousands of cell bodies, do not account for a large proportion of the total millions of neurons and billions of synaptic connections in the brain. Nevertheless, in relation to the basic biology of behavior and psychiatric illness, it does seem that aminergic systems are particularly likely to be involved, if only secondarily or incidentally, in the disturbances of mood, drive, initiative, sleep, and diurnal rhythmicity as well as sexual and feeding behavior, and hypothalamic–adrenal function which are characteristic of the major affective disorders.

In addition to the preclinical experimentation with central monoamine systems of animals, there has also been a considerable attempt to apply many of the insights and suggestions of that work to the building of clinical hypotheses and the conduct of clinical experimentation.[8][14] Several aspects of this attempt require further critical comment. First, there may have been a tendency to focus too narrowly on a few amines in the past. The dominance of the now classic studies of acetylcholine at the myoneural junction and in the peripheral parasympathetic nervous system and of norepinephrine in the peripheral sympathetic nervous system appear to have had a particularly influential restraining effect in the development of hypotheses concerning chemical synaptic transmission in the CNS. Since it is likely that there are many neurotransmitters,[13] including other amines and amino acids, they should also be considered in future hypotheses. Much of the interest in the catecholamines and indoleamines has evolved through the application of attractive unifying concepts and reliable experimental methods to both preclinical and clinical studies which have been mutually supportive, but which may have reinforced the retention of a somewhat constricted and simplistic set of hypotheses.

One very broad criticism of the amine hypotheses is that they have often not adequately taken into account the physiology of central neurotransmitters. This may have been due to the relatively primitive state of knowledge of the function of central neurotransmitters, which has lagged behind developments in the biochemical pharmacology of central synapses, although this situation is changing.[12] The development of the ''indoleamine hypotheses'' may represent one particularly flagrant example of the failure to consider what is known physiologically. These have generally followed the lead of the ''catecholamine hypotheses'' in assuming that a deficiency of serotonin equals depression and that an excess equals mania. Such a simple view seems no longer to be tenable in light of what is now known about the functional role of the indoleamines in the CNS. Thus, most behavioral and pharmacological studies suggest that an *excess* of serotonin is associated with ''behavioral–depressant'' effects, while decreased availability of serotonin as associated with a variety of ''excited'' behaviors (insomnia, hyperarousal, hypersexuality, aggression, etc.). Indeed, it might make more sense to consider the converse hypothesis: that *too much* serotonin may have something to do with some depressions.

A second criticism derives from a consideration of the metabolic regulation of aminergic synapses in the brain. Initially, amine hypotheses and even experiments were based on the grossly simplistic notion that too much amine did one thing and that too little did the opposite, and ''much'' and ''little'' were taken to mean static concentrations or ''levels'' of a substance as measured by chemical assay. One of the earliest observations contradicting that idea was that reserpinized animals are still responsive to behavioral stimulation by amphetamine, suggesting that depletion of an amine by reserpine may remove large stores not directly involved in synaptic function.

In recent years the concept has evolved that most, if not all, amine-containing nerve terminals contain multiple "pools" of transmitter, that only a small portion of the total is essential for function, and that the rest is held in storage, possibly in presynaptic vesicles.[13] Animal experimentation has made an important step forward in considering the dynamics rather than the "statics" of amines in the brain, but even the attempt to correlate "turnover" with function or with the action of a drug is fraught with difficulty, because overall turnover is heavily biased toward measuring metabolism in the physiologically relatively uninteresting large storage pools rather than in the presumptive small functional pools of neurotransmitter. This problem may be particularly severe with the indoleamines, which appear constantly to overflow onto MAO, as the ability to store serotonin at least seems to be much less than the ability to make it.

A similar consideration which is often overlooked is that synapses are highly regulated, complex, dynamic functional systems. The degree of complexity and the physiological importance of the multiple means of their regulation are only beginning to be appreciated.[13] A few of the regulatory features of synaptic metabolism include precursor availability, the activity and concentrations of rate-limiting synthetic enzymes, the availability of their cofactors, the short-term and long-term responsiveness of transmitter synthesis to functional demands, the involvement of local and more distant feedback loops built into the neuronal circuitry, the activity of postsynaptic receptors, and the role of presynaptic receptors and local hormones in modulating the rate of release of transmitter. It is also likely that regulation occurs between neurons as well as within a neuron, and that the transmitters can affect the availability of other transmitters and their synthesizing enzymes in cells with which a given neuron has synaptic relationships. One other complicating feature of central amine-containing neurons is that their morphology is not irrevocably fixed; for example, the portion of an axon proximal to a lesion can grow and sprout, leading to a paradoxical excess of terminals and an eventual *increase* in neurotransmitter in some areas. The importance of all these regulatory features is that synaptic transmission must be considered a marvelously plastic and adaptive function, which is not simply turned on or off, and which is protected by a series of redundant homeostatic mechanisms. Unfortunately, most of the hypotheses about neurotransmission in psychiatric illness have assumed that the synapses are vulnerable and brittle and that their dysfunction should be easy to detect, overlooking the fact that synapses regularly respond to perturbation by compensatory changes which tend to reestablish physiological equilibrium. In an attempt to circumvent these various complications, there has been some consideration of the idea that the important aspect of transmitter function is the amount of transmitter that reaches and interacts with a receptor, but even this approach falls short at our complete ignorance of the function of the "effectors" which are moved by the interaction of transmitter and receptor.

Another aspect of the complexity of neurotransmitters and synaptic function is that normal behavior seems to require a well-orchestrated balance of the function of many component parts of the CNS, each involving different transmitters. A useful, if oversimplified generalization is that in the CNS, as in the peripheral autonomic nervous system, there seem to be at least two fundamental types of function, which can be called sympathetic or ergotropic, and parasympathetic or trophotropic.[3][12][15] The neurotransmitters which subserve these functions in the periphery are the catecholamines and acetylcholine, respectively. In the CNS, it also appears that catecholamines are involved with functions that might be described as activation, alertness, and appetitive or consummatory activity, while acetylcholine and serotonin seem to subserve quieting, behavior-inhibiting functions. Thus, depression and mania need not represent simply the loss of one type of function, but might rather represent a change in balance between generally opposing tendencies, for example, a shift toward relatively decreased catecholaminergic function and relatively increased cholinergic or even serotonergic function in depression and the opposite in mania.

There has been considerable debate about how well each of the monoamines fits the hypothesis that it is uniquely deficient in depression and excessively active in mania.[8] In favor of both hypotheses, it is usually pointed out that reserpine may lead to depression in susceptible patients and to a reduction of activity in animals while depleting both classes of monoamines. On the other hand, other antihypertensive drugs which more specifically antagonize the catecholamines and which can enter the CNS have been associated with sedation, depression, and antimanic effects, while those which do not pass the "blood–brain barrier" (such as guanethidine) apparently have not. Furthermore, precursors of the catecholamines, but not of the indoleamines can reverse the sedation produced by reserpine in animals and man. It should be made clear that the whole idea of relying on states of drug-induced amine depletion in animals or in man as "models of depression" is potentially misleading. The problems with "reserpine models" of depression and similar pharmacological models are that drugs which can reverse the behavioral depression associated with them (especially L-dopa and amphetamine) are not effective antidepressants in patients, and that the behavioral syndrome in animals in some instances more closely resembles sedation than depression; even in man, many of the reports of so-called depression associated with antihypertensive drugs probably represent sedation and lethargy or even cases of organic brain syndrome. Furthermore, the clinical reactions are hard to interpret since antihypertensive drugs are likely to be associated with frank depressive syndromes at unpredictable and often quite delayed times, and most often in patients who appear to be particularly predisposed or susceptible "hosts" by previous psychiatric history.[16]

The effects of the currently available MAO inhibitors in depression and in preventing the inactivation of most monoamines help both amine hypotheses about equally. The clinical effects of precursor amino acids for the indoleamines are either minimal or at least controversial, and perhaps pluripotential (both antidepressant and antimanic actions are reported)[17]; nevertheless, tryptophan might have some anti-manic effect and can have a sedative effect in some circumstances.[18] While L-dopa, on the other hand, the precursor of the catecholamines, has some stimulant properties,[19] it is no more useful in treating serious depressions than amphetamine or other stimulants, and it has even been associated with depressive reactions in some Parkinsonian patients. On the whole, as a very cautious generalization, the effects of precursors tend to support the conclusion that catecholamines generally tend to favor "stimulation" and that serotonin favors "sedation." Similarly, the relatively specific inhibition of tyrosine hydroxylase (with α-methyltyrosine) produces sedation or behavioral depression and may suppress mania, while the somewhat less specific inhibition of tryptophan hydroxylase (with p-chlorphenylalanine) on the whole tends to produce behavioral activation and hyperresponsiveness or very little effect at all. While the original tricyclic antidepressants prevent the inactivation of both catecholamines and serotonin, the facts that the desmethylated forms of these drugs are more selective against norepinephrine, and that they are prominent metabolites of the original drugs may favor a catecholamine hypothesis. The effects of lithium ion are supportive of amine hypotheses in general, but do not support one amine exclusively. The metabolic effects of ECT suggest that seizures can release catecholamines and serotonin acutely, but that effects of repeated seizures are likely to be nonspecific in the case of serotonin, and small and of short duration in the case of norepinephrine.[20] Perhaps the most important support for a single amine hypothesis are the physiological and behavioral effects of the catecholamines and indoleamines or their agonists introduced into the brain, and again, the evidence clearly favors the catecholamines.[8] [12] On balance, the behavioral and pharmacological data support a catecholamine hypothesis much more consistently than an indoleamine hypothesis.[8] An alternative position would be that an indoleamine deficiency might help to explain *some* features of depressive illness, such as insomnia and possibly some aspects of agitation, while a deficiency of catecholamines would perhaps better explain decreased drive, pleasure, enthusiasm, and appetite for food and sex, particularly in retarded depressions. Since both amines undergo important diurnal variations, a deficiency of either one might underlie the diurnal pattern of depressive symptoms. Acetylcholine could also be added as another variable which might have increased functional activity in retarded depressions and decreased activity in mania and other states of psychotic agitation.[15]

Although the preceding arguments are the common ones presented in discussions of catecholamine versus indoleamine hypotheses, there are many limitations and problems associated with them. All of the amine hypotheses seem to presume that mania and depression represent opposite poles along a single mood scale, although manic–depressive illness is much more complicated than that, and there are at least several clinical types of both endogenous depressions and manias. The current amine hypotheses do not readily account for this kind of clinical variability, and instead tend to view manic-depressive illness as a one-dimensional problem of too little or too much of something in the brain.

Another fundamental problem is that the arguments based on the metabolic or behavioral actions of drugs require gross oversimplification (Table I) and selective inattention to many aspects of preclinical and clinical pharmacology. Drugs have generally been given much more credit for clinical potency and for specificity of action, clinically or biologically, than is deserved. None of the drugs does only one thing chemically or clinically, as is sometimes inferred. Furthermore, much of what is known about the actions of drugs is strongly biased because so much attention has been given to an overly restricted range of clinically relevant theories, perhaps based at least partly on a desire to provide social justification for the pursuit of basic science. The investigation of drugs has usually been done with doses and schedules that are very different from the clinical situation: doses tend to be huge and experiments are almost never done chronically, largely because it is more difficult and expensive to do so. Even though many of the behavioral effects of the drugs in normal laboratory animals treated in this way are *not* similar to the clinical effects, the corresponding metabolic effects observed under the same conditions are usually accepted uncritically. Since it often happens that metabolic effects after repeated administration are opposite, nonexistant, or otherwise dissimilar to those observed after a single dose of a drug, it is possible to be badly misled by acute experiments.

The behavioral effects of drugs in the experimental situation are often very different from the effects observed clinically. An outstanding example of this phenomenon is that large acute doses of most antidepressants tend to produce sedation in normal laboratory animals, and it has been very difficult to devise reliable laboratory behavioral tests to screen potential new antidepressant drugs. Another problem is that most of the so-called "animal models of affective illness" are really more nearly models of sedation or stimulation, thus making it very tricky to make comparisons between human disease and animal models or to make predictions about human clinical responses based on animal behavior. Clinically, too, there are some marked peculiarities of the effects of drug substances which are difficult to reconcile with the current amine hypotheses. For example, the division of somatic therapies into antidepressant and antimanic has certain inconsistencies. It is clear that the most effective antimanic agents are highly nonspecific; they are useful in many psychotic and nonpsychotic conditions and they are even useful in the management of some agitated depressions. Less easily evaluated are the occasional reports that several forms of treatment have antimanic effects which are at variance with the amine hypotheses, For example, amphetamine, tricyclic antidepressants, and ECT have all at one time or another been used to treat manic patients,[9] evidently with some success. A persistent difficulty for the current hypotheses is the slowness of clinical action of both the MAO-inhibitors and the tricyclic antidepressants (and in some cases, ECT as well), while their much-discussed metabolic effects occur quickly. While this aspect may suggest that subtle late-occurring metabolic changes should be suspected, it seems likely that this time-course may involve "nonbiological" aspects of psychological adaptation and reintegration of the recovering patient. A final theoretical and practical problem of the available antidepressants is that they are simply unsatisfactory drugs, the efficacy of which is sometimes barely demonstrable.

In reviewing the clinical metabolic studies in this field, one is forced to conclude that it is a tribute to the persuasiveness and attractiveness of current pharmacological theories concerning the biogenic amines that they have persisted in spite of conflicting and inconsistent clinical findings.[3 5 8 14 19 21-29] Even the most cautious conclusions based on the clinical literature are hard to propose without fear of contradiction. Nevertheless, they would seem to include the following points: many amines seem to be released from peripheral tissues and made more available to general metabolism and urinary excretion during states of excitement or agitation, regardless of the diagnostic lable applied (mania or agitated depression); conversely, in retarded depressive states the opposite tends to occur. Comparable events may also occur in the brain, although this point is still unclear. While it is usually assumed that changes in the CNS are likely to be more important than changes in the peripheral metabolism of amines or the activity of the autonomic nervous system, there is no *à priori* reason why this must be so. Furthermore, since similar changes in amine metabolism may also be associated with other psychiatric illness or even "stress," their specificity to affective illness is questionable. There is almost no evidence to suggest that these changes are primary and thus perhaps etiologically important in initiating the severe endogenous affective disorders, although the recent hint that changes in the rate of excretion of MHPG (3-methoxy-4-hydroxyphenylethylene-glycol, a metabolite of norepinephrine, at least part of which is derived from the brain) in the urine of a patient, followed over time may have slightly *preceded* the clinical change in mood and behavior[30] is very interesting in this regard. This approach also highlights another important methodological question of whether some of the failures to find clinical evidence of changes in the excretion or CSF levels of MHPG or other amine metabolites when comparisons were made between groups of patients may represent "false negative" findings due to scatter of data and regression to the mean, paradoxically, as the size of the groups increase. In other words, serial studies of individual patients over time may represent a more powerful (though usually more difficult) research strategy.

While the changes may be only peripheral or incidental, it is not unlikely that changes in the metabolism of the monoamines are one part of the pathophysiology of the affective disorders, and that can be true without any implication about etiology or "cause." It is on this point that room is allowed for psychosocial hypotheses about the affective illnesses. The increased understanding of the physiology of central neurotransmission should help greatly to make sense of the clinical pathophysiology of depression and mania, as it has already helped to evolve theories concerning the actions of several forms of physical treatment that really do something for affective illness and which also have clear effects on the metabolism of biogenic amines in the brain. There may be a risk of a *post hoc, propter hoc* logical fallacy in this field, as it is often accepted uncritically that responsiveness to a physical therapy implies not only the existence of an organic–metabolic etiology, but furthermore that the etiology is opposite to the metabolic actions of the treatment. It may very well be that the organic therapies merely suppress or activate central neuronal systems which mediate emergency and stress responses, tending to reestablish homeostasis, regardless of how they came into action or inaction in mania or depression, respectively. Nevertheless, even if alterations in amine metabolism have nothing to do with the cause of the illnesses, but modifying this metabolism with drugs or treatments has therapeutic value, then an understanding of the biogenic amines would indeed still be worthwhile.

The confusing state of affairs in the clinical literature on amine metabolism has led to a tendency to seek finer subdivisions of the diagnostic categories, in search for some coherence in the psychological and metabolic correlations, or some ability to make predictions about clinical outcomes or response to specific therapies. While this attempt has some merit and should be pursued, it may be premature. There is certainly a growing impression that there are several sorts of depression and mania. Unfortunately, there is as yet no universal agreement about how to categorize the affective disorders, and there are few, if any, *independent* means of arriving at a single scheme. One could attempt to evolve an hypothesis based on the metabolism of the catecholamines, serotonin, and acetylcholine with sufficient variables so as to fit any diagnostic system. On the other hand, it would be unfortunate if a basically attractive hypothesis were to be weakened by the premature accretion of excessive complications and embellishments before the basic idea is established on a firm foundation.

Have there been any practical gains in the preclinical or clinical areas of this field? It is clear that there have been enormous improvements in the laboratory techniques and analytical methods applied to both the basic and clinical study of amine metabolism. There has also been important progress in the design of clinical studies, with attention now routinely paid to the objective evaluation of behavior and mood, the use of control groups and placebo conditions, and the attempt to avoid or control as many spurious environmental and biological variables as possible. There is also more attention paid to the timing of studies as appreciation for the phasic changes in mood disorders increases. On the other hand, many hoped-for gains have not been forthcoming. For example, regardless of whether the currently available metabolic findings suggest interesting generalizations about groups of patients, it is not yet possible to base clinical decisions or predictions about a major affective illness on any known measure of amine metabolism. Another unhappy realization is that the amine hypotheses have not yet led to the prediction and rational development of a therapy which is better or safer than those known two decades ago.

For the future, it seems highly likely that a more rational understanding of the pathophysiology of the affective illnesses will include an appreciation of the function of the biogenic amine neurotransmitters of the central nervous system. Even if one of the current hypotheses is correct, and the strongest seems to be that a deficiency of central catecholamines is an important aspect of the occurrence of retarded depression, we would still be left with the riddle of what makes that so!

References

1. Jacobsen, E.: The theoretical basis of the chemotherapy of depression, in "Depression: Proceedings of the Symposium at Cambridge, September, 1959" (E.B. Davis, Ed.), p 208, Cambridge Univ. Press, New York (1964).
2. Everett, G.M., and Toman, J.E.P.: Mode of action of Rauwolfia alkaloids and motor activity. in "Biological Psychiatry" (J.H. Masserman, Ed.), pp. 75-81. Grune and Stratton, New York (1959).
3. Weil-Malherbe, H.: The biochemistry of the functional psychoses. *Adv. Enzymol.* 29: 479–553, 1956.
4. Glassman, A.: Indoleamines and affective disorders. *Psychosom. Med.* 31: 107–114, 1969.
5. Davis, J.M.: Theories of biological etiology of affective disorders, *in* International Review of Neurobiology (O.C. Pfeiffer and J.R. Smythies, Eds.), Vol. 12, pp. 145-175. Academic Press, New York (1970).
6. Himwich, H.E.. Indoleamines and the depressions, *in* "Biochemistry, Schizophrenias and Affective Illnesses" (H.E. Himwich, Ed.), Chap. 9, pp. 230-282, Williams and Wilkins, Baltimore, (1970).
7. Schildkraut, J.J.: "Neuropsychopharmacology and the Affective Disorders," 111 pp. Little Brown and Co., Boston (1970).
8. Baldessarini, R.J.: Biogenic amine hypotheses in affective disorders, *in* "The Nature and Treatment of Depression" (S.C. Draghi and F.F. Flach, Eds.), Chap. 9. John Wiley and Sons, New York (1974, in press).
9. Pare, C.M.B., and Sandler, M.: A clinical and biochemical study of a trial of iproniazid in the treatment of depression. *J. Neurol. Neurosurg. Psychiat.* 22: 247–251, 1959.
10. Ström-Olsen, R. and Weil-Malherbe, H.: Humoral changes in manic-depressive psychosis with particular reference to the excretion of catechol amines in urine. *J. Ment. Sci.* 104:696–704, 1958.
11. Weil-Malherbe, H.: The concentration of adrenaline in human plasma and its relation to mental activity. *J. Ment. Sci.* 101:733–755, 1955.
12. Baldessarini, R.J.: Biogenic amines and behavior. *Ann. Rev. Med.* 23:343–354, 1972.
13. Baldessarini, R.J., and Karobath, M.: Biochemical physiology of central synapses. *Ann. Rev. Physiol.* 35:273–304, 1973.
14. Schildkraut, J.J.: Neuropsychopharmacology of the affective disorders. *Ann. Rev. Pharmacol.* 13:427–454, 1973.
15. Janowsky, D.S., El-Yousef, M.K., Davis, J.M., and Skerke, H.J.: Parasympathetic suppression of manic symptoms by physostigmine. *Arch. Gen. Psychiat.* 28:542–547, 1973.
16. Goodwin, F.K., Ebert, M.H., and Bunney, W.E., Jr.: Mental effects of reserpine in man: A review, Chapter 4. *in* "Psychiatric Complications of Medical Drugs", (R. Shader, Ed.), pp. 73–101, Raven Press, New York (1972).
17. Carroll, B.J.: Monoamine precursors in the treatment of depression. *Clin. Pharmacol. Ther.* 12:743–761, 1971.

18. Prange, A.J., Jr., Wilson, I.C., Lynn, C.W., Alltop, I.B., and Stikeleather, R.A.: L-Tryptophan in mania. *Arch. Gen. Psychiat.* 30:56–62, 1974.

19. Goodwin, F.K., Murphy, D.L., Brodie, H.K.H., and Bunney, W.E., Jr.: L-Dopa, catecholamines and behavior: A clinical and biochemical study in depressed patients. *Biol. Psychiat.* 2:341–366, 1970.

20. Ebert, M., Baldessarini, R.J., Lipinski, J.F., and Berv, K.: Effects of electroconvulsive seizures on amine metabolism in the rat brain. *Arch. Gen. Psychiat.* 29:397–401, 1973.

21. Bowers, M.B., Jr.: Cerebrospinal fluid 5-hydroxyindoleacetic acid (5HIAA) and homovaillic acid (HVA) following probenecid in unipolar depressives treated with amitriptyline. *Psychopharmacologia (Berlin)* 23:26-33, 1972.

22. Bunney, W.E., Jr., Goodwin, F.K. and Mrrphy, D.L.: The "switch process" in manic depressive illness. *Arch. Gen. Psychiat.* 27:295-317, 1972.

23. Dunner, D.L., Cohn, C.K., Gershon, E.S., and Goodwin, F.K.: Differential catechol-*O*methyltransferase activity in unipolar and bipolar affective illness. *Arch. Gen. Psychiat.* 26:364–366, 1972.

24. Maas, J.W., Fawcett, J.A., and Dekirmenjian, H.: Catecholamine metabolism, depressive illness, and drug response. *Arch. Gen. Psychiat.* 26:246-262, 1972.

25. Murphy, D.L., and Weiss, R.: Reduced monamine oxidase activity in blood platelets from bipolar depressed patients. *Amer. J. Psychiat.* 128:1351-1357, 1972.

26. Post, R.M., Kotin, J., Goodwin, F.K., and Gordon, E.K.: Psychomotor activity and cerebrospinal fluid amine metabolites in affective illness. *Am. J. Psychiat.* 130:67-72, 1973.

27. Rosenblatt, S., Chanley, J.D., and Leighton, W.P.: Temporal changes in the distribution of urinary tritiated metabolites in affective disorders. *J. Psychiat. Res.* 6:321–333, 1969.

28. Shopsin, B., Wilk, S., Sathananthan, G., Gershon, S. and David, K.: Catecholamines and affective disorders revised: A critical assessment. *J. Nerv. Ment. Dis.* 125:369-383, 1974.

29. Van Praag, H.M., Korf, J., and Schut, D.: Cerebral monoamines and depression. *Arch. Gen. Psychiat.* 28:827–831, 1973.

30. Jones, E.D., Maas, J.W., Dekirmenjian, H., and Fawcett, J.A.: Urinary catecholamine metabolites during behavioral changes in a patient with manic-depressive cycles. *Science* 179:300–302, 1973.

Chapter 6

Genetics of Affective Disorder

MING T. TSUANG

Affective disorders are affect disturbances having three characteristics: a primary affect disturbance manifested either by extreme elation or great depression; an episodic or periodic course; and a time of apparent recovery.

Genetic Evidence

Evidence for a genetic component in affective disorder comes from an examination of both twin and family studies. A survey of available literature on twin studies appears in Table I. The pooled data from seven studies show that the overall concordance rate for affective disorder in monozygotic pairs (MZ) is 76%, whereas in dizygotic pairs (DZ), the concordance rate is 19%, a statistically significant difference. Price[1] reviewed the available literature on monozygotic pairs reared apart and showed concordance in 8 out of 12, a rate of 67%, which is very similar to the overall MZ concordance rate of 76%. The results of these twin studies suggest the presence of genetic factor in affective disorder.

A genetic factor in affective disorder is also indicated in the comparison of the rate of affective disorder in the general population with that in the

TABLE I

Twin Studies of Affective Disorders

Author	Country	Concordant pairs/Total pairs MZ (%)	DZ (%)
Rosanoff et al. (1935)	U.S.A.	16/23 (70)	11/67 (16)
Kallmann (1954)	U.S.A.	25/27 (93)	13/55 (24)
Luxenburger (1942) *	Germany	47/56 (84)	12/83 (15)
Slater (1953)	England	4/8 (50)	7/30 (23)
de Fonseca (1959)	England	15/21 (71)	15/39 (38)
Harvald & Hague (1965)	Denmark	10/15 (67)	2/40 (5)
Kringlen (1967)	Norway	2/6 (33)	0/9 (0)
Total		119/156(76)	60/323(19)
Price (1968) MZ (%) Reared apart		8/12 (67)	

* from Gedda (1951)

relatives of patients with affective disorder (Table II). In the general population, the median risk for affective disorder is estimated to be 1.1%. This single risk figure is derived from two sources. A survey of six studies[2] provides a 0.85% median risk for males and a 1.8% median risk for females. According to Spicer et al.[3] the proportion of affective disorders for males and females in the general population differs by the ratio of 0.35 for males and 0.65 for females. Multiplying the male/female median risks by their respective ratios and then adding these two products results in 1.1%, the median risk for affective disorders in the general population. When this 1.1% is compared with the risk for first-degree relatives in the pooled data of the Zerbin-Rubin study,[4] the rate is shown to be ten times higher for first degree relatives.

Table III shows that the risk for sibs increases from 12 to 26% if one parent is affected and to 43% if both parents are affected. The indication of a genetic factor in affective disorder becomes even stronger from these data.[5]

Convincing evidence of a genetic factor in affective disorder may be shown by comparative studies on the distribution of affective disorder among the biological and adopted relatives of the index patient. Studies of this kind have been done with positive results for schizophrenia,[6] [7] but, as yet nothing of this sort is available in the literature for affective disorder.

Mode of Transmission

Available evidence for genetic factors in affective disorder, however, has been sufficiently compelling as to have prompted several investigations into the mode of its transmission. A study of families of 89 manic probands[8] compared ill parent–ill child pairs (Table IV). The striking finding was that there were no ill father–ill son pairs; while there were 13 or more for each of the other combinations. This suggested the possibility that mode of transmission might be associated with X-linkage in manic patients, a hypothesis previously proposed,[9] [10] which had remained untested.

Using X-linked markers such as the Xg^a blood group and color blindness, a St. Louis group[11] showed significant evidence of linkage with color blindness loci and suggestive evidence of linkage with the Xg^a locus. Figure 1 is taken from their study of pedigrees of families with two successive generations of affective disorder (manic-depressive). This figure clearly illustrates that the affective disorder is linked with Xg^{a+} which is known to be present in X chromosomes. For example, the pedigree shows the mother is both Xg^{a+} and depressed. One of her sons, the proband, is Xg^{a+} and manic, whereas his dizygotic co-twin, who is Xg^{a-}, is well. Another son is Xg^{a+} and depressed.

Subsequent studies using the Xg^a locus,[12] color blindness,[13] and an analysis of family pedigrees[14] have replicated and confirmed Winokur's study. However, some controversy still exists regarding X-linkage of bipolar illness.

However, there are a number of studies available which are incompatible

TABLE II

Median Risk for Affective Disorder in
General Population* and First Degree Relatives**

	Number of studies	Median risk
General population	6	1.1
Parents	·9	10.3
Sibs	7	10.7
Children	5	10.9

*Slater and Roth(1969) and Spicer et al.(1973)
**Based on Zerbin-Rudin(1967); investigations
other than Kallman or Luxenburger

TABLE III

Risks for Affective Disorders in Sibs, According to Affective Disorder in Parents

	No. of probands (AD)	Total no. of sibs (corrected)	No. of sibs affected	Morbid risk
Neither parent affected	329	522	64	12 ± 1.4%
One parent affected	91	128	33	26 ± 3%
Both parents affected	6	7	3	43 ± 19%

From Winokur and Clayton (1967)

with a strictly X-linked transmission, because they indicate the presence of a number of ill father–ill son pairs. Perris[15] summarized a number of such studies[16–18] which had been conducted prior to the Winokur study, and in which a total of 32 ill father–ill son pairs were found from among a total of 168 ill parent–ill child pairs of manic-depressive psychosis. Following the publication of the Winokur study, several other studies have analyzed parent–child pairs, both of whom are affectively disordered, and found ill father–ill son combinations: Von-Greiff et al.,[19] 4 of 16 male manic depressives had affectively disordered fathers; Dunner et al.,[20] 4 of 23 male manic-depressives had affectively disordered fathers; Green et al.,[21] 4 cases of father–son illness in 35 bipolar families.

There are two possible explanations for these different findings. Perhaps, the genetic factor is not actually father-to-son transmission, but rather transmitted from the maternal side. Two of the studies cited above[19] [21] specifically investigated this possibility and were able to find no evidence of affective illness on the maternal side. The second possibility is that the transmission is not just simply X-linked, but that there are several modes of transmission.

Slater,[16] Kallmann,[23] Stenstedt,[17] and Angst[23] suggested that transmission was by single autosomal dominant gene; however, the available data from family studies, showing a rate of around 15% of first degree relatives similarly affected, did not follow any strictly Mendelian ratio of distribution, in which 100% gene penetrance would be manifested by an illness rate of 50% among first degree relatives; therefore a concept of a dominant gene of reduced penetrance (30%) with somewhat variable expression was suggested.

Yet another possible mode of transmission may be by polygenes,[24] [25] which is a hypothesis based on findings that secondary cases of affective disorder in the family tend to be bilaterally distributed on the paternal and maternal sides.

To summarize then, the genetic factor in affective disorder may be X-linked, or transmitted by a single autosomal dominant gene of reduced penetrance, or by polygenes with quasi continuous variations.[26] Affective disorder may be one kind of illness with many modes of transmission, as in retinitis pigmentosa. Another possibility is that affective disorder is not actually unitary, and thus, there are different modes of transmission corresponding to different kinds of affective disorder. This raises the question of genetic heterogeneity in affective disorder.

Genetic Heterogeneity

Traditionally, manic-depressive disorders have been considered as one illness: however, three separate studies in three countries (Sweden,[18] Switzerland,[23] United States[5]) have shown that manic-depression can and should, be divided into at least two kinds, bipolar and unipolar. Bipolar patients experience both manic episodes and depressive episodes, while the unipolar patients experience only episodes of depression.

For the Sweden study,[18] evidence of three successive depressive episodes was needed to classify patients as unipolar, while those exhibiting at least

TABLE IV

Sex Relationships in Ill Parent—Ill Child Groupings in Families of 89 Manic Probands

	No. of pairs
Ill father - ill daughter	13
Ill father - ill son	0
Ill mother - ill daughter	17
Ill mother - ill son	17

x^2 = 13.8855, d.f. = 1, P < 0.0005

From Winokur, 1970.

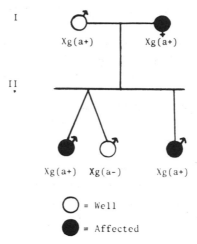

Fig. 1. Mode of transmission: Xg(a+) linkage (From reference 11).

one manic and one depressive episode were classified as bipolar. The same criteria were used for the relatives. However, cases of unspecified affective disorder and suicide among the relatives were proportionally assigned to bipolar, unipolar, and schizophrenic diagnostic groups, according to the respective ratios of these illnesses to the total of definite cases.[15] The estimated morbidity risk (Table V) for the first degree relatives in this study shows the marked difference between the two illnesses. Families of bipolar probands have a significantly higher risk for bipolar disorder, and a nonsignificant one for unipolar; likewise, families of unipolar probands show a significant risk for unipolar depression, and a nonsignificant one for bipolar. This difference strongly suggests that bipolar and unipolar affective disorders are genetically independent.

Results from the Switzerland study[23] likewise show a greater proportion of bipolar illness in family members of bipolar probands, 3.7% as compared to only 0.29% in the families of unipolar probands. Using a different methodology than the Swedish or Swiss studies, the American study[5] found that 13% of their probands with a family history of affective disorders in two generations were manic at the time of index admission. This 13% is compared with only 1.6% of probands with a totally negative family history being manic at time of index admission.

These three independent studies, then, support the existence of at least two types of affective disorder. In addition, Winokur et al.[27] (Table VI) suggest there are perhaps at least two types of unipolar depression, as manifested in early onset females (onset before age 40) and late onset males (onset after age 40). In the families of early onset females, more depression is seen in female relatives than in male relatives; in the male relatives, this deficit for depression is made up by alcoholism and sociopathy. In the families of late onset male probands there is less depression, and there is no significant difference in its distribution between males and females. Unlike the case of early onset females, there is no large amount of alcoholism or sociopathy in the male relatives of late onset males. On the basis of their findings, they propose two prototypes for unipolar depression: "depression spectrum disease" (early onset females) and "pure depressive disease" (late onset males). Subsequent studies[28-31] which have seemed to support these proposals have all been done at the same or closely related centers. Before the concept of at least two kinds of unipolar depression can become generally accepted, it will be necessary for other centers to confirm these findings.

A variety of studies have attempted to differentiate such recognized clinical diagnoses as involutional melancholia, and neurotic or reactive depression from endogenous affective disorders on genetic grounds. Stenstedt[32] and Kay[33] both studied relatives of patients with late onset depression. Using age of onset as the genetic variable, they both found that the relatives tended to have affective disorder which was indistinguishable from the main body of affective disorder. Attempts to differentiate neurotic

TABLE V

Morbidity Risk of First Degree Relatives of Bipolar (138) and Unipolar (139) Probands*

Probands' Diagnoses	Relatives' Diagnoses	No.	BZ	Morbidity Risk (%)
Bipolar	Bipolar	94.0	574	16.3 + 1.5
	Unipolar	5.3	574	0.8 + 0.4
Unipolar	Bipolar	3.3	684	0.5 + 0.3
	Unipolar	72.8	684	10.6 + 1.2

* Based on Perris, 1973

TABLE VI

Morbidity risk (%) of Depression, Sociopathy, and Alcoholism among First Degree Relatives of 100 Unipolar Probands*

Probands (100)		Relatives (529)			
Onset	Sex	Sex	Dep.	Soc. & Al.	Total
E a r l y (54)	F	F	29	6	34
		M	9	19	28
	M	F	37	6	43
		M	16	24	40
L a t e (46)	F	F	19	1	20
		M	6	3	9
	M	F	12	0	12
		M	19	2	21

* Based on Winokur et al., 1971

or reactive depression from endogenous manic-depressive disorders with family studies have likewise in the past met with little success. Stenstedt[34] found the families of neurotic depression patients to be closely interwoven with his manic-depressive families; Winokur and Pitts[35] compared the family histories of depression reaction and manic-depressive cases and could find no difference from the main body of affective disorder. Shields and Slater[36] examined the co-twins of MZ and DZ same-sex twins who had received a diagnosis of neurotic disorder, and, although some twin pairs were concordant for the-diagnosis of neurosis, the authors could find no concordance for the diagnosis of neurotic depression, leading them to conclude that neurotic depression is not a specific genetic entity.

Schizo-Affective Disorder

The evidence for heterogeneity in affective disorder leads quite naturally to the suggestion that schizo-affective disorder may be, in at least some cases, yet another genetic variant of affective disorder, rather than a subtype of schizophrenia, where it has traditionally been classified.[37] Because such cases might prove to be as amenable to lithium in clinical treatment as recurrent mania and depression, perhaps no question in psychiatry today is more urgently deserving of further investigation than the one, "Is schizo-affective disorder a subtype of schizophrenia, a subtype of affective disorder, or is it a distinct illness?"

As reviewed above available evidence supports the existence of genetic factors in affective disorder and schizophrenia. There is also evidence that the two are separate illnesses. If this line of evidence is taken to its theoretical conclusions, then, given pairs of sibs with mental disorder, namely, affective disorder or schizophrenia, they should both be suffering from the same illness, that is, for example, both schizophrenia or both manic-depression. Clinical experience however demonstrates that this does not always hold true in practice. Those cases where sibs are discordant for the diagnoses of schizophrenia or affective disorder may be used to shed light on the nature of schizo-affective disorder.

For this purpose, data[38] on 71 pairs of sibs both hospitalized for mental disorder were reanalyzed. The original diagnoses of these pairs had been made from case histories[39] by Dr. Eliot Slater, formerly the Director, MRC Psychiatric Genetics Research Unit in England without knowledge of sib relationships. On the basis of his diagnosis, the 70 patients in 35 of the 71 pairs were suffering from schizophrenia (Sc) or affective disorder (Ad), either concordantly, both schizophrenia (ScSc) or both affective disorder (AdAd), or discordantly, both illnesses being represented in the same pair (AdSc). The case histories of these 70 patients were recently presented for re-diagnosis to Dr. George Winokur, Head of the Department of Psychiatry, University of Iowa, U.S.A. Dr. Winokur was asked to diagnose the 70 cases as: schizophrenia (Sc), affective disorder (Ad), or schizo-affective disorder (Sa). For schizophrenia and affective disorder the criteria for diagnosis were essentially those of Feighner et al. (1972), but for schizo-affective disorder the criteria were that a patient presents (1) both schizophrenic and affective features; or (2) an affective episode, but who in another episode had a mixture, or only, schizophrenic symptoms.

Following this diagnostic exercise, paired sibs were grouped according to the six possible pairings of the three diagnoses: AdAd, AdSa, SaSa, AdSc, SaSc, ScSc. Because of the effectiveness of age of onset to differentiate clinical subtypes, and since the diagnostician did not use age of onset as part of his diagnostic criteria, it was used to analyze any differences among the diagnostic pairings. In some cases, when the exact age of onset was difficult to determine because onset had been insidious, it was possible to determine onset fairly well from the available information or to use the age of first

TABLE VII

Mean Ages of Onset of Sib Pairs According to Diagnoses

Sib pairs	No. of pairs/ No. of patients	Mean age of onset + S.D.
Ad Ad	11 / 22	49.0 + 15.4
Ad Sa	8 / 16	42.3 + 16.5
Sa Sa	4 / 8	37.5 + 10.0
Ad Sc	2 / 4	30.8 + 10.3
Sa Sc	5 / 10	24.9 + 7.8
Sc Sc	5 / 10	25.9 + 5.8

Ad: affective disorder; Sa: schizoaffective disorder; Sc: schizophrenia

admission as the nearest approximation of age of onset. In spite of some difficulties in determining age of onset, its advantage as a parameter is that it provides an exact numerical figure for statistical analysis. The results of the six possible pairings of the three diagnoses, along with the statistical analysis of each pair's mean age of onset, shows some definite tendencies (Table VII): the AdAd pairs have the oldest mean age of onset, while the SaSa pairs are grouped in the middle range and the ScSc pairs tend to be younger.

In Table VIII, those pairs in which both sibs were given the same diagnosis (AdAd, SaSa, and ScSc) are compared with all other possible pairs with regard to mean age of onset. In this comparison, the AdAd sib pairs show a very significant difference in mean age of onset from the ScSc and SaSc pairs, whereas the SaSa sib pairs show no difference from the AdAd and AdSa pairs, but a very significant difference from the ScSc and ScSa pairs. These findings suggest that in the AdSa and SaSa sib pairs schizo-affective disorder is more closely associated with affective disorder than with schizophrenia. Further, the schizo-affective disorder in ScSa pairs appears more closely associated with schizophrenia, as there is practically no difference statistically between the ScSc and ScSa pairs.

From these data three major groups emerge: an affective disorder group (AD=AdAd+AdSa); a schizo-affective group (SA=SaSa); and a schizophrenic group (SC=ScSc+ScSa). These three major groups, with their respective mean ages of onset, are presented in Table IX. As might be expected, there is a significant difference between the SC and the AD groups; however, there is also a significant difference between the SC and the SA groups. There is no significant difference between the AD and the SA groups.

These findings would tend to indicate that on the basis of age of onset schizo-affective disorder is more closely associated with affective disorder than with schizophrenia. Previous studies also support the possibility that schizo-affective disorder is a genetic variant of affective disorder. Clayton et al.[41] found a higher prevalence of affective disorder (21 out of 39 probands) than schizophrenia in families of schizo-affective probands. Another study[41] examined probands diagnosed as poor prognosis and good prognosis schizophrenics, using diagnostic criteria for good prognosis schizophrenia similar to those commonly used for schizo-affective disorder. Their findings showed a significant incidence of affective disorder among the relatives of the good prognosis schizophrenics, while the poor prognosis schizophrenics had a higher incidence of familial schizophrenia. A study of Cohen et al.[42] of monozygotic male twins found a significantly higher concordance rate for the schizo-affective pairs than for schizophrenia, while the pairwise concordance rates for schizo-affective disorder and affective disorder were not significantly different.

From the time when the term schizo-affective disorder was first introduced by Kasanin,[43] it has generally been thought to be a subtype of schizophrenia. However, the evidence of previous studies and the results shown in this study indicate the inadvisability of classifying schizo-affective disorder as a subtype of schizophrenia, and thus failing to recognize its affective component which may be amenable to lithium treatment. Instead, the evidence would support regarding schizo-affective disorder as a separate

TABLE VIII

Difference between Mean Ages of Onset of Concordant Pairs with All Sib Pairs

	AdAd	AdSa	SaSa	AdSc	SaSc	ScSc
AdAd	0	6.7	11.5	18.2*	24.1***	23.1***
SaSa	-11.5	-4.8	0	6.7	12.6**	11.6**
ScSc	-23.1***	-16.4**	-11.6**	-4.9	1.0	0

P: *.05 - .025; **.01 - .005; ***less than .001

TABLE IX

Difference between Mean Ages of Onset for Three Main Groups

Diag. group	Mean age of onset	Diff.	Diag. group	Mean age of onset
AD	46.2 ± 16.0	8.7	SA	37.5 ± 10.0
SA	37.5 ± 10.0	12.1***	SC	25.4 ± 6.7
SC	25.4 ± 6.7	-20.8***	AD	46.2 ± 16.2

AD = AdAd + AdSa; SA = SaSa; SC = ScSc + ScSa

***: P, less than .001

category with three subtypes: (1) an affective type; (2) a schizophrenic type; and (3) an undifferentiated type, where both affective and schizophrenic features are pronounced, or where there is insufficient information regarding affective or schizophrenic features.

With regard to these findings, the following are suggested as the different clinical approaches for patients diagnosed as schizo-affective: *Treat as affective disorder* when either (1) the age of onset is after 40 and there is a positive family history of affective disorder, or (2) the age of onset is between 30 and 40 years of age and there is a positive family history of schizo-affective disorder; *Treat as schizophrenia* when the age of onset is before 30 and there is a positive family history of schizophrenia.

Future Study

The subtypes of schizo-affective disorder suggested above are based on the parameters of age of onset and family history only. For future research, other variables, such as frequency and intensity of symptoms, clinical course, and outcome need to be considered in order to more clearly differentiate subtypes of schizo-affective disorder.

In the area of unipolar depression, further study is needed from other centers to support Winokur's differentiation of unipolar into "depressive spectrum" and "pure depressive." If possible, linkage studies for unipolar depression should also be undertaken as none are available in the literature.

Bipolar disorder presents several possibilities for future research. While bipolar linkage with color blindness and Xg^a blood type has been shown by

Winokur's group and confirmed by the Columbia study, the doubts introduced by subsequent studies need to be resolved with more data. Also linkage studies should be undertaken for blood types other than Xg^a. If indeed sex linkage can be shown, it will be interesting to identify the clinical variables which differentiate those bipolar with X-linked transmission from those that are not X-linked, thus enabling the study of a pure subgroup in bipolar disorder.

With regard to studies of lithium's effectiveness for bipolar disorder, present evidence indicates that more bipolar than unipolar respond to lithium, yet even some bipolar do not respond. Thus it is necessary that future research investigate the different clinical variables within bipolar affective disorder which account for these differences in response.

Biochemical studies on the actual mechanism of the efficacy of lithium for affective disorders should be conducted on a homogeneous group of patients who are known to be lithium respondent. Future biochemical studies on lithium should include not only patients, but also patients' relatives in order to elucidate the genetic factors which are associated with affective disorder.

If future research into psychiatric disorders is to yield meaningful results, the results of the studies presented above concerning the heterogeneous character of affective disorder will have to be taken into account. Study populations will have to be strictly defined, and represent, insofar as possible, homogenous subgroups, e.g., all patients with a diagnosis of bipolar and who are lithium respondent. A trend in this direction can be noted from the appearance of various schemes of objective research criteria (e.g., Feighner et al.[44]).

An example of research of this kind is to be found in an Iowa investigation which is currently conducting a 35 year follow-up and family study of 525 patients who were selected from among 5000 in-patients according to strict research criteria for the diagnoses of mania, depression, and schizophrenia. The study is utilizing structured interview forms, a nonpsychiatric control group, and blind interviews. On the basis of objective data regarding clinical features, course and outcome, life histories, related illnesses, and characteristics of familial association, this study's findings may be of great value for establishing criteria for diagnoses of homogeneous subgroups of affective disorder for future study.

In summary, it is imperative that future biological and psychosocial studies, whether of schizo-affective, bipolar, or unipolar disorder, be based on two research standards: (1) a diagnostically homogeneous subgroup, and (2) the clinical and genetic features of both patients and their families.

Acknowledgment

This work was supported in part by NIMH Grant 1 RO1 MH24189-01. The author wishes to express his appreciation to Dr. George Winokur, Head, Department of Psychiatry, University of Iowa, College of Medicine, for his encouragement to undertake this paper, and for his valuable criticism in the course of its writing.

References

1. Price, J.S.: The genetics of depressive behaviour, *in* "Recent Developments in Affective Disorders," (A. Coppen and A. Walk, Eds.), pp. 37–54. British Journal of Psychiatry Special Publication, No. 2. Headley, Ashley, Kent (1968).
2. Slater, E., Roth, M.: "Mayer-Gross, Slater and Roth Clinical Psychiatry" (ed. 3.). Baillière, Tindall & Cassell, London (1969).
3. Spicer, C.C., Hare, E.H., and Slater, E.: Neurotic and psychotic forms of depressive illness: Evidence from age-incidence in a national sample. *Brit. J. Psychiat.* 123: 535–541, 1973.
4. Zerbin-Rüdin, E.: Endogene psychosen, *in* Humangenetik, ein kurzes Handbuch" (P.E. Becker, Ed.), Vol. 2, pp. 446-577. Thieme, Stuttgart (1967).
5. Winokur, G., and Clayton, P.: Family history studies: II. Two types of affective disorders separated according to genetic and clinical factors, *in* "Recent Advances in Biological Psychiatry" (J. Wortis, Ed.), Vol. 9, pp. 35-50. Plenum Press, New York (1967).
6. Heston, L.L.: Psychiatric disorders in foster home reared children of schizophrenic mothers. *Brit. J. Psychiat.* 112: 819-825, 1966.
7. Kety, S.S., *et al.:* The types and prevalence of mental illness in the biological and adoptive families of adopted schizophrenics, *in* "The Transmission of Schizophrenia" (D. Rosenthal and S.S. Kety, Eds.), pp. 345–362. Pergamon, Oxford (1968).
8. Winokur, G.: Genetic findings and methodological considerations in manic depressive disease. *Brit. J. Psychiat.* 117: 267–274, 1970.
9. Rosanoff, A.J., Handy, L.M., and Plesset, I.R.: The etiology of manic-depressive syndromes with special reference to their occurence in twins. *Amer. J. Psychiat.* 91: 725–762, 1935.
10. Burch, P.R.J.: Manic-depressive psychosis: Some new aetiological considerations. *Brit. J. Psychiat.* 110: 808–817, 1964.
11. Winokur, G., and Tanna, V.L.: Possible role of X-linked dominant factor in manic depressive disease. *Dis. Nerv. Sys.* 30: 89–93, 1969.
12. Mendlewicz, J., Fleiss, J., and Fieve, R.: Evidence for X-linkage in the transmission of manic-depressive illness. *J. Amer. Med. Ass.* 222: 1624–1627, 1972.
13. Fieve, R.R., Mendlewicz, J., and Fleiss, J.L.: Manic-depressive illness: Linkage with the Xg [a] blood group. *Amer. J. Psychiat.* 130: 1355–1359, 1973.
14. Taylor, M., and Abrams, R.: Manic states. A genetic study of early and late onset affective disorders. *Arch. Gen. Psychiat.* 28: 656–658, 1973.

15. Perris, C.: The genetics of affective disorders, *in* "Biological Psychiatry" (J. Mendels, Ed.), pp. 385–415. John Wiley and Sons, New York (1973).

16. Slater, E: Zur Erbpathologie des manisch-depressiven Irreseins. Die Eltern und Kinder von Manisch-Depressiven. *Zeitsch. ges. Neurol. Psychiat.* 163: 1–147, 1938.

17. Stenstedt, A.: A study in manic-depressive psychosis. Clinical, social and genetic investigations. *Acta Psychiat. Scand. Suppl.* 79, 1952.

18. Perris, C.: A study of bipolar (manic-depressive) and unipolar recurrent depressive psychoses. *Acta Psychiat. Scand.* 42 (Suppl. 194), 1966.

19. Von-Greiff, H., McHugh, P.R., and Stokes, P.: The familial history in sixteen males with bipolar manic depressive disorder. Presented at Sixty-third annual meeting of the American Psychopathological Association, New York, New York, 1973.

20. Dunner, D., Gershon, E., and Goodwin, F.K.: Heritable factors in the severity of affective illness. Paper read at 123rd annual meeting APA.

21. Green, R., *et al.:* X-linked transmission of manic-depressive illness. *J. Amer. Med. Ass.* 223: 1289, 1973.

22. Kallman, F.J.: "The Genetics of Psychoses: an Analysis of 1,232 Twin Index Families." *Congrès International de Psychiatrie, Rapports VI Psychiatrie Social*, Paris, 1–27, 1950.

23. Angst, J.: "Zur ätiologie und nosologie endogener depressiver psychosen. *Monogr. Gesamtgeb. Neurol. Psychiat.* 112. Springer, Berlin, 1966.

24. Slater, E., and Tsuang, M.T.: Abnormality on paternal and maternal sides: observations in schizophrenia and manic-depression. *J. Med. Genet.* 5: 197–199, 1968.

25. Perris, C.: Genetic transmission of depressive psychoses. *Acta Psychiat. Suppl.* 203: 45–52, 1968.

26. Edwards, J.H.: The simulation of Mendelism. *Acta Genet. (Basel)* 10: 63–70, 1960.

27. Winokur, G., *et al.:* Depressive disease: A genetic study. *Arch. Gen. Psychiat.* 24: 135–144, 1971.

28. Woodruff, R., Guze, S., and Clayton, P.: Unipolar and bipolar primary affective disorder. *Brit. J. Psychiat.* 119: 33–38, 1971.

29. Marten, S., *et al.:* Unipolar depression: a family history study. *Biological Psychiatry*, vol. 4, 205-213, 1972.

30. Winokur, G.: Diagnostic and genetic aspects of affective illness. *Psychiat. Annu.* 3: 6–15, 1973.

31. Winokur, G., *et al.:* The Iowa 500: Familial and clinical findings favor two kinds of depressive illness. *Comprehen. Psychiat.* 14: 99–107, 1973.

32. Stenstedt, A.: Involutional melancholia. *Acta Psychiat. Neurol. Scand.* Suppl. 97, 1959.

33. Kay, D.: Observations on the natural history and genetics of old age psychoses: A Stockholm material 1931-7. *Proc. Roy. Soc. Med.* 52: 791–794, 1959.

34. Stenstedt A.: Genetics of neurotic depression. *Acta Psychiat. Neurol. Scand.* 45: 392–409, 1966.

35. Winokur, G., and Pitts, F.N.: Affective disorder: I. Is reactive depression an entity? *J. Nerv. Mental Dis.* 138: 541–547, 1964.

36. Shields, J., and Slater, E.T.O.: La similarité du diagnostic chez les jumeaux et le problème de la spécificité biologique dans les névroses et les troubles de la personnalité. *L'Évolution Psychiatrique*, No. 2, pp. 441–451, 1966.

37. *DSM-II Diagnostic and Statistical Manual of Mental Disorders*, ed. 2. American Psychiatric Association, Washington, D.C., 1968.

38. Tsuang, M.T.: A study of pairs of sibs both hospitalized for mental disorder. *Brit. J. Psychiat.* 113: 283–300, 1967.
39. Tsuang, M.T.: *A Study of Pairs of Sibs both Hospitalized for Mental Disorder.* Ph.D. Thesis, University of London, 1965.
40. Clayton, P.J., Rodin, L., and Winokur, G.: Family history studies: III. Schizo-affective disorder, clinical and genetic factors including a one to two year follow-up. *Comprehen. Psychiat.* 9: 31–49, 1968.
41. McCabe, M.S., *et al.:* Familial differences in schizophrenia with good and poor prognosis. *Psychol. Med.* 1: 326–332, 1971.
42. Cohen, S.M., *et al.*: Relationship of schizo-affective psychosis to manic depressive psychosis and schizophrenia. *Arch. Gen. Psychiat.,* 26: 539-545, 1972.
43. Kasanin, J.: Acute schizo-affective psychoses. *Amer. J. Psychiat.* 90: 97-126, 1933.
44. Feighner, J.P., *et al.*: Diagnostic criteria for use in psychiatry. *Arch. Gen. Psychiat.* 25: 57-63, 1972.

Chapter 7

Lithium Distribution in Depressed Patients: Implications for an Alteration in Cell Membrane Function in Depression

J. MENDELS
and
A. FRAZER

Research into the psychobiology of the affective disorders, to a considerable extent, has been dominated by an examination of the changes in the biogenic amines. Some of this work is discussed elsewhere in this volume (Chapters 2-4, 9) and aspects of it have been reviewed elsewhere by us recently.[1-3] While there have been a large number of studies of aminergic function in affective illness, they have not yet provided a clear-cut understanding of the underlying biology of the affective disorders. Therefore, it is important to examine other biochemical systems which contribute to alterations in neuronal function and which may be associated with changes in mood.

Electrolytes are known to play a critical role in the control of neuronal function through their actions at several loci.[4] For example, they are involved in maintaining the normal resting membrane potential; in carrying the current for the action potential; in the synthesis, storage, release, and inactivation of neurotransmitters; and in carrying the current responsible for depolarization or hyperpolarization of postsynaptic membranes. Furthermore, recent observations show that active cation transport mechanisms responsible for maintaining normal neuronal excitability may, in themselves, generate potentials termed electrogenic pump potentials.[5] In certain instances, these electrogenic pump potentials contribute to the resting membrane potential. Thus, changes in pump activity can alter the resting potential and so alter the excitability of the neuron.

Since it is a reasonable assumption that disorders of mood are associated with some alteration in neuronal function, detailed investigations of electrolyte metabolism are potentially important.

In an early study, Schottstaedt and his colleagues[6] conducted a simple, yet revealing, experiment in which they correlated changes in sodium balance with changes in mood. Normal subjects were asked to provide a daily rating of their mood, and 24-hour urinary sodium concentrations were measured. It should be noted that dietary sodium intake was not controlled in this study. They found a decrease in urinary sodium concentration in association with periods of reported ''depression.'' This decrease in urinary sodium concentration was reversed when the depression passed.

This study is of interest for several reasons. First, it was conducted in normal subjects rather than in clinically depressed patients. Second, there was no control of electrolyte intake. Third, 24-hour urinary sodium concentration is not regarded as a particularly subtle or sensitive measure. In spite of this, the initial observations of these investigators have been confirmed in a number of subsequent, more sophisticated, studies. Durell,[7] in a recent comprehensive review of the literature, concluded that clinical depression is frequently associated with sodium retention. This finding emerges when sodium metabolism is measured in several different ways including urinary sodium concentration,[6] 24-hour exchangeable sodium,[8-10] or ^{22}Na retention.[11] All of these values return toward control values with clinical recovery, i.e., clinical recovery from depression is accompanied by a negative sodium balance.

The suggestion that there is a retention of sodium during periods of clinical depression leads to a consideration of where the additional sodium may be found. Coppen and Shaw[9] suggested that there is an increase in residual sodium in depression. Residual sodium is the combination of intracellular and bone sodium. However, the methodology employed in their studies is controversial [1,7] so that their observation must be interpreted with caution. Its potential importance requires attempts at replication by others.

More recently, two groups of investigators have attempted a more direct measure of intracellular sodium concentration. Naylor *et al.* [12,13] reported that erythrocyte sodium concentration decreased on recovery from psychotic depression. In our laboratory, we have not been able to find any consistent difference in erythrocyte sodium concentration in depressed patients in comparison with hospitalized controls.* However, we have found an increase in erythrocyte sodium concentration in association with the successful treatment of depressed patients with lithium carbonate. Obviously, further work with larger groups of carefully selected and defined patients is required before we will know with any certainty the site of sodium retention during periods of depression.

Lithium

Since 1949 it has been increasingly widely recognized that lithium carbonate is an effective treatment for various stages of affective disorders. Cade's[17] original demonstration that lithium has a specific antimanic action has now been confirmed by a number of investigators[18] (see reference 19). It is also now known that lithium is an effective prophylactic agent against recurrent manic-depressive illness and perhaps against recurrent depressive illness[20] (see reference 21). There is also increasing evidence that lithium may be useful in the treatment of selected acute depressive episodes. While this claim remains controversial, it would be reasonable to conclude at this time that lithium is probably effective in the treatment of acute depressive

* We had reported the preliminary finding that erythrocyte sodium concentration was low in manic-depressive or bipolar patients.[14] However, subsequent consideration revealed several problems with that finding. The number of depressed subjects studied was small; the method used to measure erythrocyte sodium was not sufficiently precise; and the control subjects were not hospitalized in the same environment as the depressed patients. We have since studied a larger number of patients using a more accurate method for the measurement of erythrocyte sodium,[15] and have included a group of hospitalized control subjects. This is potentially important in that it has been shown that plasma sodium concentration is reduced in hospitalized patients[16] and it is possible that this occurs in the erythrocyte. This more recent work (including longitudinal studies of the same patient over time) has not revealed any significant difference in erythrocyte sodium concentration between depressed patients who are not receiving any medication and control subjects (to be published).

episodes in a subgroup of patients, particularly those with manic-depressive illness as opposed to recurrent unipolar depression (see references 22 and 23). However, there is clearly not a one-to-one relationship between the response to lithium and the diagnosis of manic-depressive illness.

The recognition that lithium exerts an important effect on abnormal mood states has provided a strong impetus to the further investigation of electrolyte metabolism in patients with affective disorders. As a univalent cation, lithium may have sodium- or potassium-like effects. For example, it may substitute for sodium in carrying the current of the action potential spike.[24,25] With time, the neurone becomes inexcitable due to the accumulation of intracellular lithium.[24,25] This occurs because of the slow rate of removal of lithium from the cell (in comparison with sodium).[26] This is probably due to its inability to substitute for sodium in stimulating sodium-potassium activated adenosine triphosphatase (Na,K-activated ATPase).[27] Lithium does have some affinity for the external site (K-site) of cation transport[26,28] and the K-site of the Na,K-activated ATPase,[27] but is less potent than K in activating these processes.

Others have suggested that lithium may interact with the magnesium ion with which it has certain physical and chemical properties in common (see reference 29). In this regard, we have noted an interaction of lithium with magnesium on prostaglandin E_1-stimulated platelet adenylate cyclase activity.[30] It is also possible that lithium may act by virtue of effects on biogenic amines.[31] These latter possibilities will not be considered in detail in this review, although its potential importance is recognized.

Lithium has a series of well-defined effects on sodium balance. In summary, the acute administration of lithium to man is followed by an initial negative sodium balance which, after a day or two gives way to several days of sodium retention.[32-34] Aronoff et al.[35] have reported that the sodium retention associated with lithium administration only occurred in those patients who showed clinical improvement and not in those whose clinical status was unchanged. We have recently found that there is a tendency for erythrocyte sodium concentration to increase with lithium administration, a finding which will be discussed in more detail later.

Summary

In this brief introduction we have made the following points:

1. Cations play a crucial role in neuronal function.

2. An alteration in cation metabolism will probably alter neuronal function and may alter mood state.

3. Lithium is a cation with properties in common with sodium (and magnesium) and may affect a number of systems which govern normal neuronal function.

4. Some direct action of lithium in its own right or some interaction between lithium and sodium may alter mood in man.

5. There is evidence that sodium metabolism is altered in patients with depression and, in particular, there appears to be a retention of sodium in association with clinical depression.

The next section summarizes a series of experiments which have been conducted in our laboratory. It may be helpful to place this material in perspective by presenting a hypothesis. *We have suggested that there may be a subgroup of depressed patients with a genetically determined abnormality in some aspect of cell membrane properties which regulate the movement of electrolytes across the plasma membrane.* While this is a preliminary hypothesis, and although other interpretations of our data are possible, we believe that sufficient information has been generated to justify further exploration and evaluation of this concept.

It is also important to emphasize that this hypothesis is not incompatible with the view that there may be a dysfunction in biogenic amine metabolism, neuroendocrine function, or in some other system in patients with affective illness. Clearly, there are many ways in which these systems might interact with each other and where an abnormality in one area may in fact be responsible for changes in other systems. Thus, this is neither an exclusive concept nor a competitive one. Rather, we hope that it might complement information being gathered from other areas of investigation and assist in the development of a cohesive, unified theory of affective illness.

As noted earlier, there is evidence that a subgroup of depressed patients will improve when treated with lithium. While clinical observations suggest that these patients are more likely to be of the manic-depressive or bipolar type, it is clear that this diagnosis in itself is not a sufficient explanation for the response to lithium carbonate. Patients with a diagnosis of manic-depressive illness, depressed phase do not respond to treatment with lithium, and a number of patients with recurrent unipolar depressive illness do respond to this treatment. Thus, we attempted to try to find a more meaningful correlation with clinical response to lithium.

The Use of the Erythrocyte as a Model for the Neurone

We elected to measure intraerythrocyte or red blood cell (RBC) lithium concentration. We reasoned that the concentration of lithium in the brain is an important variable in determining the clinical response of individual patients and that a cellular measure of lithium might correlate better with brain lithium concentration than an extracellular or plasma measure. We further hypothesized that patients who respond to treatment with lithium would have a higher intracellular lithium concentration, for a given plasma level, than patients who did not improve.

The erythrocyte was chosen as our model cell for several reasons. There appear to be qualitative similarities in cation transport in RBC's and in nerve cells. While the RBC is atypical of other mature cells in that it lacks a nucleus and depends on glycolysis rather than respiration for its energy production, it is known to possess an active transport system for sodium and potassium which has characteristics similar to the cation pump mechanisms of nerve cells. For example:

(1) Na,K-activated ATPase of RBC ghosts responds to electrolyte alterations and ouabain administration in a manner similar to that of the neuronal enzyme.[36]

(2) ATP furnishes the energy necessary for the maintenance of Na and K gradients both in RBC's and in squid nerve axons.[37,38] Whether the ATP is derived from glycolysis or respiration appears to be irrelevant.

(3) Both erythrocytes and nerve cells use one molecule of ATP for every three ions of Na transported.[39-41]

(4) Ethanol alters both brain and RBC cation transport processes and the activity of Na,K-activated ATPase, the enzyme responsible for Na and K transport,[27] to a similar degree. For example, Israel *et al.*[42] have shown that ethanol can produce similar changes in ion transport and enzyme activity in *both* brain tissue and in erythrocytes. They also suggest that changes which are presumably occurring in the brains of humans can be detected by the study of human RBC's.

It is, of course, obvious that there are quantitative differences in cation transport between nerve cells and erythrocytes.[43] However, qualitatively, the RBC may provide a useful model for studies of neuronal electrolyte distribution and transport. In this regard, we have shown that there is a superior correlation between RBC lithium concentration and brain lithium concentration than between plasma lithium and brain lithium after the discontinuation of lithium administration to rats.[44] Thus, we found that red cell lithium concentration had a correlation with brain lithium concentration of between 0.80 and 0.94, depending on the experimental circumstances. This allowed a predictability of brain lithium concentration from the knowledge of red cell lithium concentration of between 64 and 88%. In contrast, the predictability of brain lithium levels from plasma concentrations ranged from a low of 17% to a maximum of 62%, indicating the superiority of predicting brain lithium concentration from a knowledge of RBC lithium concentration. This provides some support for our contention that RBC lithium concentration provides a more useful index than plasma concentration for the prediction of the level of the cation in the brain.

Erythrocyte Lithium Concentration

Table I summarizes findings from a study in which we found that male depressed patients who responded to treatment with lithium had significantly higher RBC lithium concentrations, and RBC lithium:plasma lithium ratios (Lithium Ratio) than depressed patients who did not respond to treatment with this cation.[45] These values are independent of the dose of lithium or plasma lithium concentrations, suggesting that the higher ratio in the responders is a function of a proportionally higher RBC lithium concentration.

This finding suggests that there may be a difference in the cell membrane properties which govern the passage of lithium into or out of the cell between these two groups of patients. Furthermore, Lyttkens *et al* [46] reported a

TABLE I

Mean Plasma and RBC Li and Daily Dose of Lithium Carbonate in Patients Who Improved and Who Did Not Improve

Patients	N	Daily dose of lithium carbonate (mg)	Plasma lithium (m-equiv/1)	RBC lithium (m-equiv/1 RBC)	RBC lithium / plasma lithium
Responders	8	1572 ± 92*	1.11 ± 0.07	0.64 ± 0.07	0.56 ± 0.03
Non-Responders	6	1836 ± 186	1.02 ± 0.06	0.40 ± 0.03†	0.39 ± 0.02**

*$\bar{X}$ ± SEM

†$p < 0.02$ (Student's t test)

**$p < 0.005$ (Mann Whitney u test)

higher Lithium Ratio in manic-depressive females than in control female subjects. We have found that three male control subjects who received lithium for 17 days had lower Lithium Ratios (0.33 ± 0.02; X $\pm$ SEM) than did nine male manic-depressive patients (0.51 ± 0.04).

It is worth emphasizing that this difference in the Lithium Ratio in the responders and nonresponders, or between manic-depressive patients and controls is not likely to be the result of differences in the intake of sodium between the two groups. In a systematic evaluation of the effects of varying sodium intake on the Lithium Ratio in three hospitalized male control subjects we found that lowering sodium intake to 65 mEq/day from 165 mEq/day resulted in a 29% increase in plasma lithium. However, there was a corresponding change in RBC lithium, so that the Lithium Ratio remained *stable* (Table II). Thus, alterations in sodium intake probably did not

TABLE II

The Effect of Changing Sodium Intake on Plasma and Erythrocyte Lithium

Subject	Diet	Urine Na (mEq/day)	Plasma (mEq/L)	RBC (mEq/L)	RBC Li / Plasma Li
O.M.	Low[a]	61 ± 9[b]	0.74 ± .03	0.24 ± .02	0.33 ± .01
		(7)[c]	(5)	(5)	(5)
	High	166 ± 19	0.52 ± .07	0.19 ± .03	0.36 ± .02
		(8)	(5)	(5)	(5)
W.C.	Low	34 ± 4	0.65 ± .02	0.20 ± .01	0.31 ± .01
		(8)	(6)	(6)	(6)
	High	146 ± 11	0.55 ± .01	0.17 ± .01	0.30 ± .01
		(8)	(5)	(5)	(5)
E.T.	Low	45 ± 6	0.77 ± .01	0.28 ± .004	0.36 ± .003
		(8)	(6)	(6)	(6)
	High	138 ± 12	0.61 ± .02	0.21 ± .01	0.34 ± .01
		(8)	(6)	(6)	(6)

[a]The Na content of the "Low" diet was 55-65 mEq/day, whereas the Na content of the "High" diet was 165-175 mEq/day.

[b]X̄ ± SEM

[c]Number of observations

TABLE III

Erythrocyte Na Change with Li Administration

Mean Daily Dose of Lithium Carbonate (mg)	Number of Patients	Erythrocyte Na (mEq/L cells)					p*
		a	b	c	d	e	
>1500	7	7.8	7.9	7.9	8.4	9.1	<.001
<1500	8	8.1	8.2	8.3	8.6	8.6	NS

a & b - Baseline period divided into equal halves.

c, d & e - Treatment period divided into thirds.

* - From linear trend analysis.

contribute significantly to the difference in Lithium Ratios observed between the responders and nonresponders.

In this regard, it is of interest to note that Gibbons[8] in his study of changes in exchangeable sodium in depressives before and after treatment found that there was no difference in the results whether dietary sodium intake was controlled or not. Thus, it seems that control of diet is not always essential in studies of electrolyte metabolism.

Erythrocyte Sodium

In view of the alterations in sodium distribution associated with depression, as well as the changes in sodium induced by lithium administration, we have measured erythrocyte sodium concentration in 12 of our depressed patients. The method used for measuring erythrocyte sodium has been described in detail.[15] For each patient studied, there were at least seven days of base line values followed by a period of 21 days during which the dose of lithium was either held constant or increased. There was no significant change in the concentration of RBC sodium in any patient during the base line period indicating the stability of this measure under these conditions.

The period of lithium administration for each patient was then divided into thirds, the mean for each third was computed, and a linear trend analysis done to determine if there were any significant alterations in sodium concentration. There was a significant increase [F (linear) = $5.60; p < 0.05$] in RBC sodium concentration with lithium administration. Furthermore, as shown in Table III, the increase in RBC sodium was positively correlated with the dose of lithium.

We have also found an association between this increase in RBC sodium concentration and alterations in the patient's clinical state, i.e., those patients whose RBC sodium concentration increased with lithium administration were those who improved clinically. The patients who showed little or no increase in RBC sodium did not improve (Table IV).

Finally, we found that there was a tendency for the Lithium Ratio to be higher in patients who had a higher base line RBC sodium concentration (Fig. 1). However, even these "higher" base line RBC sodium values were well within the normal range.

These findings are compatible with the reports by Aronoff et al.[35] and Baer et al.[47] that patients who improved when treated with lithium had a greater increase in the 24-hour exchangeable sodium than patients who did not respond. While the methods of measurement are quite different, both sets of observations do lend themselves to the same interpretation. It is important to bear in mind that these findings are temporal associations or correlations, the physiological significance of which remains to be determined.

TABLE IV

Changes in Depression Ratings in Groups Subdivided by Changes in RBC Sodium

Subgroups	Nurses' Depression Score			Beck Depression Score		
	a	b	c	a	b	c
Sodium Increasers (7)*	8.4	8.2	5.8**	17.7	10.5	5.5#
Sodium Non-Increasers (8)	7.8	7.7	7.3	19.8	13.4	14.4

* Number of patients.

** F (linear) = 8.8; p<0.05.

F (linear) = 6.5; p<0.05.

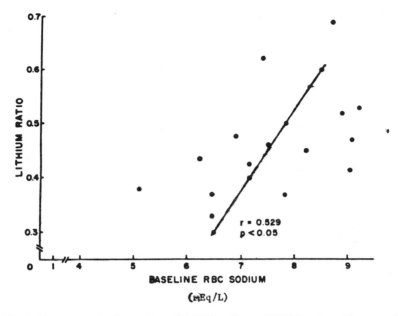

Fig. 1. Linear regression between base line RBC sodium and RBC Li: plasma Li measured on day 14.

Cell Membrane

We next considered the possibility that intrinsic factors which are responsible for the normal distribution of sodium across the cell membrane might also be responsible for the different Lithium Ratios seen in the responders and the nonresponders.

To examine the role of such factors in determining lithium distribution across the cell membrane, we conducted an experiment in which lithium carbonate was administered to two groups of sheep whose erythrocytes are known to have genetically determined quantitative differences in the membrane properties which regulate RBC sodium and potassium concentrations.[48,49] One group of sheep has a high potassium and low sodium concentration in the RBC (HK sheep), similar to humans; the second group has only about 1/9 the RBC potassium concentration of the HK sheep and a proportionately high sodium concentration (LK sheep). Several factors are believed to account for these differences in RBC cation concentrations. Firt, there is reduced Na,K-activated ATPase activity in

RBC membranes from LK sheep and a correspondingly low rate of active cation transport. Second, there is a difference in the rate of passive diffusion of cations across the RBC membranes, in that LK cells are leakier to cations than HK cells. Also, the LK cells have more exchange diffusion than HK cells.

When lithium was administered *in vivo* to these sheep, a higher steady-state concentration of lithium was observed in the LK cells than in the HK cells in spite of there being no difference between the plasma concentrations. When erythrocytes were obtained from HK and LK sheep and incubated *in vitro* with lithium (1.5 m*M*), much more lithium was found in the LK cells than in the HK erythrocytes.[50]

The following experiments were done to explore the reason for the higher concentration of lithium measured in the LK cells both *in vivo* and *in vitro*. First, washed HK and LK erythrocytes were loaded with lithium by suspending them in a phosphate buffered salt medium containing lithium (50 m*M*) at 2°C for 20 hours. The rate of loss of lithium from these loaded cells was then determined by placing them into an iso-osmotic phosphate-buffered media (containing no lithium) and incubating at 37°C. At the times specified (Fig. 2), aliquots were withdrawn and the RBC concentration of

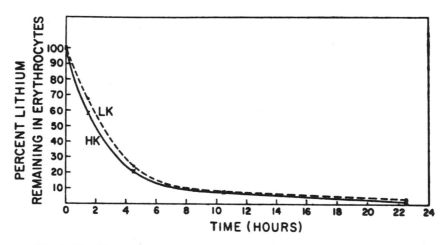

Fig. 2. The efflux of Li from HK and from LK erythrocytes *in vitro*. At time zero, the concentration of Li in the HK cells (1.66 ± 0.23 mEq/liter; X ± SEM) was not significantly different from that in the LK cells (1.39 ± .19; *p* > 0.3). Each point represents the mean of six determinations. The percent Li remaining in the LK erythrocytes was not significantly different from that left in the HK cells at any of the times of measurement.

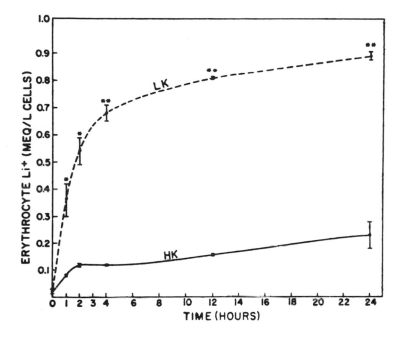

Fig. 3. The uptake of Li by HK and by LK erythrocytes *in vitro*. Each point represents the mean of three determinations ± SEM. *—significantly different from corresponding HK value, $p<0.01$; ** — significantly different from corresponding HK value, $p<0.001$.

lithium determined. It can be seen that the rate of loss of lithium from HK and from LK cells was identical; furthermore, ouabain ($1 \times 10^{-4}M$) did not alter the rate of loss of lithium from either type of erythrocyte. Thus, lithium does not appear to be actively removed from erythrocytes by Na,K-activated ATPase. Maizels,[51] also, was unable to demonstrate any active efflux of lithium from human erythrocytes.

In contrast to this, when freshly washed HK and LK erythrocytes were suspended in a phosphate-buffered salt media containing ouabain (1×10^{-4} M) and lithium (1.5 mM), and shaken at 37°C, the uptake of lithium by LK cells was significantly greater than the uptake by HK cells (Fig. 3). From these results, it appears that the greater accumulation of lithium by LK erythrocytes *in vivo* is not a consequence of reduced transport of this cation from the cell but rather is the result of a greater leak into the cell. The reason for this greater uptake of lithium by the LK erythrocyte is unknown. One factor to consider is whether the difference in intracellular sodium in these two types of cells contributes to the difference in lithium uptake, perhaps by an exchange diffusion process.

To examine this possibility, an experiment was conducted in which human red cells obtained from the same subject had their intracellular sodium concentration changed by treatment with parachloromercuribenzoate (PCMBS), essentially as described by Garrahan and Rega.[52] Cells with the desired intracellular sodium concentration were then incubated in a balanced buffer solution containing ouabain ($1 \times 10^{-4} M$) and lithium (1.5 mM) for 24 hours. At this time, the intracellular sodium and lithium concentrations were measured. As can be seen in Table V, the intracellular lithium concentration increased in asssociation with the increased intracellular sodium concentration. The same trend has appeared in a number of subsequent experiments. Nevertheless, it is clear that a considerable change in intracellular sodium is required to allow for a demonstrable increase in lithium uptake.

It is of interest to recall our finding that the RBC lithium concentration in our depressed patients was correlated significantly with their base line erythrocyte sodium concentration, i.e., the higher the base line RBC sodium concentration, the higher the Lithium Ratio at 14 days. The correlation between these two variables was 0.55. While this correlation is statistically significant, it only accounts for about 27% of the variance. Thus, while these experiments indicate that the intracellular sodium concentration is

TABLE V

The Effect of Intracellular Sodium on the Concentration of Lithium Taken Up by the Erythrocyte *in Vitro*

Erythrocyte Na[a] (meq/1)	Erythrocyte Li[a] (meq/1)
10.0	0.24
39.8	0.36
67.0	0.50
87.5	0.64

[a]Measured after 24 hours of incubation in the presence of ouabain (1×10^{-4}M) and lithium (1.5mM).

involved in determining the RBC lithium concentration, it is, in itself, not the only, or perhaps even the main, factor.

In summary, then, these experiments show that membrane factors which control sodium and potassium distributions across the erythrocyte membrane regulate, also, the distribution of lithium. Specifically, we found the distribution of lithium to be similar to that of sodium. If these results can be extrapolated to the clinical situation, they suggest that lithium might be used as a tool to identify differences in cation transfer in different patient populations.

Cation Transport

Naylor *et al.*[53] have reported that there was a lower active transport of sodium in erythrocytes from eleven psychotically depressed female patients, as compared with erythrocytes from 13 neurotic depressed patients. Not only were the neurotically depressed women less severely ill, but they were also younger. Erythrocyte sodium concentrations correlated positively with severity of the depression while erythrocyte Na,K-activated ATPase had a negative correlation with mood. They also reported that the erythrocyte potassium flux and erythrocyte Na,K-activated ATPase did not differ between psychotic and neurotic depressives during base line (pretreatment) studies. However, there were significant correlations between these two variables and depressed mood for the group as a whole, suggesting a reduction in erythrocyte cation carrier activity.

In both patient groups, the active and the passive transfer of sodium (but not of potassium) increased significantly with recovery after treatment with electroconvulsive therapy. In a subsequent study, Naylor *et al.*[54] reported that neither Na,K-activated ATPase activity nor ouabain-sensitive potassium flux was different in erythrocytes obtained from psychotically depressed or neurotically depressed females. Further investigations of the cation transport systems in patients with affective illness are indicated, with attempts to correlate the results with RBC lithium concentrations with clinical response to lithium and with nosological subgroups.

Genetic Factors

There is extensive evidence that genetic factors play an important role in the development of manic-depressive illness and perhaps other forms of affective illness.[55,56] There is also a report that patients with a positive family history of affective illness are more likely to benefit from the prophylactic effects of lithium than those without such a history.[57] Further, our finding of a significant difference in the RBC lithium concentration between two strains of sheep whose erythrocyte cation transport characteristics are determined genetically suggests that the Lithium Ratio in our depressed patients may be influenced by genetically determined differences in cell membrane function. In order to evaluate this possibility, we conducted a study in which erythrocytes were obtained from monozygotic and dizygotic twins and incubated *in vitro* at 37°C in the presence of lithium (1.5 mM) for 24 hours. At this time, a significantly higher intrapair difference score between the dizygotic twins than the monozygotic twins was found. The calculated hereditability index ranged between 0.79–0.85, indicating a substantial genetic determinant for this variable.[58]

Other Studies

Glen *et al.*[59] evaluated membrane transport characteristics in depressed patients by measuring sodium activity and pH of secreted saliva. The depressed patients had a significantly higher salivary sodium activity and lower hydrogen ion activity than did healthy control subjects. These data suggest reduced reabsorption of sodium and of bicarbonate (measured as pH) in the depressives and are consistent with the hypothesis of an alteration in the transport of cations across cell membranes.

Electrolyte transport has also been studied by measuring the rate of entry of ^{24}Na from plasma into lumbar spinal fluid. The underlying mechanisms of this sodium transport are not known; it may involve both passive diffusion and active processes.[60]

Carroll[61] reviewed findings from five studies of ^{24}Na transfer in depressives. He concluded that there may be a reduction in ^{24}Na transfer in such patients. The significance of this and its relationship to the transfer of electrolytes across the RBC membrane is unknown.

Antidepressant Drugs, ECT, and Membrane Function

Unfortunately, there are only a few investigations of the effects of antidepressant drugs on cell membrane function. For example, Tarve and

Brechtlova[62] found that imipramine inhibited quinea pig brain microsomal Na,K-activated ATPase activity. The effects of imipramine were similar to those of ouabain, but the mechanisms of inhibition appear to be different. Other investigators have reported that a series of daily electroconvulsive shocks produce *increases* in sodium and decreases in potassium concentrations in rat brain synaptosomes.[63]

Conclusion

In this chapter we have reviewed evidence which points to a possible genetically determined abnormality in some aspect(s) of cell membrane properties regulating the movement of electrolytes across the plasma membrane in a subgroup of depressed patients. Such an abnormality can clearly affect neuronal function in its own right, or may produce significant alterations in other systems (e.g., the biogenic amines). For example, Bogdanski and Brodie[64] have proposed a model of biogenic amine transport in which norepinephrine, sodium and a carrier combined in a complex at the outer neuronal surface (where sodium is high). Norepinephrine is taken up by the cell as a consequence of the downhill sodium concentration gradient, which is maintained by the activity of the sodium pump. A similar model has been proposed for serotonin uptake.[65] Although the validity of this model has been challenged,[66,67] it indicates a way in which a change in ionic gradients may alter the physiological effects of biogenic amines, providing a "bridge" between electrolyte and biogenic amine areas of investigation.

The work and ideas which have been reviewed here must be extended in a number of ways. Further information is needed about the relationship between the Lithium Ratio, diagnosis, and clinical response in a larger number of patients. It would be important to study the Lithium Ratio over months or years to determine whether or not it remains stable. We have noticed a tendency for it to rise slowly over months in a few patients and have wondered if this in any way correlates with Schou's[68] suggestion that the long-term prophylactic effect of lithium may not be fully present in all patients for many months.

We have previously noted[45] that the RBC lithium:plasma lithium ratio appears to stabilize by about the seventh day of treatment at which time it may be possible to tell whether or not a patient will respond to lithium treatment. It would be important to see if this can be determined even earlier, perhaps leading to a "predictive" test of who will or will not respond to lithium treatment. It is also possible that lithium may be used as a "marker" to detect a biological difference among groups of depressed patients; a difference that would not be apparent in the absence of the drug.

In conclusion, we have suggested that some depressed patients, perhaps manic-depressives, have a disturbance in some aspect of cell membrane function governing the passage of electrolytes into or out of erythrocytes, resulting in an increased concentration of lithium within the cell. This correlates with a reduction of symptoms in the depressed phase. There is some evidence to support the view that this regulation of lithium concentration is under genetic control. Obviously we are not suggesting that this form of affective illness is a disease of red cell membranes. Rather, the hope is that the dysfunction in this system is paralleled by similar changes in neuronal membranes at some critical site in the central nervous system.

Acknowledgments

We gratefully acknowledge the advice and assistance of Carl M. Cochrane, Ph.D. with the data analyses. Drs. Elizabeth Dorus, Ghanshyam Pandey, and Arthur Schless have collaborated in aspects of this research. Janis Baron provided valuable technical assistance. The Nursing Staff, 7 East, assisted with patient evaluation and management. Supported in part by Research Funds from the Veterans Administration and NIMH grants No. 1 RO3 MH 16920-01 and RO1 MH 25433.

References

1. Mendels, J., and Stinnett, J.: Biogenic amine metabolism, depression and mania, *in* "Biological Psychiatry" (J. Mendels, Ed.), pp. 99–131, John Wiley and Sons, New York (1973).
2. Mendels, J.: Biological aspects of affective illness, in "American Handbook of Psychiatry" (S. Arieti, Ed.), pp. 448–479. Basic Books, New York (1974).
3. Mendels, J., and Frazer, A.: Brain biogenic amine depletion and mood. *Arch. Gen. Psychiat.* 30:447–451, 1974.
4. Katz, B.: "Nerve, Muscle, and Synapse," McGraw Hill, New York (1966).
5. Thomas, R.C.: Electrogenic sodium pump in nerve and muscle cells. *Physiol. Rev.* 52:563–594, 1972.
6. Schottstaedt, W.W., Grace, W.J., and Wolff, H.G.: Life situations, behaviour, attitudes, emotions and renal excretion of fluid and electrolytes. IV. Situations associated with retention of water, sodium and potassium. *J. Psychosom. Res.* 1:287-291, 1956.
7. Durell, J.: Lithium salts and affective disorders, *in* "Factors in Depression" (N.S. Kline, ED.), Raven Press, New York (1974), in press.

8. Gibbons, J.L.: Total body sodium and potassium in depressive illness. *Clin. Sci.* 19:133–138, 1960.
9. Coppen, A.J., and Shaw, D.M.: Mineral metabolism in melancholia. *Brit. J. Med.* 2:1439–1444, 1963.
10. Shaw, D.M., and Coppen, A.: Potassium and sodium distribution in depression. *Brit. J. Psychiat.* 112:269–276, 1966.
11 Baer, L., Durell, J., Bunney, W.E., Jr., *et al.*: Sodium-22 retention and 17-hydroxycorticosteroid excretion in affective disorders. *J. Psychiat. Res.* 6:289–297, 1969.
12. Naylor, G.J., McNamee, H.B., and Moody, J.P.: Erythrocyte sodium and potassium in depressive illness. *J. Psychosom. Res.* 14:173–177, 1970.
13. Naylor, G.J. McNamee, H.B., and Moody, J.P.: Changes in erythrocyte sodium and potassium on recovery from a depressive illness. *Brit. J. Psychiat.* 118:219–223, 1971.
14. Mendels, J., Frazer, A., and Secunda, S.K.: Intra-erythrocyte sodium and potassium in manic-depressive illness. *Biol. Psychiat.* 5:165–171, 1972.
15. Frazer, A., Secunda, S.K., and Mendels, J.: A method for the determination of sodium, potassium, magnesium and lithium concentrations in erythrocytes. *Clin. Chim. Acta* 36:499–509, 1972.
16. Owen, J.A., and Campbell, D.G.: A comparison of electrolytes and urea values in healthy persons and in hospital patients. *Clin. Chim. Acta* 22:611–618, 1968.
17. Cade, J.F.J.: Lithium salts in the treatment of psychotic excitement. *Med. J. Aust.* II:349–352, 1949.
18. Schou, M., Juel-Nielsen, N., Stromgren, E., *et al.*: The treatment of manic psychoses by the administration of lithium salts. *J. Neurol. Neurosurg. Psychiat.* 17:250–260, 1954.
19. Goodwin, F.K., and Ebert, M.H.: Lithium in mania: Clinical trials and controlled studies, *in* "Lithium: Its Role in Psychiatric Research and Treatment" (S. Gershon and B. Shopsin, Eds.), pp. 237–252, Plenum Press, New York (1973).
20. Baastrup, P.C., Poulson, J.C., Schou, M., *et al.*: Prophylactic lithium: Double blind discontinuation in manic-depressive and recurrent-depressive disorders. *Lancet* 2:326–330, 1970.
21. Schou, M.: Prophylactic lithium maintenance treatment in recurrent endogenous affective disorders, *in* "Lithium: Its Role in Psychiatric Research and Treatment" (S. Gershon and B. Shopsin, Eds.) pp. 269–294. Plenum Press, New York (1973).
22. Mendels, J.: Lithium and depression, *in* "Lithium: Its Role in Psychiatric Research and Treatment" (S. Gershon and B. Shopsin, Eds.) pp. 253–267, Plenum Press, New York (1973).
23. Mendels, J.: Lithium in the treatment of depressive states, *in* "Lithium Research and Therapy" (N. Johnson, Ed.) Academic Press, New York (1974), in press.
24. Huxley, A.F. and Stämpfli, R.: Direct determination of membrane resting potential and action potential in single myelinated nerve fibres. *J. Physiol.* 112:476–495, 1951.
25. Gardner, D.R., and Kerkut, G.A.: A comparison of the effects of sodium and lithium ions on action potentials from *Helix aspersa* neurones. Comp. Biochem. Physiol. 25:33–48, 1968.
26. Wespi, H.H.: Active transport and passive fluxes of K, Na, and Li in mammalian non-myelinated nerve fibres. *Pflüg. Arch. ges. Physiol.* 306:262–280, 1969.
27. Skou, J.C.: Further investigations on a Mg ion- and Na ion- activated adenosinetriphosphatase, possibly related to the active, linked transport of Na ion and K ion across the nerve membrane. *Biochem. Biophys. Acta* 42:6–23, 1960.

28. Rang, H.P., and Ritchie, J.M.: On the electrogenic sodium pump in mammalian non-myelinated nerve fibres and its activation by various external cations. *J. Physiol. (London)* 196:183–221, 1968.

29. Williams, R.J.P. The chemistry and biochemistry of lithium, *in* "Lithium: Its Role in Psychiatric Research and Treatment" (S. Gershon and B. Shopsin, Eds.), pp. 15–31. Plenum Press, New York (1973).

30. Wang, Y.-C., Pandey, G.N., Mendels, J., *et al.:* The effect of lithium on prostaglandin E_1-stimulated adenylate cyclase activity of human platelets. *Biochem. Pharmacol.* 23:845–855, 1974.

31. Davis, J.M., and Fann, W.E.: Lithium. *Annu. Rev. Pharmacol.* 11:285–303, 1971.

32. Trautner, E.M., Morris, R., Noack, C.H., *et al.:* The excretion and retention of ingested lithium and its effect on the ionic balance of man. *Med. J. Aust.* 2:280–291, 1955.

33. Tupin, J.P., Schlagenhauf, G.K., and Creson, D.L.: Lithium effects on electrolyte excretion. *Amer. J. Psychiat.* 125:536–543, 1968.

34. Baer, L., Platman, S.R., Kassir, S., *et al.:* Mechanisms of renal lithium handling and their relationship to mineralocorticoids: A dissociation between lithium and sodium ions. *J. Psychiat. Res.* 8:91–105, 1971.

35. Aronoff, M.S., Evens, R.G., and Durell, J.: Effect of lithium salts on electrolyte metabolism, *J. Psychiat. Res.* 8:139–159, 1971.

36. Hodgkin, A.L., and Keynes, R.D.: Movement of cations during recovery in nerve. *Symp. Soc. Expt. Biol.* 8:423–437, 1954.

37. Gardos, G.: Akkumulation der kaliumionen durch menschliche Blutkorperchen. *Acta Physiol. Acad. Sci. Hung.* 6:191–199, 1954.

38. Caldwell, P.C., Hodgkin, A.L., Keynes, R.D., *et al.:* The effects of injecting "energy-rich" phosphate compounds on the active transport of ions in the giant axons of *Loligo. J. Physiol. (London)* 152:561–590, 1960.

39. Sen, A.K., and Post, R.L.: Stoichiometry and localization of adenosine triphosphate-dependent sodium and potassium transport in the erythrocyte. *J. Biol. Chem.* 239:345–352, 1964.

40. Garrahan, P.J., and Glynn I.M.: The stoichiometry of the sodium pump. *J. Physiol. (London)* 192:217–235, 1967.

41. Baker, P.F.: Phosphorus metabolism of intact crab nerve and its relation to the active transport of ions. *J. Physiol. (London)* 180:383–423, 1965.

42. Israel, Y., Kalant, H., LeBlanc, E., *et al.:* Changes in cation transport and $(Na+K)$-activated adenosine triphosphatase produced by chronic administration of ethanol. *J. Pharmacol. Exp. Ther.* 174:330–336, 1970.

43. Bonting, S.L., and Caravaggio, L.L.: Studies on sodium-potassium-activated adenosinetriphosphatase. V. Correlation of enzyme activity with cation flux in six tissues. *Arch. Biochem. Biophys.* 101:37–46, 1963.

44. Frazer, A., Mendels, J., Secunda, S.K., *et al.:* The prediction of brain lithium concentrations from plasma or erythrocyte measures. *J. Psychiat. Res.* 10:1–7, 1973.

45. Mendels, J., and Frazer, A.: Intracellular lithium concentration and clinical response — Towards a membrane theory of depression. *J. Psychiat. Res.* 10:9–18, 1973.

46. Lyttkens, L., Soderberg, U., and Wetterberg, L.: Increased lithium erythrocyte/plasma ratio in manic-depressive psychosis. *Lancet* 1:40, 1973.

47. Baer, L., Durell, J., Bunney, W.E., Jr., *et al.:* Sodium balance and distribution in lithium carbonate therapy. *Arch. Gen. Psychiat.* 22:40–44, 1970.
48. Tosteson, D.C., and Hoffman, J.: Regulation of cell volume by active cation transport in high and low potassium sheep red cells. *J. Gen. Physiol.* 44:169–194, 1960.
49. Tosteson, D.C.: Some properties of the plasma membranes of high potassium and low potassium sheep red cells. *Ann. N.Y. Acad. Sci.* 137:577–590, 1966.
50. Schless, A.P., Frazer, A., Mendels, J., *et al.:* Genetic determinants of lithium metabolism: II. An *in vivo* study of lithium distribution across erythrocyte membranes. *Arch. Gen. Psychiat.* 1974, in press.
51. Maizels, M.: Effect of sodium content on sodium efflux from human red cells suspended in sodium-free media containing potassium, rubidium, caesium or lithium chloride. *J. Physiol. (London)* 195:657–679, 1968.
52. Garrahan, P.J., and Rega, A.F.: Cation loading of red blood cells. *J. Physiol. (London)* 193:459–466, 1967.
53. Naylor, G.J., McNamee, H.B., and Moody, J.P.: The plasma control of erythrocyte sodium and potassium metabolism in depressive illness. *J. Psychosom. Res.* 14:179–186, 1970.
54. Naylor, G.J., Dick, D.A.T., Dick, E.G., *et al.:* Erythrocyte membrane cation carrier in depressive illness. *Psychol. Med.* 3:502–508, 1973.
55. Winokur, G., Clayton, P.J., and Reich, T.: "Manic Depressive Illness," The CV Mosby Company, St. Louis (1969).
56. Perris, C.: The genetics of affective disorders, *in* "Biological Psychiatry" (J. Mendels, Ed.), pp. 385 415, John Wiley and Sons, New York (1973).
57. Mendlewicz, J., Fieve, R.R., Stallone, F., *et al.:* Genetic history as a predictor of lithium response in manic depressive illness. *Lancet* 1:599–600, 1972.
58. Dorus, E., Pandey, G.N., Frazer, A., *et al.:* Genetic determinant of lithium metabolism: I. An *in vitro* monozygotic-dizygotic twin study. *Arch. Gen. Psychiat.* 1974, in press.
59. Glen, A.I.M., Ongley, G.C., and Robinson, K.: Diminished membrane transport in manic-depressive psychosis and recurrent depression. *Lancet* 2:241–243, 1968.
60. Katzman, R., and Pappius, H.M.: "Brain Electrolytes and Fluid Metabolism," pp. 75–80 Williams and Wilkins, Baltimore (1973).
61. Carroll, B.J.: Sodium and potassium transfer to cerebrospinal fluid in severe depression, *in* "Depressive Illness, Some Research Studies" (B. Davies, B.J. Carroll, and R.M. Mowbray, Eds.), pp. 247–260, Charles C Thomas, Springfield (1972).
62. Tarve, U., and Brechtlova, M.: Effects of psychopharmacological agents on brain metabolism. 3. Effects of imipramine and ouabain on the (Na+ plus K+) activated ATPase from brain microsomes and cooperative interactions with the enzyme. *J. Neurochem.* 14:283–290, 1967.
63. Escueta, A.V., and Appel, S.H.: The effects of electroshock seizures on potassium transport within synaptosomes from rat brain. *J. Neurochem.* 19:1625–1638, 1972.
64. Bogdanski, D.F., and Brodie, B.B.: Role of sodium and potassium ions in storage of norepinephrine by sympathetic nerve endings. *Life Sci.* 5:1563–1569, 1966.
65. Bogdanski, D.F., Tissari, A., and Brodie, B.B.: Role of sodium, potassium, ouabain and reserpine in uptake, storage and metabolism of biogenic amines in synaptosomes. *Life Sci.* 7:419–428, 1968.
66. White, T.D., and Keen, P.: The role of internal and external Na+ and K+ on the uptake

of (^{3}H) noradrenaline by synaptosomes prepared from rat brain. *Biochim. Biophys. Acta* 196:285–295, 1970.

67. White, T.D., and Keen, P.: Effects of inhibitors of (Na+ + K+)-dependent adenosine triphosphatase on the uptake of norepinephrine by synaptosomes. *Molec. Pharmacol.* 7:40–45, 1971.

68. Schou, M.: Lithium in psychiatric therapy and prophylaxis. *J. Psychiat. Res.* 6:67–95, 1968.

Chapter 8

A Neuroendocrine Strategy in the Psychobiological Study of Depressive Illness

EDWARD J. SACHAR

It is the thesis of this paper that neuroendocrine techniques may offer a promising approach to the study of brain function in the affective disorders. Many clinical features of depressive illness would suggest that it involves hypothalamic functions: Patients typically experience a change in mood, a loss of appetite, libido, and aggressive drive, as well as disturbances in autonomic functioning and sleep, and a curious diurnal variation in the intensity of symptoms. It is not implausible to suspect, then, that along with these apparent hypothalamic disturbances, neuroendocrine regulation might also be affected in depression. This possibility is strengthened by recent findings that the neuroendocrine cells which secrete the hypothalamic releasing hormones are themselves regulated by monoaminergic neural tracts; the monoamines involved include those which have been implicated in the chemical pathology of affective illness, particularly noradrenaline and dopamine.[1,2] If there is a disturbance in brain monoaminergic function in depressive illness, and if it affects the neuroendocrine pathways, it could be

123

expected to be reflected in abnormalities in hormonal responses.

I would like to illustrate these points by describing briefly three endocrine studies of depressed patients. The first deals with the secretion of cortisol, the second with growth hormone, the third with luteinizing hormone (LH).

It has long been known that a substantial group of depressed patients hypersecrete cortisol. Several clinical studies have suggested that this hypersecretion is more likely to occur in those who are severely depressed, actively suicidal, markedly anxious, or psychotically decompensating.[3-7] It also occurs more frequently in unipolar depressive—that is, those without a prior history of manic episodes.[8] However, it has remained unclear whether the cortisol hypersecretion represents a nonspecific stress response in these patients, or whether it is an integral feature of severe depressive illness.

To learn more about neuroendocrine regulation in these cases, we endeavored to study the precise way the "extra" cortisol was secreted in hypersecreting depressed patients, by sampling blood through a cannula every 20 minutes around the clock. Figure 1 shows in a healthy 60-year old man the typical normal plasma cortisol pattern, synchronized with the sleep–wake cycle, as described by Weitzman et al.[9] For a six-hour period in the late evening and early morning, extending two hours past sleep onset, cortisol secretion virtually ceases and plasma cortisol concentration approaches zero. Cortisol secretion then turns on in a series of discrete episodes, the largest usually occurring between 5:00 and 9:00 AM. Normally there are seven to nine such episodes in a 24-hour period, with peak cortisol concentrations reaching about 15 μg%. It appears that each secretory episode represents a burst of ACTH secretion,[10] and presumably of hypothalamic CRH secretion; the plasma cortisol pattern can be inferred, then, to reflect the pattern of hypothalamic neuroendocrine activity. Figure 2 shows the cortisol patterns in a depressed patient before and after recovery, from a study previously published.[11] Note that during illness the patient actively secretes cortisol during the period when secretion is normally minimal. Note that the number of major secretory episodes is increased to about 12, and that both at the beginning and end of episodes, plasma cortisol concentration is markedly elevated. Above all, note that the disturbance in neuroendocrine function extends through both day and night, including hours of sleep. Total cortisol secretion is approximately doubled during illness. After recovery, the cortisol program normalizes.

We have seen similar patterns in nine hypersecreting patients to date, and the data do not easily seem to fit a simple stress hypothesis: First, the disturbance is pervasive and extends through sleeping hours; it would seem more likely for stress-related hypersecretion to be manifested primarily during waking hours. Second, the disturbance occurs in apathetic unanxious patients as well, although not as commonly. Third, other laboratories have reported relative unresponsiveness to dexamethasone suppression tests in these cases.[12,13]

It is possible, then, that the hypersecretion reflects a central neuroendocrine abnormality. It is particularly relevant that there is strong evidence for a brain noradrenergic system which normally exerts tonic inhibition on CRH and ACTH secretion.[14] Depletion of the brain of noradrenaline—which can

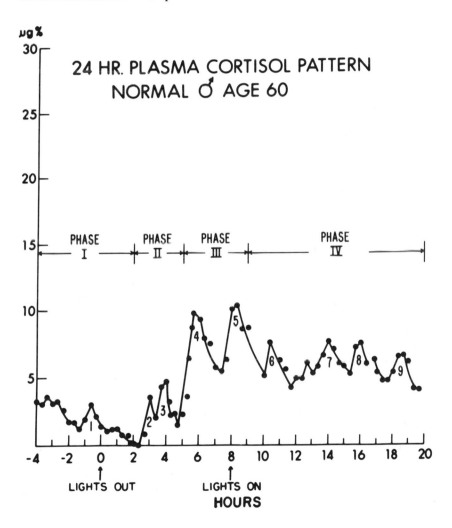

μg %

24 HR. PLASMA CORTISOL PATTERN
NORMAL ♂ AGE 60

PHASE I PHASE II PHASE III PHASE IV

LIGHTS OUT   LIGHTS ON
HOURS

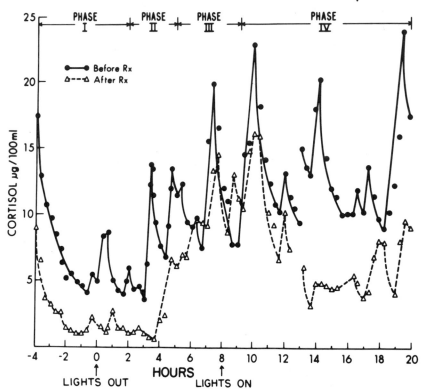

24 HR. PLASMA CORTISOL PATTERN DEPRESSED ♀ AGE 62

precipitate depressions in humans—markedly stimulates ACTH secretion in animals. The hypersecretion of cortisol, in depressed patients may, therefore, provide support for the current hypothesis that depressive illness is associated with diminished hypothalamic catecholaminergic activity.

Let us turn, now, to another catecholamine-regulated hormone: growth hormone. A potent stimulus to growth hormone secretion is a fall in blood sugar, and this is the basis for a standard test using insulin-induced hypoglycemia.[15] Brain catecholamines evidently mediate the GH response to hypoglycemia: The response is abolished or inhibited by a variety of catecholamine depletors and blockers.[16] If hypothalamic catecholaminergic activity is diminished in depressive illness, one might then expect to see reduced GH responses to hypoglycemia in depressed patients. Figure 3

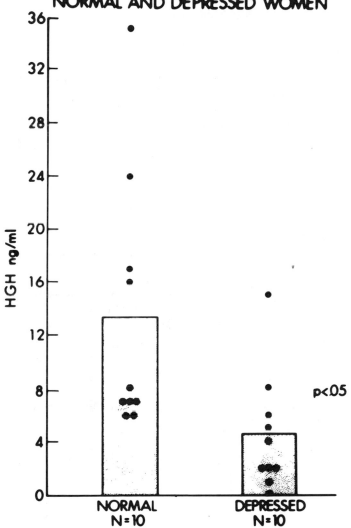

MAXIMUM HGH RESPONSES TO HYPOGLYCEMIA
IN POST-MENOPAUSAL
NORMAL AND DEPRESSED WOMEN

shows the maximal GH responses to insulin-induced hypoglycemia in postmenopausal unipolar depressed women. These data were gathered in collaboration with Drs. Gruen, Altman, and Sassin.[17] In this study, one of a series on growth hormone responses to hypoglycemia,[18,19] we focused on postmenopausal women in order to eliminate the potentiating effects of estrogens on GH responses. Despite the small sample size, the maximal GH responses of the depressed women were significantly reduced, to about one-third of the mean response of the normal women. Indeed, while all of the normal women had clinically adequate responses, more than half of the depressed women did not. Note that the ages of the two groups were virtually identical. Figure 4 shows that the hypoglycemic responses were also identical in the two groups, both in terms of absolute glucose drop and percent drop from base line. The diminished GH response in the depressed patients is, then, consistent with the concept of a central hypothalamic abnormality and with the hypothesis of diminished brain catecholaminergic activity. These findings are also consistent with reports from other laboratories of decreased GH responses to hypoglycemia in groups of depressed patients heterogeneous with respect to age, sex, and depressive subtype.[20,21]

We have also studied GH responses to the catecholamine precursor L-dopa. L-dopa stimulates a GH response in both normal and Parkinsonian

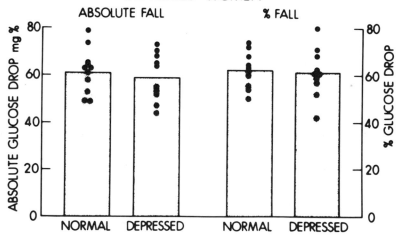

MAXIMUM HYPOGLYCEMIC RESPONSES TO 0.1 u/kg OF INSULIN IN POST-MENOPAUSAL NORMAL AND DEPRESSED WOMEN

subjects.[22,23] This response also appears to be mediated by brain catecholamines.[2] Our initial studies suggested that this GH response to L-dopa declined with age, and declined further with unipolar depressive illness.[19,24] However, most of the unipolar depressed patients were postmenopausal women, and the possible effect of the menopause on the GH response to L-dopa needed to be clarified. We have recently completed another study controlling for this variable (Fig. 5).[25] It is evident that there is an effect not only of age, but also of the menopause, and that in contrast to GH responses to hypoglycemia, there is no difference between the GH responses to L-dopa of the normal and unipolar depressed postmenopausal women.

In view of the fact that both the GH responses to hypoglycemia and to L-dopa are believed to be catecholaminergically mediated, how can we understand the abnormal GH response of depressed women to hypoglycemia but not to L-dopa? There are at least two possibilities. First, the GH response to L-dopa presumably depends on the brain conversion of *exogenous* catecholamine precursor, while the GH response to hypoglycemia calls upon *endogenous* brain catecholamines. Second, it is possible that the two stimuli act by different neurochemical pathways; one may primarily involve dopamine while the other may involve noradrenaline. We are conducting further research to clarify this latter question.

LH is also a catecholaminergically regulated hormone.[26,27] After gonadectomy or menopause, the secretion of LH and its plasma concentration rises markedly, because of the absence of feedback inhibition on brain receptors by circulating estrogens. This postgonadectomy rise in LH can be blocked by brain catecholamine depletors; it can be restored by the noradrenaline precursor DOPS.[27] If brain catecholamines are "depleted" from the neuroendocrine tracts in postmenopausal depressed women, one might expect them to have reduced LH secretion. With Drs. Altman and Gruen and Mrs. Halpern, we have gathered preliminary data from small groups of postmenopausal normal and unipolar depressed women, aged 57–65. Our findings thus far indicate that mean plasma LH concentration is significantly reduced in the depressed women, compared to age-matched normals, again supporting the view of diminished hypothalamic catecholamine activity. These results are quite preliminary, however, and we are in the process of enlarging both our normal and depressed groups.

In conclusion, the study of neuroendocrine responses appears to offer an unusual opportunity to study brain function in the intact, living organism, and may provide us with a physiological window into the hypothalamus of the patient with affective illness.

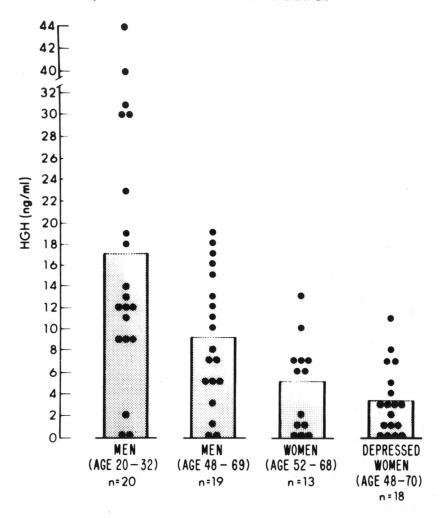

HGH RESPONSES TO L-DOPA IN YOUNG MEN, OLDER MEN, POST-MENOPAUSAL WOMEN, AND DEPRESSED POST-MENOPAUSAL WOMEN

References

1. Brown, G., and Reichlin, S.: Psychologic and neural regulation of growth hormone secretion. *Psychosom. Med.* 34:45–61, 1972

2. Martin, J.B.: Neural regulation of growth hormone secretion. *N. Engl. J. Med.* 288:1384–1393, 1973.

3. Gibbons, J.L.: Cortisol secretion rate in depressive illness. *Arch. Gen. Psychiat.* 10:572–575, 1964.

4. Sachar, E.J., Hellman, L., Fukushima, D.K., and Gallagher, T.F.: Cortisol production in depressive illness. *Arch. Gen. Psychiat.* 23:289–298, 1970.

5. Bunney, W.E., Mason, J.M., Roatch, J., and Hamburg, D.A.: A psychoendocrine study of severe psychotic depressive crises. *Amer. J. Psychiat.* 122:72–80, 1965.

6. Bunney, W.E., Fawcett, J.A., Davis, J.M., and Gifford, S.: Further evaluation of urinary 17-hydroxycorticosteroids in suicidal patients. *Arch. Gen. Psychiat.* 21:138–150, 1969.

7. Bunney, W.E., Mason, J.W., and Hamburg, D.A.: Correlations between behavioral variables and urinary 17-hydroxycorticosteroids in depressed patients. *Psychosom. Med.* 27:299–308, 1965.

8. Dunner, D.L., Goodwin, F.K., Gershon, E.S., *et al.:* Excretion of 17-OHCS in unipolar and bipolar depressed patients. *Arch. Gen. Psychiat.* 26:360–363, 1972.

9. Weitzman, E.D., Fukushima, D., Nogeire, C., *et al.:* Twenty-four hour pattern of the episodic secretion of cortisol in normal subjects. *J. Clin. Endocrin. Metab.* 33:14–22, 1971.

10. Berson, S., and Yalow, N.: Radioimmunoassay of ACTH in plasma. *J. Clin. Invest.* 47:2725–2751, 1968.

11. Sachar, E.J., Hellman, L., Roffwarg, H.P., *et al.:* Disrupted 24-hour patterns of cortisol secretion in psychotic depression. *Arch. Gen. Psychiat.* 128:19–24, 1973.

12. Stokes, P.E.: Studies on the control of adrenocortical function in depression, *in* "Recent Advances in the Psychobiology of Depressive Illnesses" (T.A. Williams, M.M. Katz, and J.A. Shield, Eds.), U.S. Department of Health, Education and Welfare, pp. 283–293, Washington, D.C. (1972).

13. Carroll, B.J.: Control of plasma cortisol levels in depression: Studies with the dexamethasone suppression test, *in* "Depressive Illness: Some Research Studies" (B. Davies, B.J. Carroll, and R.M. Mowbray, Eds.), pp. 87–148, Charles C. Thomas, Springfield (1972).

14. Van Loon, G.R.: Brain catecholamines and ACTH secretion, *in* "Frontiers in Neuroendocrinology" (L. Martini and W.F. Ganong, Eds.), pp. 209–247, Oxford University Press, New York (1973).

15. Raiti, S., Davis, W.T., and Blizzard, R.M.: Comparison of effects of insulin hypog lycemia and arginine infusion on release of human growth hormone. *Lancet* 2:1182–1184, 1967.

16. Frantz, A.G., Kelinberg, D.L., Noel, G.L., and Suh, H.K.: Effects of neuroleptics on the secretion of prolactin and growth hormone, *in* "Endocrinology" (R.B. Scow, Ed.), pp. 144–149, Excerpta Medica, Amsterdam (1973).

17. Sachar, E.J., Gruen, P., Altman, N., and Sassin, J.: Growth hormone response to hypoglycemia in postmenopausal depressed women. *Arch. Gen. Psychiat.* In press.

18. Sachar, E.J., Finkelstein, J., and Hellman, L.: Growth hormone responses in depressive illness: Response to insulin tolerance test. *Arch. Gen. Psychiat.* 24:263–269, 1971.

19. Sachar, E.J., *et al.:* Growth hormone and prolactin in unipolar and bipolar depressed patients: Responses to hypoglycemia and L-dopa. *Amer. J. Psychiat.* 130:1362–1367, 1973.

20. Mueller, P.S., Heninger, G.R., and MacDonald, R.K.: Studies on glucose utilization and insulin sensitivity in affective disorders, *in* "Recent Advances in Psychobiology of Depressive Illnesses" (T.A. Williams, M.M. Katz, and J.A. Shield, Eds.), U.S. Department of Health, Education and Welfare, pp. 235-248, Washington, D.C. (1972).

21. Carroll, B.J.: Studies with hypothalamic-pituitary-adrenal stimulation tests in depression, *in* "Depressive Illness: Some Research Studies" (B. Davies, B.J. Carroll, and R.M. Mowbray, Eds.), pp. 149–201, Charles C. Thomas, Springfield (1972).

22. Kansal, P.C., Buse, J., Talbert, O.R., *et al.:* Effect of L-dopa on plasma growth hormone, insulin, and thyroxine. *J. Clin. Endocrin. Metab.* 34:99–105, 1972.

23. Boyd, A.E., Lebovitz, B., and Pfeiffer, B.: Stimulation of human growth hormone secretion by L-dopa. *N. Engl. J. Med.* 283:1425–1429, 1970.

24. Sachar, E.J., *et al.:* Growth hormone responses to L-dopa in depressed patients. *Science* 178:1304–1305, 1972.

25. Sachar, E.J. *et al.:* Growth hormone responses to L-dopa: Relation to age, menopause, depression, and plasma dopa concentration. Submitted for publication.

26. Coppola, J.A.: Brain catecholamines and gonadotropin secretion, *in* "Frontiers in Neuroendocrinology" (L. Martini and W.F. Ganong, Eds.), pp. 129–143, Oxford University Press, New York (1971).

27. Ojeda, S.R., and McCann, S.M.: Evidence for participation of a catecholaminergic mechanism in the post-castration rise in plasma gonadotrophins. *Neuroendocrinology* 12:295–315, 1974.

Chapter 9

Clinical Pharmacological Strategies

JOHN M. DAVIS
and
DAVID JANOWSKY

There are various strategies for investigating possible biochemical factors in mental illness. These include: studying neurotransmitters and their metabolites in urine, spinal fluid, or autopsy brain; using platelets as a model for the central amine-containing neuron; using red blood cells as a model for electrolyte transport in brain; using the precursor loading strategy, etc. A different strategy for investigating the role of neurotransmitters in mental disease is to study the behavioral effects of drugs known to affect a given transmitter. However, some drugs alter transmitters acutely but cannot be used chronically due to possible severe side effects and are therefore unsuitable for routine therapy. Nevertheless, such agents might prove to be valuable tools for investigating the role of transmitters in mental disease. In this Chapter we will discuss the use of the drugs physostigmine and methylphenidate as research tools.

Classically, efforts to relate transmitters to mental disease have focused on a single disease–single transmitter concept. For example, in reference to depressive disorders, in the United States research has focused on the suggestion that low functional norepinephrine is associated with depression, and high functional norepinephrine with mania. That is, depression could be caused by low brain norepinephrine or by decreased noradrenergic function in the brain occurring through some other mechanism, such as an abnormality in receptor site, uptake, transport, or release.

However, we would like to suggest that abnormal behavior such as mania and depression may be under the control of more than one transmitter, involving a balance between transmitters. It is relevant to note that in the peripheral nervous system, most functions are controlled by a balance between noradrenergic and cholinergic factors. Thus, many central nervous system functions are controlled by a balance between transmitters, including a variety of vital functions such as thirst, hunger, sexual behavior, and temperature. Of particular interest is the fact that movement disorders, such as Parkinsonism, may well be under the control of several transmitters. It is known that Parkinson's disease is caused by low brain dopamine. However, Parkinsonian symptoms can be influenced by cholinergic factors. That is, anticholinergic drugs such as benztropine lessen Parkinsonian symptoms and cholinomimetic drugs such as physostigmine, which raise brain acetylcholine (ACH), worsen Parkinsonian symptoms. Consequently, physostigmine provides a useful therapeutic tool for investigating cholinomimetic function in man. By blocking the destruction of ACH, both peripherally and within the brain, physostigmine raises brain level of ACH and, functionally, has a cholinomimetic effect. It lasts several hours and is reversible.

Neostigmine produces the same peripheral effects as does physostigmine, but does not pass the blood–brain barrier, and so provides an active placebo which serves as a convenient control substance for these experiments. In our investigations, neostigmine did not produce any behavioral effects.[1,2] In previous experiments we have reported that physostigmine produces a lessening in manic symptoms and substitutes for such symptoms a state of psychomotor retardation. The purpose of this Chapter is to extend this series to a larger number of patients and elaborate in greater detail the psychological states produced by physostigmine. These experiments report the results of 18 physostigmine studies performed on 12 patients. In those patients where more than one physostigmine study was done, the results were averaged.

Method

The patients were pretreated with methscopolamine bromide, 0.75 to 1 mg intramuscularly, an anticholinergic agent which does not pass the blood–brain barrier. This agent partially blocks the peripheral cholinomimetic properties of physostigmine or neostigmine. An intravenous infusion was started 30 minutes after pretreatment, followed by a varying number of placebo injections, then by a sequence of doses of either physostigmine or neostigmine methylsulfate (0.25 mg or 0.5 mg, respectively). Active drug was given until behavioral change occurred or until a total of 3 mg of physostigmine or 1.5 mg of neostigmine had been administered. Only one cholinomimetic agent was given in each experiment. In a given experiment, neither the patient nor the rating nurse was aware of whether placebo, physostigmine, or neostigmine was administered. In addition, in a given experiment, neither the patient nor the rating nurse knew whether the series of injections contained placebo only or active drug, or physostigmine or neostigmine. Thus, the participants of an experiment were blind as to which drug was being administered as well as to where in the injection sequence the active drug was substituted for placebo. Patients were evaluated using the modification of the Beigel-Murphy Manic Rating Scale. The 11 items best reflecting manic severity as described by Beigel and Murphy were rated on a 0 to 5 point continuum. The Beigel-Murphy Manic Grandiosity Sub-Scale was also used to evaluate patients. Patients were rated on a 0 to 5 point continuum scale for depression using the Bunney-Hamburg Rating System. Ratings were done every 5 minutes. Further details of the administration have been described previously.[1,2] Eight patients were manic-depressives in the manic phase, while four patients fell on the borderline between mania and schizoaffective disorder and therefore were classified as atypical mania or schizoaffective manic phase.

Results

There was a marked diminishment of the manic symptoms which occurred after physostigmine but after neither placebo nor neostigmine. The manic states seemed to be replaced by the state of psychomotor retardation. Physostigmine produced an acute affect beginning roughly 10 to 20 minutes after injection and lasting approximately 90 minutes. The manic behavior markedly lessened and the patient switched from mania to a psychomotor retarded anergic state.

The quantitative aspects of the physostigmine effects will be discussed first, followed by their qualitative aspects. The Beigel-Murphy Euphoria and Manic Intensity Rating Scales are quantitative instruments developed to measure the degree of mania. Physostigmine produces marked lessening on the Beigel-Murphy Manic Intensity Scale, a decrease which is not only significant to a high degree of statistical reliability but also of considerable magnitude. Similarly, the Beigel-Murphy Euphoria Scale scores were greatly reduced (71%), again a result which is highly statistically significant at 0.001. This quantitative effect was also seen on individual symptoms. Talkativeness was reduced almost in half. The symptom, "is active," is reduced to greater than this (44%). Cheerfulness was reduced by over two-thirds, statistically a very highly reliable finding ($p = 0.0007$). Flight of ideas was reduced by over one-half. Ratings of happiness were reduced from 1.71 to 0.38, a reduction of over 78%, again a highly statistically reliable change ($p = 0.0006$). The patients were rated as being more depressed after physostigmine, the depression score increasing by over 247% over control. Grandiosity was reduced in magnitude but not to a statistically significant degree. In summary, there are large quantitative differences seen after physostigmine. In a qualitative sense, all patients appeared slowed down after physostigmine. Instead of talking rapidly, rhyming and punning, being cheerful, friendly, with a flight of ideas, they were slowed down with psychomotor retardation and slow thinking. They were often quite dysphoric. In a descriptive sense, and instead of being manic, they appeared to be psychomotor depressed. The more impressive changes were slowing down, both in thought process and in movement. Patients felt sleepy but did not go to sleep. In some cases, the patients were slowed down and felt dysphoric but did not necessarily show depressed affect in the sense of feeling very sad, crying, and so forth. Other patients felt sad and cried, some patients felt suicidal, some felt hopeless, etc.; however, this was not a constant feature. The slowing down, dysphoria, and anergia were constant features, and a variable feature was change in the direction of greater depressed affect. Some patients who were grandiose were clearly much less grandiose following physostigmine. Other patients were slowed down but still responded to direct questioning with grandiose content. That is to say, when asked a direct question, the patient may say that he does not want to talk about his grandiose ideas; however, one will get the feeling that he still maintains his grandiose ideas. Other patients were less grandiose in a more clear-cut fashion. Thus, to summarize our description of the quantitative changes, the changes on the psychomotor dimension were fairly marked; the changes on the depressive affect dimension and the psychotic grandiose thought dimension were less pronounced.

The question immediately arises as to how specific the physostigmine changes were. It is our impression that they were *moderately* specific. In support of this contention, we would like to present the arguments that deal with both extremes of the specificity issue:complete specificity or complete nonspecificity. The best argument that physostigmine possesses some specificity is that there is a large and substantial drop in the Beigel-Murphy Manic Intensity and Manic Euphoria Scales and the sub items therein. This scale was not constructed by us, but was constructed to be what hopefully is a valid measure of mania, and there is a quite remarkable change in this scale following the administration of physostigmine. The symptom changes were typical of diminishing mania. Although systematic experiments have not been done, manic patients have received high doses of sedative agents such as chlorpromazine or barbiturates or other sedatives. It is important to point out here that one is comparing the effects of acute dose of chlorpromazine versus physostigmine. Obviously, chlorpromazine has antipsychotic effect when given over several weeks, but this is not the relevant comparison. After one acute dose of chlorpromazine, manic patients can be put to sleep; however, when awakened they may still be manic, rhyming, punning, hyperactive, etc., even though they may have received such a high dose of chlorpromazine that they are markedly ataxic with slurred speech, appearing like a person who is intoxicated with alcohol or barbiturates. It is quite obvious that these patients, although highly sedated, are still manic and the mania overrides the sedation until the patient is actually asleep. In the case of physostigmine, the patients are sleepy but they are not asleep and do not go to sleep in our experimental conditions. They do not appear ataxic and do not appear similar to patients who are intoxicated with alcohol, barbiturates, etc. Similarly, when high doses of barbiturates or nonbarbiturate sedatives are given, patients either are put to sleep or they are still manic in spite of being intoxicated with these agents. Similarly, a manic intoxicated on alcohol taken on his own initiative outside of the hospital presents to the hospital as an alcohol intoxicated manic, not a psychomotor retarded depressed manic having his mania converted to psychomotor retardation due to the alcohol. In the absence of systematic investigation of any of these sedative agents, we must inject a certain amount of caution into our discussion. It seems from our experience with these patients that the physostigmine effects are much more specific antimanic than nonspecific sedation. Thus, the evidence that they are not completely nonspecific is those dimensions typically measured in mania by the Beigel-Murphy Scale are changed to a quantitatively great degree by physostigmine. Furthermore, when one gives nonspecific sedative agents, one sees intoxicated manic patients, not patients appearing like psychomotor retarded depressions similar to the physostigmine state. Indeed, parenthetically, it may be more correct and less prejudicial rather than arguing about specificity or nonspecificity of the physostigmine effects to refer to it as a cholinomimetic state or a physostigmine induced state.

Discussion

To a large extent, one's opinion of how specific physostigmine is depends on what one considers to be the essence of mania. If an investigator thinks of mania as the disease of mood where the manic episodes are characterized by rhyming and punning, talking fast, hyperactivity, ceaseless activity, euphoria, happiness, etc., the effects of physostigmine appear moderately specific. Physostigmine rather markedly reduces all these dimensions. If one thinks that the thought disorder of mania, namely, the grandiose symptoms are the essence of mania, then the effects of physostigmine are less specific. It is not known in any fundamental sense in psychiatry just what mania is, and which symptoms are pathognomonic. In this sense, the primary and secondary symptoms of mania are not known. Indeed these may only become well defined after the cause of the disorder is known.

Since the degree of specificity cannot be ascertained at this time, we refer to these findings as the effects of physostigmine on manic symptoms rather than on mania and have discussed our findings in a descriptive sense noting that physostigmine is more effective on the symptoms: rhyming and punning, talking fast, hyperactivity, ceaseless activity, euphoria, happiness, etc., and less effective on grandiosity, and leave the reader to make his own judgment as to the quantitative degree of specificity. To say the effects of physostigmine are either nonspecific because they do not affect grandiosity is to assume that the cause of mania is known and that grandiosity is pathognomonic. Similarly, to assume that physostigmine is absolutely specific because it affects symptoms like ceaseless activity, happiness, etc., is again to make an assumption as to the essential nature of mania. In our view, we avoid such assumptions and talk about the effects of physostigmine on manic symptoms considered as individual symptoms or a given quantitative rating scale as operationally defined.

The specificity issue is also clouded by the possibility that mania may not have a single unique cause. The underlying assumption of much of metapharmacological psychopharmacological theorizing is the single disease–single transmitter concept. In this case a single amine, norepinephrine(NE), would be said to be elevated in mania and this would produce the symptoms. If one could have measured this elevation of NE and correlated the symptoms with the etiological cause, one could find out which symptoms are primary and which symptoms are secondary. Another etiological possibility which may be worthy of discussion is whether a balance between two transmitters is involved, or even a complicated balance between three transmitters. In a manic patient, for example, noradrenergic, dopaminergic, and cholinergic transmitter function in some broad sense could be disordered. It could well be that the psychomotor component of mania could, in some sense, be caused by a balance between dopamine and acetylcholine and the grandiosity component could be controlled by norepinephrine. We do not assert that this data prove this. We only wish to raise these complexities in thinking about the findings. In our view, these findings are empirical evidence which may be clues to finding out the biology of mania, not a statement of a theory as a fixed entity. Physostigmine produces fairly marked behavioral changes. We are taking an empirical approach in asking what would be the possibilities of clues provided by this pharmacological research strategy.

Let us now consider what type of clue the physostigmine effects may provide. There are balances between transmitters in a wide variety of physiological systems. For example, the peripheral autonomic function is generally controlled by a balance between the sympathetic and parasympathetic symptoms. On a central level, many physiological functions are controlled by more than one transmitter and some by a balance of transmitters. Indeed it is our opinion that *most* physiological functions are controlled by more than one transmitter. Of particular relevance is the fact that many releasing factors in systems of hormonal homeostasis are controlled by more than one transmitter. Drives such as hunger, reward, thirst, and other central nervous system regulatory systems are often controlled by balances between transmitters. Of particular relevance to depression is the fact that self-stimulation has been shown to be controlled by cholinergic as well as noradrenergic factors. On a human level, there is excellent evidence that physostigmine worsens Parkinsonian symptoms and anticholinergic agents benefit Parkinsonian symptoms. The cause of Parkinsonian symptoms, of course, is low dopamine but cholinergic factors clearly modulate this movement disorder. Interpolating this to mania, it would seem reasonable to hypothesize that physostigmine, in lessening mania and substituting psychomotor retardation, modulates some aspect of the manic process. If the manic process were controlled by a balance between two transmitters that functioned in an exactly opposite way, then one should have an equal turning off of all degrees of mania. Since the turning off is more pronounced in some rather than other symptoms, it may suggest that the cause may be compli-

TABLE I

Effects of Intravenous Physostigmine and Neostigmine on Various Symptoms in Acute Shizophrenics

	Change Score (Baseline-Physostigmine) 8 Subjects	p=	Change Score (Baseline-Neostigmine) 7 Subjects	p=
INHIBITION SCALE*	8.87±2.04	< .002	-1.17±2.50	NS
Lethargy	1.39±.19	< .00005	-.39±.33	NS
Has slow thoughts	.93±.40	< .003	.25±.14	< .06
Does not want to say anything	.43±.27	< .075	-.36±.29	NS
Withdrawn	.77±.28	< .02	-.14±.22	NS
Apathetic	.16±.26	NS	-.23±.29	NS
Lacks energy	1.10±.30	< .004	.24±.39	NS
Drained	1.16±.33	< .005	.17±.41	NS
Hypoactive	1.22±.29	< .002	.05±.40	NS
Lacks thoughts	.53±.38	NS	-.14±.20	NS
Depressed	.23±.46	NS	-.09±.29	NS
Psychomotor retardation	1.42±.25	< .0003	-.37±.39	NS
Emotional withdrawal	.70±.25	< .02	.47±.44	NS
ACTIVATION SCALE**	-2.80±.99	< .02	.83±1.31	NS
Cheerful	-.47±.24	< .05	-.16±.27	NS
Friendliness	-.64±.25	< .02	.06±.25	NS
Interacting	-.93±.35	< .02	.07±.32	NS
Talkativeness	-.84±.37	< .03	.29±.38	NS
OTHER				
Irritable	-.32±.38	NS	-.11±.16	NS
Dysphoric	.92±.47	< .05	.16±.41	NS
Hostile	-.32±.15	NS	.24±.24	NS
Wants to be alone	.13±.20	NS	-.13±.22	NS
Crying	.04±.17	NS	0.00±0.00	NS
Sad	.21±.45	NS	-.04±.27	NS
Sleepy	.76±.32	< .03	.23±.47	NS
Psychotic	-.06±.34	NS	-.23±.50	NS
Angry	-.27±.17	NS	.21±.21	NS
Had unusual thoughts	-.07±.16	NS	-.26±.27	NS

*"Inhibition Scale" includes sum of the following items.
**"Activation Scale" includes cheerful, friendliness, interacting, talkativeness scores.
Statistically significant differences between Baseline-Physostigmine Change Scores and Baseline-Neostigmine Change Scores occurred for the Inhibitory Scale and the Activation Scale.

cated. If one were to hypothesize that dopamine would be a transmitter more likely to be involved in a motor process, in a more broad sense, speed of thinking, moving, etc., then one might think of physostigmine affecting dopaminergic cholinergic balance; and this pharmacological effect dissecting out this component of the manic process. Our results would be consistent with this but do not prove this.

One of the problems in thinking about the physostigmine effect is that one is comparing the very acute affect of physostigmine lasting on the order of an hour with other psychotropic drugs which produce their effects after several weeks. The normalization of mania with lithium takes several weeks to occur. The antipsychotic effect of phenothiazine takes several weeks, indeed up to one or two months, to get a maximal effect. If one compared the hour after receiving lithium or an hour after receiving Thorazine with physostigmine, one would find that lithium produces minimal effect and Thorazine a sedative effect. Had physostigmine been given for a longer period of time, it might produce a lessening of grandiosity. In other words, an alternate interpretation of the data is that the motoric aspects of mania change more quickly than the cognitive or thought disorder aspects, i.e., grandiosity. It may involve loss of face for a patient who held grandiose ideas to suddenly change his mind and decide that these ideas are untrue. This may take several days or weeks of medication. To summarize our discussion so far, we have noted that the effects of physostigmine are more specific on the motoric than the grandiosity aspects of mania. One interpretation would be that the motoric is under control of a dopaminergic–cholinergic balance while the grandiosity is under control of the noradrenergic system. Another possibility would be that the motoric effects are more susceptible to change and will change in more rapid fashion than the grandiosity effects. In thinking about this latter possibility it is relevant to note the experiments of Roundtree[3] using an irreversible cholinesterase inhibitor [Diisopropyl fluorophosphate (DFP)] which increases brain acetylcholine for a longer period of time. Two hypomanic patients improved with DFP and continued to be normal after its administration. One hypomanic patient became less manic and was slightly depressed after courses of DFP, but relapsed on DFP withdrawal. Another nearly remitted hypomanic patient became markedly manic after DFP withdrawal. Roundtree also found that DFP caused the anergic syndrome in controls. Upon reviewing his case material, it would seem that DFP on chronic cases does produce normalization of both content as well as process. This study, of course, was an uncontrolled study on a small group of patients, so a certain degree of caution is advisable in interpreting these results. At the present time, we see no reason to prefer one of these alternate explanations versus the other.

References

1. Janowsky, D.S., El-Yousef, K., Davis, J.M., and Sekerke, H.J.: Parasympathetic suppression of manic symptoms by physostigmine. *Arch. Gen. Psychiat.* 28:542–547, 1973.
2. Janowsky, D.S., El-Yousef, K., Davis, J.M., and Sekerke, H.J.: Antagonistic effects of physostigmine and methylphenidate in man. *Amer. J. Psychiat.* 130:1370–1376, 1973.
3. Roundtree, D.W., Nevin, S., and Wilson, A.: The effects of diisopropyl fluorophosphonate in schizophrenic and manic depressive psychosis. *J. Neurol. Neurosurg. Psychiat.* 13:47–62, 1950.

Chapter 10

Review of Clinical
Research Strategies
in Affective Illness*

BERNARD J. CARROLL

In this final chapter I will present a clinical review of our research strategies in the affective illnesses. I will not attempt to deal with the individual papers presented in any great length because each of them has its own methodological problems, issues, and precautions which need to be taken into account in any comprehensive review. Instead, I will give some general but I think important reflections on the way we are going about our present clinical research — and I do wish to make it clear that I include myself in any criticisms which are made.

To begin with, there is a large body of clinical research in depression which I want to mention in order to put it to one side. I am referring to the strategy of using normal subjects in order to evaluate the biological con-

*From a paper presented to American Association for the Advancement of Science Symposium "Implications of Some Recent Biological Studies of Depressive Illness," San Francisco, California, February 27,1974.

comitants of mood variations. Many publications based on this strategy can be found in the literature, where volunteers, for example, have been subjected to artificial stress situations, where the spontaneous mood fluctuations of normal subjects have been followed longitudinally, or where real life stress has been experienced by normal people such as those undergoing cardiac surgery, awaiting operations for carcinoma, or awaiting the death of a child suffering from a fatal illness. One example of this work is the data of Schottstaedt, who measured urinary sodium and potassium excretion in normal subjects in relation to their spontaneous mood fluctuations. I have never had any confidence that this strategy would prove to be very helpful in the study of clinical depressive illness. On the other hand, work of this kind certainly is important if for no other reason than to underline the need for careful control groups when we do study patients with depression. This strategy of using normal subjects and their minor mood fluctuations derives from an old idea in psychiatry which can be traced from Adolf Meyer and Lange through Mapother and Aubrey Lewis up to Kendell today — this is the idea that clinical depression as seen by psychiatrists is nothing more than an extension of the normal mood lowering which can be experienced by anybody.[1-3]

My own feeling is that in the clinical situation we are dealing with an illness which is *categorically distinct from normal mood lowering* and it seems to me that recent statistical studies particularly have confirmed that this is so.[4-7]

At the same time however, we are all aware that in clinical practice the distinction between endogenous and neurotic depression is not always an easy one. The framework which I currently tend to favor is that presented recently by Donald Klein (Table I).[8] Most of us realize now that apparently endogenous depressions may in fact be preceded by episodes of environmental stress which could be regarded as precipitants. To take this into account Klein proposed a new term (endogenomorphic depression) where the emphasis is on the *clinical form* of the illness so that the question of the presence or absence of precipitants becomes of secondary importance. In contrast to this group (which is that chiefly studied by biological psychiatrists) are patients with true neurotic depressions. These are described as patients with chronic characterological problems — dependent, insecure, immature, with poor coping ability — and they present clinically with an angry, anxious, demanding and brittle, or fluctuating clinical picture rather than with profound mood lowering, pessimism, and loss of pleasure of the first group. They are often precipitated into this state by relatively minor life stresses rather than by major psychological losses. As Klein describes them, they do

TABLE I

Types of Depression

1. Endogenomorphic
   True endogenous
   Precipitated

2. Neurotic
   Chronic characterologic

3. Reactive
   Continuum with normal disappointment

not respond to antidepressant drugs and indeed must be recognized and treated with appropriate psychotherapy. By contrast, patients in the endogenomorphic group will not respond to psychotherapy alone but do show good responses to antidepressant medications. The third category which Klein describes is called reactive depression. By this he means a clinical picture of despair, loss, dejection, and disappointment, essentially on a continuum with normal disappointment reactions, only rather more severe and in response to a major life stress. One other important distinction between the second and third groups is that these reactive depressions are seen as occuring in previously healthy individuals. In addition, they tend to be self-limited disorders which resolve spontaneously in six to eight weeks and which will therefore often be found to show an apparent response to placebo as well as to tricyclic medications. These remarks by Klein come to us as a long-overdue reminder that the ''non-endogenous'' depressives are not a single population. Similarly the ''endogenous'' or ''endogenomorphic'' group is not homogeneous, as evidenced most clearly by the growing use of the categories bipolar and unipolar depression.

If we accept then that we are primarily interested in uncovering the biological aspects of the endogenous or endogenomorphic depressions and if we take several steps back from this problem to ask ourselves, ''Suppose we knew nothing about the biology of depression, suppose there were no body of knowledge from which we could proceed at the moment, how would we go about formulating the right questions?'' Well, without wishing to be too gloomy, I think that we must concede a point made some years ago by Mandell and Spooner — that we do not yet have the appropriate paradigmatic framework for relating brain function to behavior and experience.[9]

This is a problem which applies across the whole of biological psychiatry, not merely in the field of depression. What it imposes on us is the need to design limited, modest, and answerable studies and to avoid grand designs aimed at major conceptual issues in psychiatry. It also imposes on us the need to be *flexible* in our research strategies, so that we can move from one strategy to another or, even better, combine a number of strategies in an integrated, interdisciplinary way.

For some years the biogenic amine theory was considered a viable, potential framework for organizing our thinking and research strategies in this area. It is now 15 years since the theory was first outlined[10] and we have not yet identified, in depressed patients, unequivocal and consistent, let alone unique physiological abnormalities which complement the pharmacologically derived amine theory. Without the theory we would not be where we are today in our understanding of depression: It has been extremely fruitful in gererating many critical studies, at both the clinical and basic laboratory levels. Nevertheless, it has not yet proved to be very helpful to clinical psychiatrists and we should do well to consider it as no more than an indirect clue, vague and tentative, to help us begin our investigations.

I regard it as a healthy sign that we are now beginning to examine the theory in a critical way because that implies that maybe we feel able to discard the theory without too much anxiety over what to replace it with. In its original form the theory has outlived its usefulness and we will be submitting ourselves to a restrictive orthodoxy if we rely on it exclusively for our future research strategies.

In some ways it might even be better (or more honest) for us to stop describing what we do as "clinical research," and to say simply that we are engaged in a search for biologically relevant parameters in the affective disorders. I say this chiefly to underline the point that we are still at an exploratory and largely descriptive stage of knowledge and that except in the strict pharmacological area we are still a long way from the study of *mechanisms* in the pathophysiology of these illnesses.

The amine theory was developed essentially from chance observations in the area of clinical pharmacology. What we did with these observations was, in effect, to try to reason backward from knowledge about the actions of the antidepressant drugs in order to construct a theory of the development of depressive illness. As I see it, the pharmacological information may very well be merely "end point" information and it may not be at all possible to infer the mechanism of illness simply from a knowledge of what the drugs do. The danger of this kind of backward reasoning from pharmacology to mechanism can be seen very well in another clinical situation, that of cardiac failure. Suppose that we knew as little about the biology of heart failure as we do about the biology of depression and suppose that a new drug digoxin was found by chance which could relieve the symptoms of cardiac failure in many patients. If we gave this drug to the basic pharmacologists and asked them to determine how it helped the failing heart they would give us answers dealing with myocardial membrane electrolyte transport and calcium coupling and so on, and while this would be useful information it would really not take us very far toward the understanding of heart failure *as a clinical problem*. In other words, it would tell us nothing about what preceded the development of heart failure and would give us no information necessarily about such important factors as hypertension or valvular disease. Similarly, with depression, nobody doubts that the biogenic amines may very well have a lot to do with what Gerald Klerman[11] calls the "final common pathway" for the expression of depressive behavior, but this is only a very small part of the overall clinical problem.

This is one reason why I have great sympathy for the average clinical psychiatrist as he tries to cope with authoritative sounding statements of the amine theory from our invisible college. What we say sounds elegant and consistent, but the average psychiatrist has a hard time indeed relating what we say to anything that he can observe clinically in his patients. Even more revealing perhaps is the fact that despite the great amount of clinical research which has been done in the last 15 years, we are not ourselves much more sophisticated than the average psychiatrist is in matters such as the use of tricyclic antidepressants or monoamine oxidase inhibitors!

One other point about clinical research: it is easy for us to forget the fact that clinical research is very much a *derivative* occupation. In other words, when the fundamental biological nature of a clinical problem is poorly understood, then the research strategies and experimental techniques which clinical investigators use are influenced strongly by the prevailing climate of interest and success in the basic disciplines. We are sometimes amused to recall for example, that about 25 years ago electrophysiology, cybernetics, and systems theory were regarded as *the* paradigmatic disciplines in terms of which behavioral disorders would eventually be understood. We no longer think in these terms, but 25 years is not such a long time ago. In the last 10 years, neuropharmacology has become *de rigueur* for biological psychiatrists. We may have had developed for us better techniques for our clinical studies but we are still very much applying ideas and methods simply because they have become available. If you doubt that statement, then try to find one paper dealing with biological psychiatry in, say, Eugene Garfield's lists of most-cited papers. You won't find any.

This brings me to Carroll's first law of clinical research: "Research, like politics, is the art of the possible'' (with apologies to Sir Peter Medawar).[12] And I would stress again that what is ''possible'' has at least as much to do with ideas as it has to do with techniques.

Taking a positive view of our recent clinical research efforts, there does seem to have been a genuine increase in sophistication, so that we are asking better questions and presumably thinking better about the issues. In effect, we have been learning slowly but inevitably to ask *physiological questions*.

As a reflection of this increased sophistication, it is now possible to see on every level a change in the design of experimental work. Across the board we are now using dynamic, functional strategies rather than simply looking at biological variables in a static, noninterfering way. For example, we no longer attempt to obtain information simply by collecting EEG records, instead we are studying evoked potentials and contingent negative variations. In the electrolyte area we are no longer simply measuring, for example, whole body sodium and potassium at one point in time but have moved to the study of turnover rates of sodium or the rates of entry of sodium and potassium from plasma to cerebrospinal fluid. On the endocrine front, we no longer collect 24-hour urines for 17-hydroxycorticosteroid measurements and hope to tell very much from this exercise. Instead, we have become aware of the dynamic, physiological, integrated aspects of the hypothalamic–pituitary–adrenal system and we have begun to study this system with stimulation and suppression procedures given at critical times of the 24-hour cycle. With respect to the biogenic amines we no longer collect only urine for the measurement of amines and their metabolites but have moved to an intensive study of the cerebrospinal fluid, especially with the probenecid technique, which gives us an approximation of turnover rate. Most people will remember Klerman's famous joke about urine collections for clinical amine studies[13]: he said that trying to understand brain chemistry through the study of urine was like trying to find out the secret plans of the Supreme Soviet by analyzing the sewage from the Kremlin. Well in some ways the cerebrospinal fluid is still the sewer of the brain but at least it is a good deal closer to where the action is.

As one reviews the vast body of clinical investigations in depression there are two basic kinds of study which can be identified. One kind are pharmacological studies derived more or less directly from the amine theory. The other kind are studies of functional physiological disturbances designed without the direction of any overriding hypothesis, for example, studies of glucose metabolism, salivary gland function, or electrolyte balance and distribution.

Precisely because the amine theory was derived from pharmacology, the best strategies to emerge from it have been pharmacological ones. In particular, many hypothesis-oriented therapeutic trials of considerable elegance have been possible. Unfortunately, the results of these studies are not generally encouraging for the theory. For example, treatment of depressed patients with amine precursors has given us some valuable information but has not provided any kind of definitive treatment for depression. Neither dopa or tryptophan is a consistently effective antidepressant agent, and combinations of the two are not any more useful.[14,16] In the case of 5-hydroxytryptophan there is still the possibility that a subgroup of depressed patients may respond but we need a lot more information before deciding that this is really so.[17,18] Similarly, inhibitors of amine synthesis have been used in the exploratory treatment of mania and once again, the results have been equivocal. α-Methyl-*para*-tyrosine which blocks the production of both dopamine and norepinephrine has been used in this way and more recently, the dopamine β-hydroxylase inhibitor fusaric acid (which blocks only norepinephrine synthesis) has been tried.[15,19] The inhibitor of serotonin synthesis, parachlorophenylalanine, apparently has not been used in the experimental treatment of mania by any investigative group. In large measure this reflects the preoccupation which the United States workers have had with the catecholamine side of the theory and their relative neglect of indoleamine mechanisms until quite recently.

There is *no* clinical information on the effects of parachlorophenylalanine in depressed patients, although this probably should have been a high priority study over the last eight years. Inhibition of catecholamine synthesis by α-methyl-*para*-tyrosine has been shown to worsen the clinical state of depressed patients,[20] a finding which is consistent with the theory. However, only a small number of patients has been studied in this way and we do not know how generally applicable these results are. Very recently a different strategy with amine synthesis inhibitors has been reported and the findings are not straightforwardly in agreement with the work described above. Shopsin and Gershon[21] gave α-methyl-*para*-tyrosine to depressed patients *after* they had recovered with imipramine, and while they continued to take the tricyclic drug. The synthesis inhibitor did not affect the clinically recovered state of these patients. When *para*-chlorophenylalanine was given in a similar way, however, a dramatic return of depressive symptoms was produced.

This work represents a refreshing new strategy, since it aims to test directly in patients our assumptions about the mode of action of the antidepressant drugs. I would hope that it becomes more widely adopted, so that many groups may gain experience with these phenomena.

Even more surprising perhaps is that over the years that the amine theory has been with us there have been very few studies of the classic receptor-stimulating and -blocking agents in clinical situations. The serotonin receptor-blocking agents, methysergide and cinanserin, have been used in a desultory way with manic patients and the results are by no means clear cut at this point in time,[22-27] One would have expected that a fairly straightforward question such as this could have been well and truly resolved by now. Even worse, if we were really serious about the amine theory we would have established by this time whether or not the classic catecholamine receptor-blocking drugs have effects which are consistent or not with the theory: for example, we would have established what are the clinical effects of phenoxybenzamine and phentolamine on the one hand and propranalol on the other. In fact, however, there is only the most fragmentary information available[28,29] about these questions which, at least in principle, are critically important to the amine theory. Similarly, the catecholamine receptor-stimulating agents, apomorphine and clonidine, have been available for a good number of years and we have absolutely no published information about their clinical effects in depression or mania.

Perhaps as a group we have not pursued these questions of receptor function and blockade because we suspected that the results would not agree with the amine theory. Let me emphasize again that I do include myself in this criticism — I think we must all accept that we have not rigorously pushed our testing of the amine theory to its clinical limits.

Another curious and paradoxic tendency can be observed over the last few years in our research strategy development. I am referring to an uneasy feeling which I have that *unexpected findings are unwelcome,* and yet these are precisely the findings which could generate most interest and excitement at a time when the steam is running out of our old framework. What this reflects is a very real conceptual inertia which prevents us from being flexible in our research strategies. To be fair, there is also a certain amount of what I might call programmatic inertia, that is, because of the way in which investigations are funded it does take some time before new approaches can be followed up vigorously, since work which is already in progress needs to be completed.

As examples of some of these more or less unwelcome unexpected findings let me mention the following: some new antidepressant drugs, notably Iprindole, have been found, by chance, and have been shown not to have the same kind of neurochemical profile that the earlier antidepressant drugs possess.[30] I am not aware that many of us are excitedly following up on the theoretical possibilities contained in these observations. In the area of mania, there have been one or two reports that the amphetamines can have a paradoxic antimanic effect rather like their effect with hyperkinetic children.[31,32] Once again, I don't see us pursuing these very tantalizing leads in any vigorous manner. Some years ago two groups in Yugoslavia reported that they were able to induce experimental dysphoria and depression with the use of repeated injections of apomorphine[33,34]; So far as I am aware, nobody in this country has shown the slightest interest in that finding. Closer to home, the very important and innovative observations of John Davis and David Janowsky about the effects of physostigmine in mania[35] are now two years old and yet only two groups have attempted to replicate their work.[36,37]

From these examples, I think it is fair to say that as a group we tend to undervalue experimental results which do not easily fit in our present way of thinking. While it is true that at certain periods a systematic, planned, hypothesis-directed series of investigations is essential for the acquisition of knowledge, nevertheless many of the important advances in science come about *divergently*, that is, they develop from precisely the kind of unexpected and difficult-to-handle observations that I have just been mentioning.

When we look at the way in which the experimental design of clinical studies in depression has developed, we see several distinct and important stepwise refinements (Table II). From anecdotal case material and from casual unplanned observations a suggestion or an idea develops which is then submitted to further testing. For most exploratory studies, a simple control group design is commonly the next step, that is, the biological variable which one suspects may be related to depression is examined both in

TABLE II

Experimental Designs

1. Casual observations
   Anecdotal case material

2. Simple control group design

3. Clinical phase design ($\pm$ control groups)

4. Longitudinal studies
   Recurrent depression
   Cycling depression and mania
   Periodic catatonia

5. Prospective, provocative, longitudinal high risk groups

a group of depressed patients and in a control group or contrast group of other psychiatric inpatients. This constitutes a preliminary screening device which can eliminate biological variables not specifically connected with depressive illness or which may be artifacts induced for example, by the hospital diet or other irrelevant factors. If the results of this second phase are encouraging, then the very common third stage of a clinical phase experimental design will be carried out. In this case, patients are studied both when depressed and following treatment; in addition, control groups or contrast groups may be included in order to maintain a check on nonrelevant artifacts. One usually expects to find that a biologically important variable will be abnormal during the phase of illness but not in the recovery phase and that it will be essentially normal in the contrast groups. We have learned now to keep in mind the possibility however, that some biological disturbances within a population of depressed patients may remain abnormal after treatment; that is, they may signify a continuing biological disturbance associated with the predisposition to develop further episodes of illness.[38] As a refinement on the simple clinical phase design longitudinal studies are now commonly carried out within individual subjects. With this design, biological variables are measured not simply before and after treatment but daily or even several times a day. This strategy was developed particularly for the study of manic-depressive patients with rapid cycles. A final general strategy, which could be used more than it is at present, is that of studying groups of susceptible or predisposed individuals in a prospective and provacative way. For example, persons from families with a high genetic loading for depressive illness who are undergoing stress experiences such as bereavement or surgery or who are being treated with agents such as corticosteroids which can induce affective changes could be studied in a prospective manner in order to observe the development of biological changes in relation to the time of the appearance of affective change.

How many biological variables need one study with these designs? In the case of the simple clinical phase design, only one or two biological variables will usually be considered. Sooner or later however, it becomes essential to move beyond the study of a small number of variables to a multivariate design. Only in this way can we hope to integrate and cross-validate the large number of experimental findings which have proliferated from the more simple studies. For example, there are subgroups of depressed patients described who are abnormal with respect to their cerebrospinal fluid 5-hydroxyindoleacetic acid concentrations, or with respect to their cortisol production rates, or with respect to their barbiturate sedation thresholds or with respect to their sodium turnover rates, or with respect to their growth hormone secretion, and so on. What we dont't know is how many of the patients in these groups overlap with each other so that we can build up a profile of common or independent biological disturbances within subgroups of patients. In designing these multivariate studies we want as much as possible, to study central rather than peripheral variables but it is not always possible to obtain well-understood variables relating directly to central nervous system function. We need also to keep in mind the possibility that when many variables are being examined together some of them will be serially dependent one on another whereas others will be physiologically independent.

As well as considering the selection of biological variables which seem most useful to study we need also to think about the collection of behavioral data simultaneously. In general, we have moved beyond the stage of making simple clinical statements, "the patient is depressed"; "the patient is severely depressed"; "the patient is not depressed." Also, we have almost stopped using global ratings of overall depressive severity although there is a return to this method with the increasing recent popularity of the visual analog rating method.[39,40] To replace simple clinical statements or global clinical judgements there has developed what could almost be described as a rating scale industry for the study of patients in clinical investigations. There is a large number of rating scales, structured interviews and questionaires available for decision making and classification. Unfortunately, there is no general agreement among investigators about which scales are the most useful nor do we always think as hard as we perhaps should about the issues of reliability and validity when we apply, in our own clinical context, rating instruments which have been developed elsewhere.[41] In addition to rating scales which evaluate objective behavior we need also to keep in mind the need for some assessment of nonspecific psychological variables which Dr. Sachar summarizes under the term "breakdown of ego defense mechanisms."[42] This term refers to features of psychological anxiety, somatic anxiety, feelings of loss of control, fluid delusions, depersonalization, and so on, which are not specific to any particular psychiatric illness and which may in themselves be associated with some biological changes. They are, if you will, "control variables" which need to be taken into account both within the groups of depressed patients whom we study as well as in our contrast groups of patients.

Since the simple clinical phase design continues to be the one used by most groups, especially for exploratory studies, it is important that several serious problems with this design should be emphasized. The most important is that it does not allow us to take into account the factor of *duration of illness*. In practice most of the patients whom we study in the hospital have already been ill for varying time periods which range from a week or less to several months or even as much as a year before we see them, and it is quite possible that the *initiating biochemical events may not persist* from the phase of onset into the phase of established illness. Adaptation and plasticity in the nervous system are real phenomena, and a highly relevant example of these adaptive changes can be seen in the following animal study carried out by Smookler and Buckley.[43] They exposed rats to repeated sessions of daily stress in order to induce a neurogenic hypertension. Once it was established, the hypertension continued for at least six months while the stress was continued. When they examined biological variables related to the continuing stress they found that plasma corticosterone levels were elevated early during the experiment, for the first four weeks, but that for the following five months the corticosterone concentrations in plasma were not elevated significantly and tended to fluctuate around the control level. Similarly with the other stress index of increased rate of turnover of brain norepinephrine: the turnover rate, like the plasma corticosterone levels, was elevated during the first four weeks but beyond that time was no different from the turnover rate seen in control animals, *although the hypertension continued throughout the experiment*.

Since we are now beginning to think about at least some depressive ilnesses as being related to life stress,[44,45] this example becomes potentially very instructive. At the very least, it suggests that we need to consider carefully this question of duration of illness, and that a highly rewarding strategy may be the study of patients *in the process of becoming depressed* rather than simply the study of patients with established illnesses. Very little work of this kind has been carried out apart from the rare cycling patients who have been studied, for example, by Jenner [46] and other patients with rapid switches from depression to mania who have been followed longitudinally.[47–50] We need to apply this strategy to the more usual patient with recurrent unipolar depression, especially for promising variables such as the urinary MHPG excretion.[48,50]

A second problem with the simple clinical phase design is that it really does not help us to distinguish an abnormality which is simply an epiphenomenon from one which has real etiological importance. It is often possible for example, to demonstrate abnormalities which are regularly present during illness and absent during recovery, often through consecutive episodes of depression within the one subject. To complement such findings we need to know what is happening during the interval periods and especially to know what changes first, the mood and behavior of the patient or the biological variable which we happen to be measuring. Once again, there is little attention being given to this issue of longitudinal followup.

I have emphasized several times the importance of longitudinal research designs marked by frequent measures of both clinical state and biological variables. In the special situations where this strategy has been used the results obtained have been impressive, for example, in the study of premenstrual mood change and endocrine variables[51] and in the study of rapidly switching bipolar manic-depressives.[47-50]

In these studies we are looking for biological variables which change *before* the appearance of behavioral changes in the patients. Such a temporal relationship has in fact been identified in the investigations mentioned above. When we obtain such findings it is very tempting to believe that we have identified a biological variable which is etiologically important.

It must be pointed out, however, that the temporal precedence of biological change over behavioral change is not in itself sufficient to establish etiological significance for the biological variable. We may still be observing nothing more than an epiphenomenon, not secondary to the behavioral state but secondary to another, primary etiological process. A very good example of this problem of interpreting longitudinal data can be found in the report of Hullin and Court.[52] In this study fasting blood lipid concentrations were observed to fluctuate between the clinical phases of mania and depression; moreover, the plasma lipid changes clearly preceded the behavioral changes in a way that is very similar to the more recent MHPG data.[48,50] We do not have any reason to believe that shifts in plasma lipid concentrations cause the behavioral switches in manic depressive illness, yet if we did not know better the longitudinal data could suggest that this might be the case.

To underline this point Carroll's second law of clinical research may be stated as follows: "Regard as an epiphenomenon any biologic variable which changes in a strongly concordant way with daily clinical state — until it is proved to be otherwise," because that is exactly what we should expect an epiphenomenon to do.

In clinical psychiatric research units we have become rather selective with regard to our admission policies and we usually insist on stringent criteria for the diagnosis of primary affective disorders.[53] While it is no doubt important to do so we should realize that this policy forces us to ignore a group of patients who could possibly teach us a great deal about the biology of depression. These are patients with mood changes secondary to organic disease. The outstanding patients in this category are those with pituitary–adrenal disorders such as Cushing's disease and Addison's disease. The clinical association between these conditions and mood disorders has been known for many years; yet these patients have not been studied by the techniques developed recently in the primary affective disorders. What about their MHPG excretion, for example, or their cerebrospinal fluid amine metabolite responses to probenecid, or their responsiveness to antidepressant drugs?

Similarly, other patients with focal neurological disease and affective change are understudied at the present time. They could provide information of great interest in much the same way that patients with temporal lobe disease have done in the field of schizophrenia. The report of S. M. Wolff and his colleagues in 1964 is a classic in this respect.[54] They described a patient with a hypothalamic tumor who had recurring episodes of profound withdrawal and depression associated always with marked activation of the hypothalamic–pituitary–adrenal system.

By studying patients with secondary organic mood changes it may be possible, in principle, to identify the outlines of the pathogenetic pathways. For example, if variable A is found to be abnormal in both primary and secondary depressions then we may expect that A is related to the "final common pathway" for depressive behavior. Similarly, if variable B is abnormal in primary affective illness only while variable C is abnormal in both categories, then C may be related to the "final common pathway" while B may represent a functional disturbance which precedes C in the primary cases. Such information about B could be very difficult to obtain of we study only patients with primary affective disorders.

While these logical considerations may be attractive and although they are valid in principle, nevertheless in practice we should expect that our results will not be so easy to interpret, mainly because of the heterogeneity of these clinical conditions.[55] [56]We can expect continuing progress but it will most likely be serendipitous as well as divergent from our present research themes.

Accordingly, there are two predictions which I give without elaboration. Ten or 15 years from now the scientists looking back with amusement on our current preoccupation with neuropharmacology may well be a group of protein chemists who decide to get interested in electroshock. The other group who will be laughing all the way to Stockholm will be those who resolve the present constraints on psychosurgery and who reestablish responsible, high quality depth recording and stimulating procedures in the human limbic system.

References

1. Mapother, E.: Discussion on manic-depressive psychosis. *Brit. Med. J.* ii: 872–876, 1926.
2. Lewis, A.J.: Melancholia: a clinical survey of depressive states. *J. Ment. Sci.* 80:227–378, 1934.
3. Kendell, R.E.: *"The Classification of Depressive Illnesses."* Oxford University Press, London (1968).
4. Eysenck, H. J.: The classification of depressive illnesses. *Brit. J. Psychiat.* 117:241–250, 1970.
5. Pilowsky, I., Levine, S., and Boulton, D.M.: The classification of depression by numerical taxonomy. *Brit. J. Psychiat.* 115:937–945, 1969.
6. Kiloh, L.G., Andrews, G., Neilson, M., and Bianchi, G.N.: The relationship of the syndromes called endogenous and neurotic depression. *Brit. J. Psychiat.* 121:183–196, 1972.
7. Spicer, C.C., Hare, E.H., and Slater, E.: Neurotic and psychotic forms of depressive illness: Evidence from age-incidence in a national sample. *Brit. J. Psychiat.* 123:535–541, 1973.
8. Klein, D.F.: Pharmacological response as a basis for syndrome identification. Paper presented to American College of Neuropsychopharmacology, 12th Annual Meeting, Palm Springs, Dec. 7, 1973.
9. Mandell, A.J., and Spooner, C.E.: Psychochemical research studies in man. *Science* 162:1442–1453, 1968.
10. Jacobsen, E.: The theoretical basis of the chemotherapy of depression, in *Depression: Proceedings of the Symposium at Cambridge, September 1959* (E.B. Davies, Ed.) p. 208, Cambridge University Press, New York (1964).
11. Klerman, G.L.: Drug therapy of clinical depressions-current status and implications for research on neuropharmacology of the affective disorders. *J. Psychiat. Res.* 9:252–270, 1972.
12. Medawar, P.B.: "The Art of the Soluble," Methuen, London, 1967.
13. Klerman, G.: *In* "Antidepressant Drugs of Non-MAO Inhibitor Type," p. 152. U.S. Public Health Service, Workshop Series of Pharmacology Unit, N.I.M.H., N.I.H., Washington, D.C. (1966).
14. Carroll, B.J.: Monoamine precursors in the treatment of depression. *Clin. Pharmacol. Ther.* 12:743–761, 1971.
15. Bunney, W.E., Jr., Brodie, H.K.H., Murphy, D.L., and Goodwin, F.K.: Studies of alpha-methyl-*para*-tyrosine, L-DOPA and L-tryptophan in depression and mania. *Amer. J. Psychiat.* 127:872–881, 1971.
16. Dunner, D.L.: Amine precursors in depression: studies combining L-DOPA and L-tryptophan. American College of Neuropsychopharmacology, 12th Annual Meeting, Palm Springs, December 7, 1973.
17. vanPraag, H.M., and Korf, J.: Monoamine metabolism in depression: Clinical application of the probenecid test. *in* "Serotonin and Behavior" (J. Barchas and E. Usdin, Eds.) pp. 457–468, Academic Press, New York (1973).
18. Sans, I.: L-5-Hydroxytryptophan-(L-5-HTP) Therapy. *Fol. Psychiat. Neurol. Jap.* 26:7–17, 1972.

19. Sack, R.L., and Goodwin, F.K.: Catecholamines in mania: effect of a DBH inhibitor. American Psychiatric Association, Annual Meeting, Detroit, 1974.

20. Gershon, E., Bunney, W.E. Jr., Goodwin, F.K., and Murphy, D.L., *et al.*: Catecholamines and affective illness: Studies with L-DOPA and alpha-methyl-*para*-tyrosine, *in* "Symposium on Brain Chemistry and Mental Disease-Texas Research Institute-1970" (B. Ho, and W.M. McIsaac, Eds.) pp. 135–161, Plenum Press, New York (1971).

21. Shopsin, B.N., Wilk, S., Goldstein, M., and Gershon, S.: The use of imipramine, alpha-methyl-*para*-tyrosine and *para*-chlorophenylalanine in hospitalized depressives. American College of Neuropsychopharmacology, 12th Annual Meeting, Palm Springs, December 7, 1973.

22. Dewhurst, W.G.: Methysergide in mania. *Nature (London)* 219:506–507, 1968.

23. Haskovec, L., and Soucek, K.: Trial of methysergide in mania. *Nature (London)* 219:507–508, 1968.

24. Coppen, A., Prange, A.J., and Whybrow, P.C.: Methysergide in mania. *Lancet* ii:338–340, 1969.

25. McCabe, M.S., Reich, T., and Winokur, G.: Methysergide as a treatment for mania. *Amer. J. Psychiat.* 127:354–356, 1970.

26. Kane, F.J.: Treatment of mania with cinanserin, an antiserotonin agent. *Amer. J. Psychiat.* 127:354–356, 1970.

27. Itil, T.M., Polsan, N., and Holden, J.M.C.: Clinical and electroencephalalographic effects of cinanserin in schizophrenia and manic patients. *Dis. Nerv. Syst.* 32:193–200, 1972.

28. Rockwell, F.V.: Dibenamine therapy in certain psychopathologic syndromes. *Psychosom. Med.* 10:230–237, 1948.

29. Atsmon, A., Blum, I., Wijsenbeek, H., Maoz, B., Steiner, M., and Ziegelman, G.: The short-term effects of adrenergic blocking agents in a small group of psychotic patients. *Psychiat. Neurol. Neurochir. 74:251–258,* 1971.

30. Fann, W.E., Davis, J.M., Janowsky, D.S., Kaufmann, J.S., Griffith, J.D., and Oates, J.A. Effect of iprindole on amine uptake in man. *Arch. Gen. Psychiat.* 26:158–162, 1972.

31. Kulcsar, I.S.: Amphetámine sulphate in mania. *Lancet* i:1164, 1966.

32. Medical Research Council Brain Metabolism Unit: Modified amine hypothesis for the aetiology of affective illness. *Lancet* ii:573–577, 1972.

33. Tesarova, O.: Experimental depression in people caused by apomorphine and phenoharman. *Pharmakopsychiat.* 5:13–19, 1972.

34. Benesova, O., and Benes, V.: Experimental study on the mechanism of depressogenic action of apomorphine and reserpine. *Activ. Nerv. Super.* 14:269–272, 1972.

35. Janowsky, D.S., El-Yousef, M.K., Davis, J.M., Hubbard, B., and Sekerke, H.J.: Cholinergic reversal of manic symptoms. *Lancet* i:1236–37, 1972.

36. Carroll, B.J., Frazer, A., Schless, A., and Mendels, J.: Central cholinergic mechanisms in mania. *Lancet* i:427–428, 1973.

37. Shopsin, B. and Gershon, S.: Rebound phenomena in mania following physostigmine. American College of Neuropsychopharmacology 12th Annual Meeting, Palm Springs, December 6, 1973.

38. Coppen, A., Prange, A.J., Whybrow, P.C. and Noguera, R.: Abnormalities of indoleamines in affective disorders. *Arch. Gen. Psychiat.* 26:474–478, 1972.

39. Aitken, R.C.B.: Measurement of feelings using visual analogue scales. *Proc. Roy. Soc. Med.* 62:989–993, 1969.

40. Folstein, M.F., and Luria, R.: Reliability, validity and clinical application of the visual analogue mood scale. *Psychol. Med.* 3:479–486, 1973.

41. Carroll, B.J., Fielding, J.M. and Blashki, T.G.: Depression rating scales: A critical review. *Arch. Gen. Psychiat.* 28:361–366, 1973.

42. Sachar, E.J., Kanter, S.S., Buie, D., Engle, R., and Mehlman, R.: Psychoendocrinology of ego disintegration. *Amer. J. Psychiat.* 126:1067–1078, 1970.

43. Smookler, H.H., and Buckley, J.P.: Relationships between brain catecholamine synthesis, pituitary adrenal function and the production of hypertension during prolonged exposure to environmental stress. *Int. J. Neuropharmacol.* 8:33–41, 1969.

44. Paykel, E., Myers, J.K., Dienelt, M.N., Klerman, G.L., Lindenthal, J.J., and Pepper, M.P.: Life events and depression. *Arch. Gen. Psychiat.* 21:753–760, 1969.

45. Leff, M.J., Roatch, J.F., and Bunney, W.E. Environmental factors preceding the onset of severe depressions. *Psychiatry,* 33:293–311, 1970.

46. Jenner, F.A., Gjessing, L.R., Cox, J.R., *et al.*: A manic-depressive psychotic with a persistent forty-eight hour cycle. *Brit. J. Psychiat.* 113:895–910, 1967.

47. Rubin, R.T., and Overall, J.E.: Manifest psychopathology and urine biochemical measures: multivariate analysis in manic-depressive illness. *Arch. Gen. Psychiat.* 22:45–57, 1970.

48. Bond, P.A., Jenner, F.A., and Sampson, G.A.: Daily variations of the urine content of 3-methoxy-4-hydroxyphenylglycol in two manic-depressive patients. *Psychol. Med.* 2:81–85, 1972.

49. Bunney, W.E., Murphy, D.L., Goodwin, F.K., *et al.*: The "switch process" in manic-depressive illness. *Arch. Gen. Psychiat.* 27:295–317, 1972.

50. Jones, F. de L., Maas, J.W., Dekirmenjian, H., and Fawcett, J.A.: Urinary catecholamine metabolites during behavioral changes in a patient with manic-depressive cycles. *Science* 179:300–302, 1972.

50. Janowsky, D.S., Berens, S.C., and Davis, J.M.: Correlations between mood, weight, and electrolytes during the menstrual cycle: A reninangiotensin-aldosterone hypothesis of premenstrual tension. *Psychosom. Med.* 35:143–154, 1973.

52. Hullin, R.P., and Court, G.: Fasting blook lipid concentrations in manic-depressive psychosis. *Brit. J. Psychiat.* 117:275–285, 1970.

53. Feighner, J.P., Robins, E., Guze, S.B., Woodruff, R.A., Winokur, G., and Munoz, R.: Diagnostic criteria for use in psychiatric research. *Arch. Gen. Psychiat.* 26:57–63, 1972.

54. Wolff, S.M., Adler, R.C., Buskirk, E.R., and Thompson, R.H.: A syndrome of periodic hypothalamic discharge. *Amer. J. Med.* 36:956-967, 1964.

55. Blumenthal, M.D.: Heterogeneity and research on depressive disorders. *Arch. Gen. Psychiat.* 24:524–534, 1971.

56. Akiskal, H.S., and McKinney, W.T.: Depressive disorders: Toward a unified hypothesis. *Science* 183:20–29, 1973.

Chapter 11

Postscript

J. MENDELS

The papers presented at this symposium and published in this volume cover a broad range of material relevant to our understanding of the psychobiology of the affective disorders. One of the inherent limitations in a symposium of this type is that no matter how well each contributor may present his material, there are inevitably areas of overlap. Of greater significance to the reader is the fact that there is important information which has not been covered by one or another of the contributors. The purpose of this postscript is to try to reduce the latter problem by briefly summarizing some data not adequately covered elsewhere in this volume. I do not mean to provide a complete and comprehensive review of all additional material, but to high-light some areas of interest, some strategies, data and theories which may serve as a useful guide to the reader who is interested in pursuing this subject further. A number of reviews covering different aspects of the psychobiology of affective disorders have been published in recent reviews. These may provide a useful point of departure.[1-16]

It is important to bear in mind that the syndrome of depression almost certainly consists of a *group* of clinical conditions rather than a single illness.[17-19] The etiologies of these illnesses probably range from being exclusively genetic to complex environmental-psychological responses, with perhaps the most important involving interactions between biological and psychological systems. Thus, it would be naive to look for a single biology or etiology for the affective disorders. Attention must be directed to the possibility that a particular observation, while not significantly related to the syndrome as a whole, may be of importance for a subgroup of patients. There are multiple examples of this in general medicine including the many different causes for anemia, cough or chest pain.

The attempts to divide depressed patients into meaningful groups have, to date, mainly been based on symptom profiles and attempts to develop specific nosological categories. These attempts have given rise to such terms as endogenous, reactive, neurotic, psychotic, involutional, agitated, and so forth. More recently, attempts have been made to separate patients into meaningful groups on the basis of family history, specific biology, or the response to a particular form of treatment. At times these approaches will overlap, as for example in the designation bipolar and unipolar depression. This system, originally described by Leonard and later elaborated on by Perris, involves dividing depressed patients into those who have had both manic and depressive episodes (the bipolar or manic-depressive patients) and those who have had recurrent depressive episodes without evidence of mania or hypomania (unipolar). There are a number of differences including family history, symptomatology, clinical course and biology between these two groups of patients. While this appears to be a useful approach, it may require further modification, in that it seems possible that each of the two categories may contain more than one type of depression.

Maas has discussed earlier in this volume the possibility that we may be able to separate patients on the basis of the relationship between a particular biochemical change and the response to a specific form of treatment. An example of this is contained in our efforts to define the possible antidepressant effects of lithium carbonate (see Chapter 1). Further expansion of this strategy, together with a more detailed evaluation of the variations in individual metabolism of tricyclic drugs and the way in which these differences and the subsequent wide range in plasma levels of the tricyclics relate to clinical response, [20,21] offers exciting promise for the future.

Biogenic Amines

Investigation of, and speculation about, the role of the biogenic amines in the mediation of mood and in the pathogenesis of the affective disorders has occupied a great deal of attention in the past decade. Several aspects of this line of investigation have been considered by a number of the contributors to this volume. It may be useful to briefly summarize the issues.

In the early and mid-1960s it was hypothesized that clinical depression was associated with a functional deficiency of norepinephrine or serotonin at crucial receptor sites in the brain, whereas mania would be associated with a functional excess of these amines.[1,2,22,23] In the main, the initial theories were based on the investigation of the pharmacological action of the antidepressant drugs as well as of drugs which were thought to induce a depression-like syndrome in some individuals. This line of investigation has flourished in the past decade and hundreds if not thousands of reports have appeared. It appears that almost all of the clinically useful antidepressant drugs will, with acute administration, increase the amount of norepinephrine or serotonin available at neuronal receptor sites. A potentially important exception to this generalization is the drug iprindole. While it is a tricyclic compound like many others used in the treatment of depression, and while it has been reported to have an equivalent antidepressant effect to imipramine,[24] it does not potentiate monoaminergic activity.[25]

It is important to note that most of the studies of the pharmacological effects of the antidepressant drugs involved the *acute* administration of the drug under consideration with a subsequent examination of changes in monoaminergic systems. However, most clinicians are of the opinion that the antidepressant drugs do not exert any significant antidepressant effect until they have been given for two or three weeks. Consequently, it may be more important to consider the *chronic* effects of these compounds before attempting to make correlations between pharmacological actions and clinical activity. Relatively few studies of the chronic effects of antidepressant drugs have been conducted to date—a rather striking oversight. In those studies which have been conducted, it appears that the chronic effects may be quite different from the acute effects, in that several compensatory changes occur which may be the result of a feedback mechanism.[26] Thus, the initial potentiation of aminergic activity may disappear with chronic drug administration, raising questions about its importance for the therapeutic actions of these drugs. Thus, some investigators have reported a reduction in brain concentrations with both norepinephrine and serotonin with chronic tricyclic administration,[27,28] and Post and Goodwin note in Chapter 4 of this volume that chronic administration of tricyclic antidepressants to depressed patients is associated with a further reduction in the probenecid associated increase in lumbar spinal fluid 5-hydroxy-indoleacetic acid (5HIAA), when these patients are clinically well. This suggests a possible decrease in serotonin turnover in these patients. In a similar experiment, Bowers[29] has shown that the tryptophan induced increase in lumbar spinal fluid 5HIAA in a group of depressed patients was lower after the successful treatment with amitriptyline than it was before treatment when they were depressed. Again, this would imply that chronic treatment with amitriptyline is associated with a reduction in serotonin turnover in depressed patients.

While a number of factors could be responsible for these findings, one that has particular appeal at this time is a possible change in the sensitivity of post-synaptic receptors associated with chronic tricyclic administration. Aspects of this are discussed by Dr. Frazer in Chapter 2. A variety of recent studies has demonstrated that the chronic administration of psycho-tropic drugs is associated with an alteration in receptor sensitivity. Thus, agents which on acute administration enhance adrenergic transmission will produce receptor subsensitivity on chronic administration. For example, we have shown[30] that the chronic administration of imipramine produces a decrease in the stimulatory effects of norepinephrine on brain adenosine $3',5'$-monophosphate (cyclic AMP) accumulation. Similar observations are now being made by other investigators.

In the further exploration of the amine hypothesis of depression, several distinct experimental strategies have been adopted. In brief, these include the following:

i. The measurement of the concentration of amine metabolites in the urine or lumbar spinal fluid of depressed and manic patients. The lumbar spinal fluid studies are discussed by Post and Goodwin. Insofar as the urinary studies are concerned, Robins and Hartmann[31] have recently con-cluded that this approach has not produced any consistent findings support-ing the view that there is a reduction in amine metabolism in depressed patients. Changes suggestive of increased aminergic activity have been noted in manic patients. However, the latter may in part be due to the increased psychomotor activity commonly found in such patients. More recently attention has focused on the measurement of $3',4'$-methoxy-hydroxy-phenylglycol (MHPG). It has been suggested that MHPG is the main metabolite of brain norepinephrine and that the meas-urement of its concentration in the urine will provide a more reliable index of brain norepinephrine metabolism than is provided by the measurement of other norepinephrine metabolites.[32] Not all investigators agree that a significant percentage of urinary MHPG is derived from the CNS[33] and studies of urinary or lumbar spinal fluid MHPG concentrations in depressed patients have not produced consistent findings.[34-37]

It is probably fair to conclude that the study of the concentration of amine metabolites in patients with depression and mania has in itself not confirmed the biogenic amine hypothesis of affective disorders. Probably the most consistent finding is of a reduced concentration of 5HIAA in the lumbar spinal fluid. However, here, too, are contradictory reports and controversy over the origin of the lumbar fluid 5HIAA, and the significance of such a finding. A possibility is that only a subgroup of depressives have reduced levels of 5HIAA. However, this does not mean that their depression is due to reduced central serotonergic activity.

The absence of consistent findings is not in itself a refutation of the hypothesis, given the number of problems with this strategy, including the fact that many of the metabolites reflect peripheral action of the monoamines and that variables such as physical activity, anxiety or age may significantly influence the results.

ii. The administration of the amino acid precursors of norepinephrine, dopamine, and serotonin to patients with depression and mania. Depressed patients have been given relatively large doses of (L-dihydroxy-phenylalanine (L-DOPA) in an attempt to overcome the hypothesized deficit in noradrenergic activity or L-trypotophan, to increase serotonergic activity. Most investigators have reported that the administration of L-DOPA to depressed patients has not produced any significant clinical improvement,[38] although some have noticed an increased activation or even hypomanic behavior in some of their patients, but without significant alleviation of the depressive affect.[39] Similarly, while Coppen and his colleagues[40,41] have reported that L-tryptophan is perhaps as effective an antidepressant as imipramine or electroconvulsive treatment, most other investigators[38] have not found it to have any significant antidepressant effect. It is of interest to note that two groups of investigators have recently reported that L-tryptophan may have significant anti-manic effects.[42,43] The concurrent administration of L-trypotophan with monoamine oxidase (MAO) inhibitors has been reported by several investigators to enhance the antidepressant effect of the latter.[44-46] The pharmacological basis for this enhancement remains uncertain.

iii. The depletion of central nervous system monoamines. An extrapolation of the biogenic amine theory is that sufficient depletion of one or other amine might be expected to induce a clinical depression. This is an extension of the original suggestion that reserpine will induce clinical depression in some individuals because of reduced noradrenergic and serotonergic activity. However, as we have discussed elsewhere,[47] there are important questions about the reserpine-induced syndrome and the extent to which it does cause clinical depression. Furthermore, reserpine is a non-specific drug which affects a large number of biological systems, and the evidence to date suggests that its effects on dopamine may be more important for the development of the behavioral syndrome than its effects on norepinephrine or serotonin. In an effort to pursue this line of investigation, investigators have given animals and humans newer compounds which cause a more selected depletion of individual monoamines.

Alpha-methyl-paratyrosine (AMPT) will block the synthesis of both dopamine and norepinephrine.[48] Medical and schizophrenic patients who are given sufficiently large amounts of AMPT to produce a significant reduction of peripheral and presumably central catecholamine synthesis became sedated and, in some instances, anxious, but do not develop clinical depression.[48-52] There is one report[53] that AMPT may have some anti-manic effect, but this suggestion must be regarded as tentative. Fusaric acid, a specific inhibitor of dopamine-β-hydroxylase, will reduce the conversion of dopamine into norepinephrine. It has been given to manic and hypomanic patients without clinical improvement.[54] Indeed, several of the patients deteriorated further.

Parachlorophenylalanine (PCPA), an inhibitor of tryptophan hydroxylase, will reduce serotonin synthesis.[55,56] In man it produces a number of non-specific behavioral effects including tiredness, restlessness and anxiety and, in some instances, confusion, agitation and paranoid ideation.[47] In an interesting preliminary report, Shopsin and Gershon[53] noted that a small number of depressed patients who had responded to either imipramine or to a monoamine oxidase inhibitor and who were subsequently given PCPA, suffered a rapid and significant return of symptoms, in spite of the continuation of the antidepressant medication. Similar patients given AMPT showed no clinical change. If these findings are confirmed in larger groups, it would suggest that serotonin may play a more important role in the development of depression than norepinephrine. However, this must be viewed with caution in that a very small number of patients have been studied and because of the possibility of complex interactions between the two drugs being given to these patients.

In summary, it would seem that the strategy of amine depletion has in itself not produced any convincing evidence supporting the hypothesis that depletion of norepinephrine or serotonin is central to the development of clinical depression. One would have to consider the possible importance of other systems which may interact with changes in amine function.

In Chapter 9, Davis and Janowsky point to the possible role of acetyl-choline in the genesis of affective disorders, and discuss possibly important interactions between cholinergic and adrenergic systems. Their evidence is based in part on the remission of manic symptoms following the intravene-ous administration of physostigmine, a centrally active anticholinesterase inhibitor. We[57] have attempted to replicate their findings and, while we have noted changes in our patients' clinical state, have suggested some alternative explanations for the changes with emphasis on alterations in activity rather than in thinking or mood.

Neuroendocrinology

Dr. Sachar (Chapter 8) has discussed some studies of neuroendocrine function in depressed patients and how this might advance our understand-ing of the psychobiology of depression. In particular, he has pointed to possible links between changes in monoamine metabolism and endocrine activity. This strategy is of particular importance and will probably be elaborated on in future work involving not only monoamines and endocrine function, but also the other systems which are of concern to investigators in this area. Thus, for example, changes in electrolyte distribution (which in themselves may be secondary to some other abnormality, *e.g.* an aspect of cell membrane activity) can have a profound effect on biogenic amine function.

In discussing his finding that some depressed women have an abnormal growth hormone response to hypoglycemia but not to L-DOPA administra-tion, Dr. Sachar suggests that this may be a reflection of the fact that the growth hormone response to hypoglycemia is dependent upon endogenous brain catecholamines, whereas the response to L-DOPA is dependent upon the conversion of the exogenous catecholamine precursor. This is an in-teresting suggestion. It is also important to consider the possibility that other systems may also be involved. As we have pointed out, serotonergic systems may be involved in the growth hormone response to hypog-lycemia, and Dr. Sachar's finding may, therefore, be indicative of an alteration in serotonin metabolism.[58]

Investigators have paid relatively little attention to the possible impor-tance of an association between some aspects of sex hormone function and depression.[59] There are a number of observations which should be noted. Thus, depression is more common in females than males and is more likely to occur at times of significant endocrine change including the premenstrual period, post-partum, at the menopause, or in association with the administration of oral contraceptives. Alterations in levels of estrogen or progesterone or the ratio of estrogen to progesterone may have a significant effect on a variety of important functions, including the level of the enzyme, monoamine oxidase. This could in turn lead to alterations in aminergic activity.

Much of the work described in this volume is aimed at the discovery and definition of biological alterations in patients with depression or mania. The fact that there is a particular biological change in a depressed patient or, for that matter, in a group of depressed patients, does not in itself mean that the change is directly associated with the etiology or development of the illness. Such changes may be secondary to the illness itself or to some other biological alteration which may or may not have been discovered. Indeed, the secondary changes may obscure the more important primary dysfunction. Furthermore, some of the changes which have been described in depressed patients may not be specific for that condition. For example, there are reports of a reduction in 5HIAA in the lumbar spinal fluid of some depressed and manic patients, as well as reduced accumulation of 5HIAA after probenecid administration. However a number of schizophrenic patients have also been reported to have low lumbar fluid 5HIAA levels or reduced accumulation after probenecid administration.[60,61] This suggests the possibility that a reduction in lumbar 5HIAA (and presumably, but not certainly, a reduction in central serotonin turnover) may be a non-specific occurrence in psychiatric illness. It is also possible that this finding may be associated with psychotic as opposed to neurotic forms of psychiatric illness. Thus, we have noted that lumbar fluid 5HIAA levels tend to be lower in psychotic than neurotic patients.[62] Furthermore, the reduction in slow wave sleep which occurs in many depressed patients is most profound in psychotic depressives.[63] Some investigators believe that serotonin plays an important role in the mediation of slow wave sleep.[64] It is possible that the reduction in central serotonin activity may in general be associated with psychosis and not specifically with depression. It is also possible that it may simply be a manifestation of severity of illness rather than psychosis *per se*. This type of consideration will have to be elaborated in further investigations.

Several of the biologic theories of depression are based on the view that depression and mania are *opposite* conditions. This may be an oversimplistic way of conceptualizing the relationship between these two clinical states. Not only do many manic patients have signs and symptoms of depression during their manic episodes, but depressed and manic patients have a number of biological changes in common. These include reduced levels of platelet monoamine oxidase; reduced erythrocyte concentrations of catechol-o-methyl-transferase; reduced levels of 5HIAA after probenecid administration; reduced levels of 5HIAA in the lumbar fluid and reduced accumulation of homovanillic acid and 5HIAA after probenecid administration; reduced levels of tryptophan concentration in lumbar fluid; reduced rate of transfer of sodium into the CSF. Both groups of patients have been reported to show an increase in the amplitude of the average evoked response and to have similar changes in sleep. There is also the possibility that some depressed patients may respond to treatment with lithium which is clearly an effective anti-manic drug. These and other considerations have led to an alternative way of conceptualizing the relationship between mania and depression.[17,65-67]

A number of abnormalities which have been described in depressed or manic patients have been found to persist after clinical recovery. These include a reduction in slow wave sleep; in the low level of platelet MAO and erythrocyte COMT; the low levels of CSF 5HIAA and perhaps HVA and MHPG, among others. It is possible that these changes may not be related to the clinical state of depression (or mania) *per se*, but reflect some enduring underlying characteristic (perhaps of genetic origin) and be manifestations of a predisposition to the development of an affective illness. It is also possible that they may be part of an effort to adapt to some other unrecognized abnormality and thus be adaptive and not pathological.

In conclusion, the past decade has seen a considerable increase in interest in the psychobiology of the affective disorders. Much of the work which has been done remains controversial and needs elaboration and expansion. New concepts must also be sought.

References

1. Bunney, W.E., Jr., and Davis J.M.: Norepinephrine in depressive reactions. A review. *Arch. Gen. Psychiat.* 13:483-494, 1965.
2. Schildkraut, J.J.: The catecholamine hypothesis of affective disorders: A review of supporting evidence. *Amer. J. Psychiat.* 122:509-522, 1965.
3. Coppen, A: The biochemistry of affective disorders. *Brit. J. Psychiat.* 113:1237-1264, 1967.
4. Schildkraut, J.J., and Kety S.S.: Biogenic amines and emotion. *Science* 156:21-30, 1967.
5. Curzon, G.: Tryptophan pyrrolase—A biochemical factor in depressive illness? *Brit. J. Psychiat.* 115:1367-1374, 1969.

6. Lapin, I.P., and Oxenkrug, G.F.: Intensification of the central serotoninergic processes as a possible determinant of the thymoleptic effect. *Lancet* 1:132-136, 1969.

7. Davis, J.M.: Theories of biological etiology of affective disorders, *in* "International Review of Neurobiology." (C.C. Pfeiffer and J.R. Smythies, Eds.), pp 145-175. Academic Press, New York (1970).

8. Schildkraut, J.J.: "Neuropsychopharmacology and the Affective Disorders." Little, Brown and Co., Boston (1970).

9. Davis, J.M., and Fann, W.E.: Lithium. *Ann. Rev. Pharmacol.* 11: 285-303, 1971.

10. Davies, B., Carroll, B.J., and Mowbray R.M., (Eds): "Depressive Illness: Some Research Studies." Charles C. Thomas, Springfield (1972).

11. Baer, L.: Electrolyte metabolism in psychiatric disorders, *in* "Biological Psychiatry." (J. Mendels, Ed.), pp 199-234. John Wiley and Sons, Inc., New York (1973).

12. Bunney, W.E., Jr., and Murphy D.L.: The behavioral switch process and psychopathology, in "Biological Psychiatry." (J. Mendels, Ed.), pp. 345-367. John Wiley and Sons, Inc., New York (1973).

13. Mendels, J., and Stinnett J.: Biogenic amine metabolism, depression and mania, in "Biological Psychiatry." (J. Mendels, Ed.) pp. 99-131. John Wiley and Sons, Inc., New York (1973).

14. Durell, J.: Sodium and potassium metabolism. Lithium salts and affective disorders, *in* "Factors in Depression" (N.S. Kline, Ed.) pp. 67-96. Raven Press, New York (1974).

15. Mendels, J.: Biological aspects of affective illness, *in* "American Handbook of Psychiatry" (S. Arieti, Ed.), pp. 448-479. Basic Books, New York (1974).

16. Mendels, J., Stern, S., and Frazer, A.: Biological concepts of depression, *in* "Proceedings of the First International Symposium on Depression" (D. Gallant, and G. Simpson, Eds.), Spectrum Publications, Inc., New York (in press).

17. Mendels, J.: "Concepts of Depression" John Wiley and Sons, Inc., New York (1970).

18. Klerman, G.L.: Clinical research in depression. *Arch. Gen. Psychiat.* 24:305-319, 1971.

19. Robins, E., and Guze, S.: Classification of affective disorders: The primary-secondary, the endogenous-reactive, and the neurotic-psychotic concepts, *in* "Recent Advances in the Psychobiology of the Depressive Illnesses." (T.A. Williams, M.M. Katz, and J.A. Shield, Eds.), pp. 283-293. DHEW Publication #70-9053, 1972.

20. Asberg, M.: Plasma nortriptyline levels—Relationship to clinical effects. *Clin. Pharmacol. Ther.* 16:215-229, 1974.

21. Asberg, M.: Individualization of treatment with tricyclic compounds. *Med. Clin. No. Amer.* 58:1083-1091, 1974.

22. Pare, C.M.B., and Sandler M.: A clinical and biochemical study of a trial of iproniazid in the treatment of depression. *J. Neurol. Neurosurg. Psychiat.* 22:247-251, 1959.

23. Prange, A.J., Jr.: The pharmacology and biochemistry of depression. *Dis. Nerv. Syst.* 25:217-221, 1964.

24. Imlah, N.W., Murphy, K.P., and Mellor, C.S.: The treatment of depression: A controlled comparison between iprindole (Prondol) and imipramine. *Clin. Trials J.* 5:927-931, 1968.

25. Rosloff, B.N., and Davis, J.M.: Effect of iprindole on norepinephrine turnover and transport. *Psychopharmacologia* 40:53-76, 1974.

26. Carlsson, A., and Lindqvist, M.: Effect of chlorpromazine or haloperidol on formation of 3-methoxytyramine and normetanephrine in mouse brain. *Acta Pharmacol. (Kobenhaven)* 20:140-144, 1963.

27. Schildkraut, J.J., Winokur, A., and Applegate, C.W.: Norepinephrine turnover and metabolism in rat brain after long-term administration of imipramine. *Science* 168:867-869, 1970.

28. Alpers, H.S., and Himwich, H.E.: The effects of chronic imipramine administration on rat brain levels of serotonin, 5-hydroxyindoleacetic acid, norepinephrine and dopamine. *J. Pharmacol. Exper. Therap.* 180:531-538, 1972.

29. Bowers, M.B.: Amitriptyline in man: Decreased formation of central 5-hydroxyindoleacetic acid. *Clin. Pharmacol. Therap.* 15:167-170, 1974.

30. Frazer, A., Pandey, G., Mendels J., *et al.*: The effect of triiodothyronine in combination with imipramine on [³H]–cyclic AMP production in slices of rat cerebral cortex. *Neuropharmacology* 13:1131-1140, 1974.

32. Robins, E., and Hartman, B.K.: Some chemical theories of mental disorders, *in* "Basic Neurochemistry" (R.W. Albers, G.S. Siegel, R. Katzman, *et al.*, Eds.) pp. 607-644. Little Brown, Boston (1972).

32. Maas, J.W., and Landis, D.H.: *In vivo* studies of the metabolism of norepinephrine in the central nervous system. *J. Pharmacol. Exper. Therap.* 163:147-162, 1968.

33. Costa, E., and Neff, N.H.: Estimation of turnover rates to study the metabolic regulation of the steady-state level of neuronal monoamines, *in* "Handbook of Neurochemistry" (A. Lajtha, Ed.) Plenum Press, New York (1970).

34. Gordon, E.K., and Oliver, J.: 3-methoxy-4-hydroxyphenylethylene glycol in human cerebrospinal fluid. *Clin. Chim. Acta.* 35:145-150, 1971.

35. Post, R.M., Gordon, E.K., Goodwin, F.K., *el al.*: Central norepinephrine metabolism in affective illness: MHPG in the cerebrospinal fluid. *Science* 179:1002-1003, 1973.

36. Shopsin, B., Wilk, S., Gershon, S., *et al.*: Cerebrospinal fluid MHPG: An assessment of norepinephrine metabolism in affective disorders. *Arch. Gen. Psychiat.* 28:230-233, 1973.

37. Schildkraut, J.J.: Depression and biogenic amines, *in* "American Handbook of Psychiatry" (S. Arieti, Ed.), Basic Books, New York (in press).

38. Mendels, J., Stinnett, J., Burns, D., *et al.*: Amine precursors and depression. *Arch. Gen. Psychiat.* 32:22-30, 1975.

39. Murphy, D.L., Brodie, H.K.H., Goodwin, F.K., *et al.*: Regular induction of hypomania by L-DOPA in "bipolar" manic-depressive patients. *Nature* 229:135-136, 1971.

40. Coppen, A., Shaw, D.M., Herzberg, B., *et al.*: Tryptophan in the treatment of depression. *Lancet* 2:1178-1180, 1967.

41. Coppen, A., Whybrow, P.C., Noguera, R., *et al.*: The comparative antidepressant value of L-tryptophan and imipramine with an without attempted potentiation by liothyronine, *Arch. Gen. Psychiat.* 26:234-241, 1972.

42. Murphy, D.L., Baker, M., Goodwin, F.K., *et al.*: L-tryptophan in affective disorders: Indoleamine changes and differential clinical effects. *Psychopharmacologia* 34:11-20, 1974.

43. Prange, A.J., Jr., Wilson I.C., Lynn, C.W., *et al.*: L-tryptophan in mania. *Arch. Gen. Psychiat.* 30:56-62, 1974.

44. Coppen, A., Shaw, D.M., and Farrell, J.P.: Potentiation of the antidepressive effect of a monoamine-oxidase inhibitor by tryptophan. *Lancet* 1:79-81, 1963.

45. Pare, C.M.D.: Potentiation of monoamine-oxidase inhibitors by tryptophan. *Lancet* 2:527-528, 1963.

46. Glassman, A.H., and Platman, S.R.: Potentiation of monoamine oxidase inhibitor by

tryptophan. *J. Psychiat. Res.* 7:83-88, 1969.

47. Mendels, J., and Frazer, A.: Brain biogenic amine depletion and mood. *Arch. Gen. Psychiat.* 30:447-451, 1974.

48. Spector, S., Sjoerdsma, A., and Udenfriend, S.: Blockade of endogenous norepinephrine synthesis by α-methyl tyrosine, an inhibitor of tyrosine hydroxylase. *J. Pharmacol. Exper. Ther.* 147:86-95, 1965.

49. Sjoerdsma, A., Engelman, K., and Spector, S.: Inhibition of catecholamine synthesis in man with α-methyl tyrosine, an inhibitor of tyrosine hydroxylase. *Lancet* 2:1092-1094, 1965.

50. Charalampous, K.D., and Brown, S.: A clinical trial of α-methyl-paratyrosine in mentally ill patients. *Psychopharmacologia (Berlin)* 11:422-429, 1967.

51. Gershon, S., Hekimian, L.J., Floyd, A., Jr., *el al.*: α-methyl-*p*-tyrosine (AMT) in schizophrenia. *Psychopharmacologia (Berlin)* 11:189-194, 1967.

52. Engelman, K., Horwitz, D., Jequier, E., *et al.*: Biochemical and pharmacologic effects of α-methyltyrosine in man. *J. Clin. Invest.* 47:577-594, 1968.

53. Shopsin, B.N., Wilk, S., Goldstein, M., *et al.*: The use of imipramine, AMPT and PCPA in hospitalized depressives. Presented at the *American College of Neuropharmacology, 12th annual meeting,* Palm Springs, December 1973.

54. Sack, R.L., and Goodwin, F.K.: Inhibition of dopamine-β-hydroxylase in manic patients: A clinical trial with fusaric acid. *Arch. Gen. Psychiat.* 31:649-654, 1974.

55. Koe, B.K., and Weissman, A.: *P*-chlorophenylalanine: A specific depletion of brain serotonin. *J. Pharmacol. Exper. Ther.* 154: 499-516, 1966.

56. Jequier, E., Lovenberg, W., and Sjoerdsma, A.: Tryptophan hydroxylase inhibition: The mechanism by which *p*-chlorophenylalanine depletes rat brain serotonin. *Mol. Pharmacol.* 3:274-278, 1967.

57. Carroll, B.J., Frazer, A., Schless, A.P., *et al.*: Cholinergic reversal of manic symptoms. (Letter) *Lancet* 1:427-428, 1973.

58. Mendels, J., Frazer, A., and Carroll, B.J.: Growth hormone response in depression. (Letter) *Amer. J. Psychiat.* 131:1154-1155, 1974.

59. Janowsky, D.S., Fann, W.E., and Davis, J.M.: Monoamines and ovarian hormone-linked sexual and emotional changes: A review. *Arch. Sexual Behavior.* 1:205-2 8. 1971.

60. Bowers, M.B., Heninger, G.R., and Gerbode, F.: Cerebrospinal fluid 5-hydroxyindoleacetic acid and homovanillic acid in psychiatric patients. *Internat. J. Neuropharmacol.* 8:255-262, 1969.

61. Ashcroft, G.W., Brooks, P.W., Cundall, R.L., *et al.*: Changes in the glycol metabolites of noradrenaline in affective illness. Presented at the *Fifth World Congress of Psychiatry,* Mexico City, 1971.

62. Mendels, J., Frazer, A., Fitzgerald, R.G., *et al.*: Biogenic amine metabolites in cerebrospinal fluuid of depressed and manic patients. *Science* 175:1380-1382, 1972.

63. Mendels, J., and Hawkins, D.R.: Sleep and depression: Further considerations. *Arch. Gen. Psychiat.* 19:445-452, 1968.

64. Jouvet, M.: The role of monoamines and acetylcholine—containing neurons in the regulation of the sleep-waking cycle, *in* "Reviews of Physiology" (R.H. Adrian, E. Helmreich, H. Holzer, *et al.*, Eds.) pp. 166-307. Springer-Verlag, Berlin (1972).

65. Whybrow, P.C., and Mendels, J.: Toward a biology of depression: Some suggestions from neurophysiology. *Am. J. Psychiat.* 125:1491-1500, 1969.

66. Court, J.H.: The continuum model as a resolution of paradoxes in manic-depressive psychosis. *Brit. J. Psychiat.* 120:133-141, 1972.

67. Mendels, J., and Frazer, A.: Reduced central serotonergic activity in mania: Implications for the relationship between depression and mania. *Brit. J. Psychiat.* (in press).

Subject Index

A

Acetylcholine (ACH), 30, 74, 76, 78, 134, 139, 166
Addison's disease, 155
adenine ^{3}H, 13
adenosine 3′,5′–monophosphate (c–AMP), 10, 13, 15, 29, 62, 164
adenosine triphosphatase (ATPase), 29, 106
sodium–potassium ATPase, 104, 106, 111, 113, 117
adenylate cyclase, 10, 11, 12, 15, 104
adrenocorticotrophic hormone (ACTH), 124, 126
adrenergic transmission, 164
aminergic "Pools", 75
amitryptyline, 31, 32, 33, 164
amphetamine, 3, 33, 74, 151
animal models, 79
anti-cholinesterase inhibitor, 166
apomorphine, 16, 17, 18, 19, 21, 22, 150, 151
autosomal dominant, 89

B

benztropine, 134
biogenic amine
depletion, 76
storage, 39
theory, 146, 150, 164
biogenic amines, 7, 29, 32, 40, 58, 69, 79, 80, 81, 101, 104, 105, 117, 147, 148, 162, 167
CSF metabolites, 47, 163

C

calcium, 29
catecholamines, 9, 11, 16, 35, 72, 74, 76, 77, 126, 129, *see also biogenic amines*
catechol-O-methyl transferase (COMT), 168
cations, 105, 106, 112, *see also sodium, potossum, calcium*
chlorpromazine, 31, 136
cinanserin, 150
clonidine, 150
clorgyline, 35
color blindness, 87
cortisol, 124, 126
Cushing's disease, 155

D

deprenyl, 25
bipolar, 2, 12, 13, 21, 22, 36, 37, 38, 40, 89, 90, 97, 105, 162
depression
classification, 162
endogenous, 144, 145
prophylaxis, 70
reactive, 144, 145
unipolar, 2, 12, 13, 15, 19, 21, 22, 38, 40, 89, 90, 96, 97, 105, 124, 129, 162
depression spectrum disease, 91, 96
desmethylimipramine, 3, 31
dexamethasone, 125
L-dihydroxyphenylalanine (L-dopa), 9, 16, 17, 18, 19, 21, 22, 77, 149, 167
dizygote, 85, 116

173